To Roger ~
with love
Jayne
September ~ 1986 ~

Thank you for your
love, concern & support ~

LEADING A SUNDAY
CHURCH SCHOOL

Leading A Sunday Church School

by

Ralph D. Heim

Professor of Christian Education and English Bible
Gettysburg Seminary

THE MUHLENBERG PRESS • PHILADELPHIA

PREFACE

Leading a Sunday Church School is offered as a textbook for college, seminary, university, and training-school students; also as a manual for pastors, directors, and superintendents. Its place is different from that of the many ten-short-chapter books on Christian education. They serve a large group of persons but they often disappoint those to whom this volume is addressed. Conversely, of course, this will displease those who do not wish to go below the surface of things to consider reasons instead of merely discover solutions. It is prepared chiefly for workers who are interested in advanced study.

Within that sphere, the book is meant to aid in lifting the level of Sunday Church School work by doing two things. The first is to provide a ready compendium of helps, based on intelligent understanding of the task, regarding the major phases of Sunday Church School leadership. The second is to focus on those matters a current philosophy of Christian education which perhaps has not been made articulate in such a connection before.

The author's major aim regarding that philosophy is to show its implications. But that makes it necessary for him to describe and analyze the theory. In that endeavor, he cannot conceal a sympathy for it. He does not believe there is any possibility of synthesizing the two major opposing schools of philosophy in the field of Christian education. He thinks it is necessary to make a positive choice of one or the other although there is no need to be an extremist who cannot see good in the old along with the new, or vice versa. So, while the educational orientation here aims to go only far enough to get beyond vacillation and confusion while staying clear of anything that resembles radicalism, it is somewhat to the left of center.

The work began with a one-page outline in 1927 and since that time scarcely a month has passed without some addition. It has grown principally by the stimulating interchange in college and seminary classrooms, but that is not all. Pastors and superintendents of Sunday Church Schools in summer camps, leadership school classes, and conventions, as well as by private conferences and correspondence, have contributed generously. Many schools have been observed in action; also students annually have been reporting their observations and discussing their field experiences. Naturally, the conclusions of personal experience and reading have been included. Recently a hundred pastors and other workers wrote letters in response to inquiries concerning selected problems. Finally, during four years, a mimeographed edition was used in three schools and at least a hundred students wrote an evaluation of each chapter.

Manifestly it is impossible to offer proper acknowledgments and render due thanks in any complete fashion. One can say only that deepest gratitude is expressed herewith to each person who has helped in any manner, directly or indirectly.

There have been those who have said that certain things recommended in these pages might work well enough in the big city church but not fit the small rural church. The answer is: wait, see, and try! Things like these have been done and are being done now, in one place or another. In many cases, small and rural churches offer the best of all opportunities to do creative work in Sunday Church Schools. Furthermore, ideals constitute an essential factor in any educational situation. A leader who has a good mental picture of a school as it might be can be imbued with ideals that will make him more eager in effort, resourceful in practice, and correct in appraisal. He has done in advance some of the thinking which is a part of each leadership task.

The word *leader* is used with several connotations. Usually it refers to an officer or executive charged with "leadership responsibilities" of the type involved in organization, administration, and supervision. In some chapters though, notably X through XIII, it may mean the teacher or even the pupil who is leading in some learning enterprise.

The word *activities,* which is used so frequently here, may be misunderstood. It is always to be taken as referring to *any* form of human behavior, not only to that which is chiefly muscular.

The word *approach* has the significance of orientation—the outlook from which you view Christian education, the direction you take in working at it, your standards for evaluating it. It is at once the golf-player's "stance," "carry through," and rulebook.

Finally, an injunction for teachers who use this as a textbook. It came from a student who said: "More and more I am impressed by the fact that those of us who are studying these new educational processes must, also, 'learn by doing.' "

In concluding a work of this sort one remembers one's own deeply appreciated educational leaders—so many of them. It is a privilege to be able to mention three: Doctor Paul H. Heisey, Doctor Loyal H. Larimer, and Doctor John P. Schneider. To those revered teachers, along with all our fellow leaders in Christian education everywhere, the book is dedicated for anything it may contribute toward progress in Sunday Church School work.

RALPH D. HEIM
GETTYSBURG, PENNSYLVANIA
JANUARY 22, 1950.

CONTENTS

LIST OF DIAGRAMS

Chapter I

KNOWING THE SUNDAY CHURCH SCHOOL
OF YESTERDAY AND TODAY

It was in 1780 that Robert Raikes gathered the first pupils for his educational experiment which became the present Sunday Church School. Since that time hundreds of millions of devoted men and women have worked in behalf of that institution. Today in the United States every fiftieth person one meets on the street is a Sunday Church School worker.

In what activities does a leader of those men and women engage? *What must a pastor, director of Christian education, or superintendent of a Sunday Church School do, and how can he do it most effectively?*

These leaders often are impatient to have a brief directive on what to do next Sunday morning. Yet there is something better than that. It is to possess the background of understanding against which the Sunday morning task becomes meaningful. Then the leader is able to determine for himself what procedures will be most effective in his particular situation.

For that purpose the leader needs some general knowledge about the whole field of educational work in the church, including the history and fundamental theory of Christian education. Hence Chapters I and II are included here. This first chapter undertakes to answer the question, "How did the Sunday Church School come to be and what is its present status?" The second presents a particular theory of Christian education which has been gaining currency for several decades.

I

HISTORY OF THE SUNDAY CHURCH SCHOOL

Christian education in the Sunday Church School is related to an age-long development. All mankind is and doubtless always has been religious. Thus religious education in the broad sense of the term is as old as human life and institutions; older than preaching, sacred music, even the Bible itself, older than anything but the most elementary theology and worship.

Pre-Christian and Non-Christian Relations

While the special interest here is the Protestant Sunday Church School, there will be value in noticing briefly its relations with pre-Christian, non-Christian, and non-Protestant practices. Also worth while is a quick view of the whole Christian educational development which preceded the school of today.

"Primitive" is the term applied to the religion of uncultured peoples whether they are of ancient or of modern times. At present the adherents of primitive religion, numbering a few million, are distributed more or less generally over the earth. Surprisingly, their religious education has characteristics of special interest to present-day Christian educators. In it learning is by doing, by participating in life instead of verbalizing about it. Also it has a practical purpose and an immediacy of aim which relate to persons.

Egyptians, Assyrians, Babylonians, Greeks, and Romans had more or less elaborate systems of religious education. Hindus, Jains, Buddhists, and Sikhs in South Asia; Confucianists, Taoists, and Shintoists in East Asia; as well as Zoroastrians and Mohammedans in West Asia still have active programs.

Jewish education is the direct forerunner of Christian education. Undoubtedly a considerable amount of instruction in the worship of God and some teaching about his will and nature were given in the tents of the patriarchs. More ample work for Jewish education began in the time of Moses. The work continued through the times of the kings and prophets. With the return of Ezra after the exile a new era began. Synagogues were established and the people were directed to assemble in them for instruction as well as worship.

Later, wherever a synagogue was founded a school was set up, particularly for young boys. The report of Paul's experience under his teacher Gamaliel in Jerusalem indicates that higher education was established there. The strong educational program of Judaism today—especially in weekday schooling—is in harmony with the long history of that faith.

A study of non-Christian forms of religious education in their historical development reveals certain characteristics. Aims of all education were religious, so there was no sharp distinction between "religious" and "secular" education. Study was largely for boys. Sacred scriptures were the major element in the curricular subject matter. Memorization was a chief method. Much religious education was informal. Formal efforts were centered about the home and the temple, so the teachers were chiefly parents and priests. All these faiths, when virile, had programs of education which were in one way or another closely associated with life.

Christian Education before the Sunday Church School

The Christian religion was inaugurated by means of teaching. From the beginning it won adherents by educational procedures and fostered the spiritual growth of its members through the educational method. Its practice throughout its history has been in harmony with the spirit and manner of Christ. While his work was not confined to teaching, he was pre-eminently a teacher.

The work of Christ

It must be recognized that the Master had a twofold practice in his teaching ministry. There was group work with public assemblies, large and small, and there was private effort with the individuals whom he had always around him, especially his chosen twelve. In both types of work he proceeded chiefly in an informal way. He would teach as opportunity offered—in a temple court, in a synagogue, in a private home, along the public highway, by the seaside, from a boat. Even with the twelve, his teaching was usually occasional although there were instances when he seems to have taken them aside for some special instruction in the work they were to do.

As for Christ's more particular teaching methods, counseling and discussion techniques were favorites. We marvel at his artistic and effective use of storytelling. His first recorded utterance is a searching question and by that means he frequently probed to the heart of a matter. He used also what more recently has been called the project, laboratory, or learning-by-doing way when, for example, he sent out the twelve to get some experience in the work they would be doing later.

Before the Reformation

The continuing ministry of Jesus in Christian education was carried forward first by the apostles and later by certain leaders formally designated as "teachers." Even Peter, James, John, and Paul were essentially teachers. The journeys of Paul were pre-eminently teaching expeditions after the manner of the present-day missionary who meets individuals alone or in casual groups.

The first formal effort of the church to instruct its membership is known as the catechumenate. It provided systematic instruction in Christian doctrine to prepare members for admission into the church. Usually the students were adult converts or young people approaching maturity. The period of instruction lasted three or four years and culminated in baptism and admittance to the sacrament of the altar. As some form of higher training became necessary particularly for the clergy, catechetical schools—forerunners of modern Christian colleges—were established beginning about A.D. 200.

It will be seen that the early church did not undertake an extensive program of education particularly for its children. The elders lived and learned chiefly in the atmosphere of the Christian community and the children grew in the faith through the informal influence of the home.

For the remaining centuries before the Reformation, the chief educational work of the church was done in seven types of schools: monastic, conventual, bishops', cathedral, parish, song, and chantry schools. All were established mainly for the perpetuation of the clergy or orders and were conducted at the institutional seats of the church. Children of a neighborhood might attend, although attention was concentrated on those who came to live at the institution and enter lifetime church vocations. Before the Reformation, too, several universities had been established. The first, Bologna, had as many as five thousand students enrolled by the year 1200.

The Reformation

Modern Christian religious education began with Martin Luther. He was an educator by profession, beginning as an instructor at the University of Wittenberg in the autumn of 1508 and continuing until his death in 1546.

In the theological principles which Luther enunciated—notably *sola gratia* (by grace alone) and *sola fide* (by faith alone) but also the Christian vocation and the spiritual priesthood of all believers—he gave to Protestant Christian education its orientation in both form and content. In considering the great goal of education to be a Christian man fitted to discharge all the activities of life in a Christian way, he was proposing the life-centered emphasis in the teaching of religion. Because he observed and understood child life as very few before him had done, he paved the way for further study of the child's religious nature and for a rational, interesting, and joyous method of Christian education in harmony with the child's own tendencies.

Luther's translation of the Bible into the common language of the German people gave impetus to the use of modern translations. His interest in worship and his productions as the first Protestant hymnist are only a little less important. His Small Catechism is one of humanity's chief heritages among manuals for religious instruction.

Luther recognized very clearly the place of the home in any complete program of religious education. He saw the need for adapting and grading lessons to the nature and experience of the pupils. He advocated the desirability of supplementing biblical with extra-biblical materials. He favored rational methods of instruction rather than mere memorization. He saw the value of pictures, storytelling, dramatization, discussion, and play in education.

America before the Sunday Church School

The first Christian educators in America were the monks who accompanied Ponce de Leon to Florida in 1521 and endeavored to Christianize the natives. Similar work was undertaken by such men as Jacques Marquette along the Mississippi River as early as 1673. From that day to this, Roman Catholic education has been prominent on the American scene. At present there are Sunday schools in almost every Catholic church, some two hundred major and minor seminaries, a similar number of colleges, two thousand high schools and academies, and eight thousand elementary schools.

Protestant Christian education began with the colonization of the Atlantic seaboard. Three types of education developed there. In the South the children of the well-to-do were tutored in their homes or sent to private schools like the Latin schools in England, while the poor boys were bound out to artisans as apprentices. In the middle colonies, such as New York and Pennsylvania, parochial schools flourished. The New England colonies developed their educational endeavor along lines which resulted in the present free public school system.

Thus there was no uniformity as to the type of school attended by American colonial youth. Yet in all, religion was the outstanding feature of the curriculum. Until the approach of Revolutionary times, the Bible and the catechism were the chief materials used. The content of the other texts, *Hornbook* and *New England Primer,* was largely religious. Further, religion dominated not only elementary and secondary education but also motivated higher education. The three colleges or universities first founded—Harvard (1636), William and Mary (1693), and Yale (1701)—had the training of ministers as their chief purpose.

As the time of the Revolution approached, education began to be secularized. Increasing study of grammar, history, geography, and arithmetic displaced the emphasis on religion. New textbooks were introduced in which the religious element was abridged. This

trend finally resulted in a sense of need which favored the acceptance and fostered the growth of the Sunday school movement when
it reached America.

Beginnings of the Sunday Church School

There had been Sunday schooling before, but the modern Sunday Church School movement was inaugurated by Robert Raikes
of Gloucester, England, in July of 1780. Raikes was born in 1735,
just after the last of the original American colonies had been
settled. He was an aristocrat who lived in a fine house and dressed
so stylishly that he acquired a reputation for vanity. Yet he had also
a Christian spirit which expressed itself in genuine concern for
the poor and criminal classes of the city.

Historians give a dark picture of social conditions in England
at the time the Sunday school arose. The rural masses—about two-
thirds of the entire population—were coarsely clothed, poorly
housed and fed, and illiterate. In towns and industrial cities, such
as Gloucester where Raikes lived, conditions were even more de-
plorable. The result was a prevalence of vice and crime which
the ruling classes sought to suppress by drastic laws with severe
penalties.

Robert Raikes sympathized with the victims of that social system and sought to alleviate their sufferings. He interested himself
especially in prisoners of the Gloucester jails. Those were the days
before prison reform in England or anywhere else. Hardened crim-
inals and prisoners for debt mingled, starving and destitute, in filth
and risk of contagion.

Raikes went personally to aid many with gifts of food, clothing,
money, and other ministrations of mercy. Yet he realized that something more fundamental than charitable contributions must be
undertaken. Ignorance was largely the cause of the lamentable
situation, he concluded. If he could educate the children, especially
of the poor, he might remedy the current social ills.

At that time very few children were going to school, for there
was no system of popular education in England. Also, since child

labor was not forbidden, most of the children in Gloucester worked in pin factories. They spent their weekdays in long hours of labor and running wild on the streets, while on Sunday they were turned loose to carouse.

Raikes for a long time pondered his dream of teaching the children before the possibility of using Sunday for this purpose came to him. One day when walking home from an early service at the cathedral, the word "try" suddenly came so forcibly to his mind that he felt it was a divine command.

He acted at once and engaged as the first teacher a Mrs. Meredith who lived in Sooty Alley, one of the worst slum districts of the city. In her kitchen the first effort to have a school was made. But, because of her inability to handle the boys even with the aid of Mr. Raikes and his cane, that first venture did not succeed. For the teacher of his second school Raikes secured a Mrs. Critchley who had managed an inn near the county jail. She proved equal to the task and was the first successful teacher of the first permanent Sunday school in Robert Raikes' experiment.

Mr. Raikes not only paid the salary of Mrs. Critchley but also supplemented her work. His first and most important task was to secure pupils. When possible, he enlisted the co-operation of parents. More often he went out where the boys were playing and talked with them, urged them to come, even bribed them with gifts. He particularly appealed to the boys whom he had befriended in the jails.

In the sessions of the school, Mr. Raikes would tell stories from the Bible and speak of moral precepts whose worth and importance he sought to impress upon his charges. For especially fine work he was ready to give rewards such as combs, pennies, and New Testaments.

In the early schools, the program seems to have centered around learning to read, learning to say the Church of England catechism, and attending church services. Children were to come soon after ten in the morning and stay until twelve. Then they were to go home until one. Upon their return they would read a lesson and be conducted to church. After church they repeated the catechism till half-past five. When dismissed, they were to go home without making a noise, and by no means to play in the street.

Gradually the plans and methods were altered. The paid teachers were supplanted by volunteers. More Bible study and the memorization and singing of Dr. Watts' hymns were included. The age of the pupils was limited from about six to twelve or fourteen. Girls were permitted to attend as well as boys. The pupils were classified into grades.

By 1787 Raikes described his procedure as follows:

"The hour of assembly on Sunday mornings prescribed in our rules is eight o'clock . . . . Twenty is the number allotted to each teacher, the sexes kept separate. The twenty are divided into four classes; the children who show any superiority in attainment are placed as leaders of these small classes, and are employed in teaching the others their letters, or in hearing them read . . . . Their attending the service of the church once a day has to me seemed sufficient." [1]

Raikes' experiment of "botanizing in human nature," as he called it, was carried on quietly and carefully for three years. Meanwhile, the first school in Southgate Street had expanded to perhaps one hundred pupils, and others had been established in various parts of the city. By that time the outcome had proved so beneficent that Raikes began to publicize his plan.

The results of the publicity were instantaneous. There was such great need that public-spirited people everywhere were ready to try any plan which gave some promise of success. Thus the interest in Sunday schools swept over England. Before Raikes died in 1811 educational leaders from far and wide had come to Gloucester to study the movement, which rapidly extended to all the British Isles, to America, and elsewhere.

American Development

Attempts at the Sunday schooling of children in America were reported as early as 1665 in Roxbury, Massachusetts, and 1674 in Norwich, Connecticut. Sunday schools of the type originated by

---

[1] Ernest H. Hayes, *Raikes the Pioneer* (London: The National Sunday School Union, 1930), p. 70.

Robert Raikes were introduced in 1785. In that year William
Elliott in Accomack County, Virginia, organized a school in his
own home "for the purpose of teaching his own children how to
read the Bible."

At first the church itself was slow to promote the Sunday school
and in some cases opposed it. Not until about 1830 did several
denominations adopt it as their chief teaching agency and lend their
influence to the movement. Thus the earlier Sunday schools were
promoted by organizations of philanthropically minded lay people.

The first such organization, originating in Philadelphia, 1790,
was known as the First Day or Sunday School Society. A merger of
similar societies, soon established in all leading cities, formed the
American Sunday School Union in 1824 and led to the most romantic of all Christian educational developments in the United States.
In 1830 it was resolved: "That the union, in reliance upon divine
aid, will within two years establish a Sunday school in every destitute place where it is practicable throughout the valley of the
Mississippi." Seventy-eight "dollar-a-day" missionaries in the next
two years organized 2,867 schools. Encouraged by such results, the
Union has continued its missionary work to the present time.

Among the materials of instruction in the American Sunday
school, catechisms held first place during the quarter-century 1790-
1815. The use of catechisms did not decline rapidly until after
1850 and they are still used in many schools. Yet the Bible has
become central although extra-biblical materials have been included
since the beginning of this century.

At first the memorization of the Book was the chief method in
vogue. A report of the New York Sunday School Union states that
"individuals ten or twelve years of age would commit to memory,
in a single quarter, from 800 to 1,350 verses, and an amount of
18,859 verses was recited in one school during a given year."

In those instances pupils were allowed to make a more or less
random selection of the materials to be memorizd. Some "rhyme
and reason" were introduced by the coming of "selected" lessons.
Of this type of material, "Selected Scripture Lessons" of the Ameri-

can Sunday School Union, prepared in 1825, attained the widest usage. Some questions having been offered for the aid of teachers in presenting those lessons, the question-and-answer method began to supplant the memorization method and the next development was "question books." There followed from 1840 to 1870 the so-called "Babel Period" in Sunday school curriculum in which there were many personal, community, and denominational efforts to solve the problem of basic helps.

It was in 1872 that the National Sunday School Convention in Indianapolis adopted the International Uniform Lesson plan. These lessons, improved in 1918 and again revised for the period beginning 1945, continue in wide usage. The next step was "graded lessons." There had been grading of instruction even in the days when the catechism was the chief material, but there had been no adequate provision at any time until the International Sunday School Association provided for closely graded lessons in 1908 and group graded lessons in 1922. The denominations were working at the task concurrently.

From the beginning music had a place in the American Protestant educational program. The earliest attempt at a volume of hymns for children was that of Isaac Watts, whose *Divine and Moral Songs for Children* was issued in 1715. This, with Charles Wesley's *Hymns For Children* (1763), and the old *Bay Psalm Book* of 1640 provided the musical element in the curriculum until *Union Hymns* was published in 1835 by the American Sunday School Union. After that time a number of such titles appeared. Then followed the revivalistic song period and after that the development of the denominational and interdenominational hymnals most favored at present.

One of the most important developments in Christian education was the rise of leadership education. There had been some books for this work beginning in 1839, with the publication of *The Teacher Taught* by the American Sunday School Union, and there had been recommendations for promotion of the work as early as 1827. Probably Bishop John H. Vincent in Joliet, Illinois, 1857, conducted the first teacher training class in the United States. Four years later, at Freeport, Illinois, he was chairman of a Sunday school teachers' institute. In 1872 he was influential in introducing religious educational training into what is now Northwestern University and in 1874 initiated a summer training assembly at Chautauqua, New York. Thus began the leadership education program with all its ramifications of classes, schools, conferences, camps, institutes, assemblies, and correspondence, college, university, and seminary courses.

Allies of the Sunday Church School

It became apparent early that the Sunday Church School unaided is not adequate to provide sufficient religious development for the youth of the land. Earnest leaders, therefore, devised and promoted additional agencies which might serve as allies.

One group of these was undertaken for the benefit of the young people of the church. The Y.M.C.A. appeared first in London in 1844 and the first American branch was established in 1851. The Y.W.C.A. also came to America (New York, 1858) from England. The first young people's society was the Christian Endeavor founded in 1881. The boy and girl club movement had its origin with "The Knights of King Arthur" started in 1892. Boy Scouts, founded in England in 1908, came to America in 1910. Girl Scouts were founded in 1912 and Campfire Girls in the same year. The camp movement had special impetus given it by Mr. John L. Alexander beginning in 1914.

For the younger children of the church, the more recent introductions are the Vacation Church School and the Weekday Church School. The former developed according to three types, more or less simultaneously in Wisconsin, Pennsylvania, and New York. The type which became most prevalent, sometimes called "Boville," originated in New York City in 1901. The typical weekday school has been the "released time" type fostered in Gary, Indiana, beginning in 1914, by ministers of that city and the superintendent of public schools. However, on March 8, 1948, the Supreme Court of the United States rendered a decision which has put the program

in a confusion of which the far-reaching implications cannot yet
be estimated.

The "Modern Movement" in Christian Education

An upsurge of unusual effort in Christian education beginning
early in this century has come to be called the modern movement
in Christian education. There had been forerunners extending back
into the eighteen hundreds. Dr. G. B. Smith, in a book called *Religious Thought in the Last Quarter Century,* mentions three important movements which "constituted a basis for the development of
religious education." They are scientific study of the Bible, the child
study movement, and recognition of the social character of the
educational process.

Upon such foundations the modern movement began to establish itself. The Sunday Church School prospered and young people's
societies flourished. Soon the two new agencies, Daily Vacation
Bible School and Weekday Church School, arose. Approximately
coincident, too, was the rapid development of departments of religious education in colleges and universities. By 1925, there were
as many as ten thousand students taking courses in such departments. A large number of significant books was written for their
use. On other levels, too, there were important developments in
leadership education.

Like all new movements, this one met opposition, faced handicaps, and possessed weaknesses, but has had impressive results.
Many of the workers it prepared are still doing effective work for
the cause. Every major denomination revised its curricular series
more or less in harmony with principles which grew out of the
movement. Many of the college, university, and seminary departments remain and minister to students who will be avocational if
not vocational workers in the church. The leadership education
movement goes on, manned at many points by people trained under
this movement. A large quantity of literature was produced which
is only now being superseded. A spirit of scientific study and research was initiated which gives promise of continuing to refine

programs and procedures. The movement promoted weekday and
vacation schools of which the latter are thriving still. The developmental approach which the movement fostered is winning its way
into current Christian teaching.

When an enterprise has something to do with such results, it
possesses values which cannot ultimately be overcome. This one has
been tested, refined in part, and purged in part, just as it has been
proved in part. There is promise that the modern movement may
mark the middle of the century as well as its beginning with as
mighty a fervor and even greater increase of effectiveness in Christian education.

PRESENT STATUS OF THE SUNDAY CHURCH SCHOOL

The Sunday Church School continues to be the principal agency
in the educational work of the church. That whole work is now
to be surveyed briefly.

Nature and Place of Educational Work in the Church

When the church is educating, what is it doing? Broadly, the
church educates whenever it employs the learning-teaching process.
In more typical thinking, education is equated with instruction
as one of several general methods by which the church achieves its
purpose. Then education seems merely parallel with preaching,
conducting worship, handling church finances, and the like. Actually, in direct or indirect fashion, education is co-extensive with all
methods since all have their learning-teaching aspects. In a local
church there is little or nothing that can be done without some
learning and teaching. Consequently the educational work of the
church is a comprehensive, incessant task which permeates the
whole body of ecclesiastical effort.

More specifically, the process is now conducted in many agencies. One thinks first of Sunday, weekday, and vacation church
schools. There are also young people's societies and fellowships,
confirmation classes, women's societies, men's brotherhoods. On the
advanced level there are leadership education classes and schools,

training schools and seminaries, as well as universities. There may be mentioned further, clubs and camps, besides pastoral counseling, lay evangelism, the pulpit, the press, the radio, and the home. Mention should be made also of parochial or Christian day schools.

In more recent times, the educational work of a congregation is coming to be considered in terms of a Church School. A Church School may be defined as a congregation at work educating itself. A few congregations have been developing one unified educational organization and program integrated as a part of the total congregational organization and program—one Church School in which the conscious educational work of the congregation is done in various types of sessions. Such a school is described in Chapter V. Often, though, "Church School" is merely a term to cover a multitude of agencies in each of which some isolated educational work is attempted. In this book "Sunday Church School" applies to any Sunday school although it looks forward ideally to the Sunday sessions of a true Church School.

Education—the learning-teaching process as a way of working —has a secure and growing place in the church program. We may think of local congregations in terms of workers, money, or organizations. As for the church at large, we may think of workers engaged, publications used, money spent, or organizational machinery involved. In any case, the large significance of education is apparent.

The church accomplishes its total purpose in six ways, of which education is a fundamental one. Those six ways are: education, evangelism, fellowship, merciful work, stewardship, and worship. The church would cease to be itself if any one were neglected or eliminated. It is easily possible, though, to recognize the fundamental character of education. Indirect values may be considered first. Evangelism requires education for the evangelist and he evangelizes largely by educational means. Fellowship takes place most fully in the educational agencies of church work and rests upon backgrounds of teaching which unite the group and facilitate fellowship activity. The merciful work of the church is supported by education of the givers and the workers. Stewardship awaits teaching to promote and guide it. Education in worship is essential to its finest expression. By those indirect values as well as direct ones the educational program nurtures and energizes, and so ministers indispensably to the growing spiritual life of the people.

Characteristics of Current Christian Educational Work

Enough has been said to indicate that a strong new spirit is stirring in Christian education. The modern movement reached a peak about 1930 and seemed to lose strength during the following decade but in the late 1940's it had a renascence. This revived movement has certain trends of theory and practice. Some have had a long history, others developed earlier in the modern movement, still others are products of the more recent revival. A few have been selected for special consideration to introduce the chapters which follow as well as to describe educational work in the church on its more advanced, if not customary, levels.

Meeting needs

The church is increasingly aware of need for extending the reach of its educational program. The program is too slowly gaining larger numbers although there is almost boundless opportunity. Enrollments are far from satisfactory. Until about 1945 the Sunday Church School had been losing numbers for a decade. Until recently the membership of the Weekday Church School on released time was increasing. The Vacation Church School and young people's societies are growing still. Yet all of these allies are reaching less than half as many people as the Sunday Church School, and its membership still includes only about one-sixth of the population in the United States.

Similar facts appear in a study of the *scope* of the Christian educational program. Protestant Christians on the average have not more than an hour a week in formal Christian education. Thus, just as a goal for the reach of the educational program might be a threefold multiplication of numbers, the objective with regard to scope might be three hours instead of one.

The church is showing determination to act in these matters. Major denominations are renewing their efforts at enlistment and the search for more time is expressing itself vigorously in such patterns as the widespread endeavor for weekday Christian education. Subsequent chapters show how similar developments are taking place with regard to needs for improved materials and methods, better organization and equipment, more competent leadership under supervision, fuller understanding of basic theory.

Focus on persons

Current Christian education puts its emphasis on the life of persons in private and in social relationships.

Earlier in the century some Christian educators defined Christian life too narrowly. They viewed it largely in terms of ethical conduct without sufficient reference to ultimate realities. Now there is a trend toward a better balance with some danger of going to the opposite extreme. For example, one man already comments that the place of worship is making steady gains while the enterprise of teaching is on the wane.

It does appear that, regarding primary purposes, there was a permanent shift away from transmission of biblical information and theological concepts, the continuation of cultic techniques and the prolongation of institutions. Yet those were not relegated to oblivion. They have become only subordinate in the contributory sense. The focus is upon persons in life's relationships achieving a Christian way of living.

In this focus on persons, Christian educators assume that normal persons are capable of Christian living; that, indeed, they can find fulfillment only through that type of living. Also, normal persons can progressively enter and engage in Christian living by a learning-teaching process. To be sure, there is that devil's proverb, "Religion is caught, not taught." Truly religion is not solely a matter of verbal instruction for there are examples of faith, hope, and love which pupils can see and, admiring, unconsciously follow. But that is teaching!

Further, all normal persons are open to growth in Christian living by educational means at all stages of life and in every situation, a fact which places a twofold responsibility upon the church. First, her workers are to view the whole world of men, women, young people, and children as their constituency. Second, as long as there is one who is not living the Christian life at his highest possible level, the task is unfinished.

While the church has rather completely apprehended the first responsibility, to win all the un-Christian to the faith, it has not so fully conceived the second task of guiding every member in the fullest development of his capacities at every age level and in every circumstance. In particular, there is a false tendency to assume that there is an adult experience of Christianity to which a child must be advanced by various stages and then, when he gets there, his Christian education is ended.

In this emphasis on persons, group affiliations are not neglected. Indeed, twentieth-century Christian education has had a keen consciousness of the social implications of the Christian life. We are concerned about the whole individual, not only his inner self but also all his socially significant dimensions. We seek to develop Christians who, among other things, are devoted to the social good and capable of working at the improvement of social conditions. For some time there have been pressures which threatened to alter that social outlook. Still, though, Christian education seems to continue upon the view that, while Christ came to redeem individuals, the individual and society develop reciprocally.

Throughout, then, the current emphasis is not, as of old, on the maintenance and dissemination of the end products of past religious experience, social institutions, and the like. It is on current life, the actual present activity of growing persons as it undergoes interpretation, analysis, appraisal, control, and consequent change. The North American Study puts it well: "Current Christian living is regarded as the growing point of the Christian movement in which the movement is being recreated . . . where the living God and man meet each other in the expanding experience of a growing reality and a growing Christian experience." [2]

The Church as School

Originally, education was a function of the whole church. Then the Sunday Church School arose outside the institutional life of the church itself. This has resulted in a separateness of organizational provision for that educational enterprise and a disjunction of thought regarding Christian education generally. It seems sometimes to be conceived as a function which may or may not be employed, church schools being looked upon as auxiliaries if not optional ones.

Now, however, education is being viewed more widely as a function of the entire church in all its activities. The Church School is the requisite work of the church in educating itself, a Sunday Church School being the congregation operating for educational purposes in one organizational form.

Comprehensiveness

Current Christian education is comprehensive in outlook and practice. Once "Christian education" may have connoted no more than Sunday Church School classes. Now it connotes also weekday and vacation schools, young people's societies, the home, the college, the press, and many others. Furthermore, it is not a series of agencies alone but chiefly a method used throughout the entire range of church work.

Christian education is not for study and instruction alone, but also for worship, fellowship, and service. Nor is it Bible study alone, for it uses materials from many sources, particularly current experience. It is not only for children but for all persons from earliest to eldest years. Further, it deals with all fundamentals— God, man, immortality, moral responsibility, sin, freedom, the highest good, and salvation as well as lesser things.

---

[2] *A North American Study in the Field of Religious Education,* published for the Madras Conference by the Presbyterian Committee of Publication, Richmond, Virginia, 1938, p. 48.

Finally, Christian education is for all phases of life. It involves the whole person in all his relationships. It concerns the individual and the social order. It includes past, present, and future. It is for every aspect of personality—knowledge and judgment, feeling and appreciation, character and conduct. Yet it is not for isolated experience only, but for an integrated totality of Christian experience.

Developmental approach and creative use of techniques

There are no generally accepted words to describe the particular philosophy and related technique which have been developed within twentieth-century Christian education. Various persons speak of new, modern, scientific, pupil-centered, life-centered, experience-centered, creative or activity education. None of those quite meets the requirements. In particular, "progressive Christian education" cannot be used because the progressive education movement has accumulated too much opprobrium because of its actual or fancied excesses.

"Developmental approach" suggests growth, change, development all along the line. Twentieth-century Christian education views its work in precisely that way. Its task is cumulative pupil experience in Christian living for personal growth and the ongoing process of the social order. Thus the term "developmental approach" is used here, tentatively and experimentally, for the type of educational theory which characterizes the modern movement at its present stage.

"Creative," properly understood, describes the special character of the technique which is now in the ascendancy. Creative means that the learner works within a learning situation which is developed as far as possible by himself for a purpose which is his own. He meets the learning situation in a way which he develops for himself, albeit under guidance and with whatever assistance is necessary. The result achieved is creative, too, in the sense of something novel to the degree which may be fitting for all interests concerned.

Scientific method, normal procedure, and the Spirit's activity

Christian education relies on several supporting sciences, including general education, psychology, and sociology. In general, Christian educators assume that whatever truth educational research may disclose about the ways in which human beings learn will guide procedure in this area. They proceed as if pupils are dependent for learning in the field of religion on the same psychological equipment which is employed in any other field; that, except as special laws or equipment may be discovered, whatever is true about the psychology of childhood, adolescence, and adulthood anywhere will apply here. Lately, too, they are employing the findings of sociology, for example the principles of group dynamics, in Christian education.

This is not to say that the proponents of Christian education view it humanistically as a man-made process alone, a boot-strap for lifting oneself into the Kingdom. They simply believe that the Holy Spirit works in an orderly manner and that devoted students of life working from either the religious or from the secular angle have discovered, consecrated workers have observed, and earnest pupils have come to know the Spirit's ways in some degree. There is regeneration, salvation, sanctification, renewal. The Holy Spirit accomplishes all, but he does it as leaders, learners and he come into appropriate relationships of the type we call educational. Thus man in his lostness is met by God's graciousness in an educational matrix.

Emphasis on Christian specifics

Among more recent trends in Christian education is an increased appreciation of worship, church, Bible, and theology. A majority of Christian educators always upheld their importance. However, some of those who favored a "life-centered" approach tended to equate culture and religion. Developments, particularly in the last decade, have served to correct some of the more superficial and romantic views. Now it is more widely recognized that Christian personality finds essential aids to growth in those specifics. Scripture, devotional literature, and historic faith, institutions, and concepts can be brought into functional relations with current religious experience. Indeed, the great resources out of past experience, while not used for their own sakes, must be used for the directing and activating of current Christian living.

The above catalogue does not by any means exhaust current characteristics of Christian education. At least as many others could be mentioned, including such things as the unit concept in curriculum, the functional way of using the Bible, the ecumenical idea, the employment of audile and visual materials and equipment, newer developments in children's and youth work, a new emphasis on adult work, and efforts at the promotion of Christian family life. Many of them will be developed in later chapters.

The Sunday Church School in the Present Program

Within all Protestantism, the Sunday Church School holds first place among the agencies in the educational work whose current characteristics have been described. Putting it otherwise, in the Church School, the Sunday sessions are of primary significance.

Sunday Church School work now engages more leaders and learners than any other form of educational enterprise. Speaking in round numbers, there are some five million workers and fifty million pupils in the world's five hundred thousand Protestant Sunday Church Schools. More than half of these are in the United States; others distributed in all continents and many of the isles. There is something like one Sunday Church School member for each fifty persons in the world's population.

In relation to other agencies, the Sunday Church School not only reaches the largest number of persons. It also represents the most highly developed form of Christian educational endeavor with the longest background of experience. It has the most carefully worked out curricular materials and provides the most elaborate leadership education program. It is the most universally understood and fully recognized form of Christian educational endeavor.

When the church evaluates the Sunday Church School, it finds various weaknesses. A major one was never more devastatingly described than in 1839 when Frederick Adolphus Packard wrote *The Teacher Taught*. His words are still only too relevant: "It is to be feared that of a large proportion of our Sunday-school children it may be justly said that they are bewildered with verbal mysteries, where there is no refreshment of truth for the eye, and are wearied with wandering from shadow to shadow, where there is all the fatigue of continual progress, without the advance of a single step in real knowledge." [3]

Yet Sunday Church School leaders cannot permit their agency to lose its place for any lesser program. Such high values as these are to be conserved:

It furnishes a definite setting for commitment to Christ and growth therein.
It is the major agency for fostering acquaintance with the Bible.
It serves as an important recruiting ground for the church.
It provides a period of public worship and fosters private devotions.
It makes Christian social fellowship available.
It has international scope.
It develops leadership for the whole church.
It is a major ally of the home in the moral and religious development of youth.
It provides the major portion of Christian literature.
It gives many persons their first experiences in Christian service.
It broadens experience, increases understanding, and deepens motives.
It has an impressive record of guiding and stimulating Christian conduct.

Unquestionably the Sunday Church School must be altered and expanded, or possibly replaced sometime for more effective educational results within Protestantism. Yet what has been done in Christian education during the nineteenth and twentieth centuries, it has had a large share in doing. Also, for what is yet to be done it will be needed for a long time. There is no more appropriate summary in appraisal of the Sunday Church School than the words

[3] Frederick Adolphus Packard, *The Teacher Taught* (Philadelphia: American Sunday School Union, 1839), p. 16.

of Dr. Paul Veith in *The Church and Christian Education* where
he writes of our attempt to do with a fifty horsepower machine "a
work which requires many hundreds of horsepower." [4]

---

[4] Paul H. Veith, *The Church and Christian Education* (St. Louis: The
Bethany Press, 1947), p. 294.

Chapter II

UNDERSTANDING WHAT CHRISTIAN EDUCATION IS

What is Christian education, anyhow? That, possibly, is the major question of a Sunday Church School leader who is developing the background for wise consideration of his task.

The nature and purpose of Christian education have been redefined during recent decades. In the same period the understanding of religion itself was being clarified by scientific study of its racial origin, its social function, and the psychological experience of it. Likewise, the whole field of education was undergoing similar study with important results in philosophy and practice. Christian education felt the effects of both those movements as it underwent its own reconstruction and emerged in its present form.

The resulting type of Christian education, "developmental approach," is described below in definitions of religion, education, religious education, and Christian education.

Two terms will be used frequently, namely, "activity" and "abundant life." "Activity" usually suggests only physical behavior —muscular movement. Indeed, it is sometimes used with that meaning in educational literature still current. In these pages, however, the term is applied not only to any overt act but as well to any inward thought, feeling, or purpose. The life of an individual or group is viewed as a system of activities, so defined.

"Abundant life" stems from the words of Jesus, John 10:10, "I am come that they might have life, and that they might have it more abundantly." As the term is used here it is meant to be consonant with the ultimates of Christian idealism. Thus the abundant life of self and others is regarded as the proper goal and standard, or purpose and measure, of human enterprise.

WHAT IS RELIGION?

Among the great body of Christians, religion means various degrees and combinations of activities like the following: restraint from the more grievous breaches of the ten commandments; practice of daily devotions and attendance at public services of worship; participation in church activities; giving to the program of the church and to charitable causes; acceptance of certain beliefs; some concern about those who are not in the fold; and the expectation of a future life.

Religion has been more exactly defined in the long course of its history and many characteristic definitions might be quoted. However, for the sake of better adaptation to the purpose here, this further venture is made: *the religion of an individual or group is that system of activities which, whether they are primarily intellectual, emotional, or volitional, arises in the relationship of that individual or group to its gods or God.*

This definition recognizes religion as an experience between a man and his deity or deities as he conceives them. It views the religious experience as one which involves the whole man who is now theologizing about his beliefs, now adoring the beloved deity, now giving a cup of cold water to a thirsty fellow man, now restraining his acquisitive tendencies. It further recognizes that religious experience may be known as either an individual or a group phenomenon. In addition, the definition does not view religion as a disjointed, fragmentary, or partial relationship with deity. It recognizes that there is properly some coherence and correlation among the religious activities of a man or group.

Then, too, a true religious experience should involve all the life of an individual or group in a whole "way of living" where all life's activities are included directly or indirectly within the God-relationship. Among truly religious men, life is co-extensive with religion and religion with life, both alike God-related in every aspect. The proposed definition can include such an understanding and, most important for present purposes, it recognizes the present tendency among educators to think of life in terms of activities and of educational objectives as furthered activities of life.

WHAT IS EDUCATION?

In *A Living Universe* Principal Jacks urges that everyone should attempt to define education. The reading of educational literature suggests that almost everyone has tried, for definitions are truly legion.

Typical Definitions

Following are some results of that effort by representative thinkers:

The true aim of education is the attainment of happiness through perfect virtue.—Aristotle

Education in its widest sense means just this: acquiring experience that will serve to modify inherited adjustments.—Bagley

Under the term education, used in its widest sense, must be included those changes which, from birth to death, are wrought in the individual by the process of learning.—Chapman and Counts

The object of education is the realization of a faithful, pure, inviolate, and hence, holy life.—Froebel

Education, then, is the process which seeks to adjust the individual to his physical, mental, and moral environment.—Klapper

Education is the leading out of the individual into a full-orbed, efficient, and rightly integrated personality; able to express himself fluently and with precision in his mother tongue; equipped to make a living while he lives the more abundant life; serviceable to society; comfortably at home with himself and with his fellows; and *en rapport* with the ultimate spiritual realities that lie behind the visible phenomena of the universe.—Marsh

Education means the natural, progressive, and systematic development of all the powers.—Pestalozzi

Education is nothing but the formation of habits.—Rousseau

Education is preparation for life.—Spencer

Education means the universal distribution of extant knowledge.—Ward

An analysis of those and other definitions of education reveals that they vary at many points. We can think of education as science or product, schooling or total learning-teaching process, planned or incidental, in character formal or informal. Other points at which definitions of education differ have to do with aim, content, and method. But the most significant differences arise at the point of approach—the pupil's or teacher's way of looking at the educative process and his general way of going about it. The traditional approach emphasizes *transmissive preparation for life* while the developmental approach is concerned with *creative experience in living*.

Traditional Approach

Traditional approach gets its name not only because it is, superficially, the older point of view, but chiefly because of its tendency to be static in character. That tendency is most apparent in the matter of aim. Certain achievements of the race must be preserved: items of knowledge, practice, institution, and aesthetic and moral value. Those "traditions" are to be sustained by oncoming generations. So, the social purpose of the educational system is to put youth in possession of them and prepare youth to sustain them. In its goal for the pupil himself, traditional approach aims at his competence in adulthood.

The twofold purpose of traditional education—social preservation and personal preparation—is achieved by a process of transmitting the racial heritages in which the content is largely organized subject matter, the techniques are chiefly memoriter, and the control is authoritarian. Pupils are to store up items of knowledge as if in a psychic refrigerator where they may go at will and get the mental eggs preserved there. More recently, too, there has been added the concept that you can do with traditional attitudes and skills what it had been more anciently thought you could do with ideas. If pupils are but trained in certain ways as children, they will act accordingly when they have grown up. That training is meant to provide, at one and the same time, for the maintenance of society and the mature living of the individual.

Something of that traditional view, although so greatly modified already by its counterpart that it scarcely can be seen in its purity, may be said to dominate popular educational thinking today. It has elements of truth. No one would wish to let the great heritages be lost. A transmissive element and a preparatory aspect can never be omitted properly from any educational program. There must be some mastery of fact or there are no materials with which to build intelligent judgments and perform requisite functions. We need certain emotional and executive habits established by long and frequent exercise in order to carry us along in our daily avenues.

Yet this is not an adequate philosophy of education. It does not fit the needs of dynamic personalities growing individually within a changing society. They want satisfaction and achievement that are real and they want them now as well as in the future. They are concerned primarily about the moving present. The past has values largely as it contributes to the present. As for the future, it is, indeed, a rather dim unknown for which their best preparation is to become experienced total persons.

Developmental Approach: Creative in Character

What is here termed developmental approach has been called "this new education," even "this new-fangled nonsense." Nothing could be farther from the truth unless it be defined falsely—and it has been—as "this kind of education in which they let the children do as they please."

This is actually the oldest of all forms of education. It is also the most common form since it is the educational way of the home, the street, the farm, and the shop. It can be misunderstood and mismanaged. Yet those who use it wisely are working in a long line of competent thinkers and practitioners. Furthermore, recent carefully conducted researches prove its worth.

The approach has been named "developmental" because development is its watchword. It is a way for the constant growth of the learner and the continuous development of the social order. In more respects than one, it is "the continuous reconstruction of experience."

Re-creation of inheritances

Developmental approach was described above as emphasizing creative experience of living. Toward social inheritances it holds the sort of creative attitude expressed in this paragraph:

It is our obligation, as it was the obligation of our fathers in the Christian movement, to reinterpret Christian faith in terms of the living experience of our own day, to discover its wider and deeper implications, and to bring it into effectual relation with the issues of contemporary living. In doing so, we should constantly remind ourselves that there are depths of meaning in the Christian gospel that far outrun our limited capacities to apprehend them. Nor should we seek to bind our own conceptions of Christian faith upon the future. Rather, we should, by the understanding and appreciation of the great historic symbols, seek to use them without being bound by them and to free those who will come after us to explore the depths and the heights of Christian truth which belongs to the centuries and which cannot be fully stated within the limited framework of any given historic period.[1]

Original personal results

Developmental approach holds the same attitude with respect to the pupil himself. For one thing, it has no fully preconceived notion as to his present behavior or future status, although it does have standards and ideals for him. It wants his way to be illuminated by the clear light of the revelation that is in the life and teachings of Jesus Christ. Then it wants him to be himself at his best now and in succeeding days, growing stage by stage into the better that he can become. In doing so, his unique qualities are not to be thwarted but encouraged to the extent compatible with long-range good for himself and others. His results are to be creative, at least as he views them.

Dynamic motivation

Developmental approach waits as long as possible on dynamic motivation. Persons are dynamic; they have drives that thrust them out for satisfactions both egoistic and altruistic. Inner compulsion, the personal outreach of the activating force within, is to be the fundamental stimulus to pupil effort. To be sure, this principle dare not be allowed to end in anarchy. Children can become bored or frightened by too much freedom. Coercion is certainly needed in emergency and in actual or anticipated danger. Yet the ideal is

[1] *Christian Education Today* (Chicago: The International Council of Religious Education, 1940), p. 12.

independent decision in the place of obedience; inner control instead of outward compulsion; self-imposed discipline. While the leader need not and dare not abdicate, he is primarily a helper instead of an authority, one who counsels and encourages instead of dictating. The matter was well understood by an intermediate who was pleading, "Why don't they let you do what you're interested in? Then you'd do the work yourself and they'd just need to help you. That's it, why don't they just help you instead of always telling you?"

Pupil purpose and self-directed procedure

Of necessity, then, developmental approach has high regard for the pupil's own goals. It wants him to judge where his own well-being lies and it allows his sense of need, interest, and desire to determine his work as fully as possible. Obviously the leader has a significant responsibility at this point. Since the pupil has not seen and cannot evaluate with complete wisdom all the values that he might serve, the leader will help him see and give proper weighting to all that may be pertinent to a disciple of Jesus Christ.

Developmental approach also encourages the pupil to devise his own ways of working. This is not an individualistic task by any means. There will be much discussion in the group as it arrives democratically at the formation of policies, the teacher being a member of the group. Within the proper limits of that social setting, the pupil is allowed to have his say in planning, controlling, executing his program. Then, in completing his own particular share of the total task, he is expected to add his personal touch.

The pupil does not need to recapitulate the whole history of racial trial and error. He may utilize every resource of racial accumulation—that crystallization of past experience called knowledge not being excluded. His own experience through which alone he can truly learn can be enlarged and interpreted by reliving to a degree the experience of others. Yet the pupil uses the achievements of the past not merely to memorize, copy, or imitate them. He chooses from among them in a way which is creative experience in itself; then he adds his original contribution.

The pupil is to have, throughout, whatever measure of guidance is needed. However, the school is a learning laboratory in which leaders arrange situations so that pupils may have the most fruitful, creative experience. It is essentially a place for living—living at its best in a social center, a library, and a workshop. The teachers handle certain mechanical elements of the whole process. They guide the program to, and keep it on, its principal track. They make resources available. Meanwhile, they seek progressively to render themselves as unnecessary as reasonably possible. Thus the pupil is permitted to make a creative quest, although a guided one.

Social emphasis

Such an emphasis on the pupils' own activity might easily be misinterpreted or misconducted as an antisocial or unsocial enterprise. Actually, though, developmental approach emphasizes social integration. The community's needs and desires are always to be reckoned with. There is to be constant use of group procedure in arriving at the truth. The democratic way of planning and attaining personal self-realization is to be stressed. Items in school management are to be carried by the pupil to the full extent of his enlarging ability. Social experiences are to be viewed as being particularly fertile for learning just as social graces and services are given high priority among objectives.

If it be said that all this overestimates the nature of man, Christian education has its characteristic reply. Our confidence in man's worth may have been shaken just as the greatness of God has been re-affirmed. Yet, when we rise from our reading of the Gospels, how can we accept a theology of pessimism and engage in a program of despair?

Summarizing, the developmental approach puts the pupil truly in the midst creatively. Relying as it does upon his activity at each step, it is essentially guided self-education. Self-control, self-reliance, and individual initiative while sharing and progressively exercising social responsibility are essential bases. It is meant to advance enkindled life, foster awakened intellect, and increase productive capacity while accomplishing spiritual re-formation and social reform toward increasingly abundant life.

Developmental Approach: As Life's Experience

The fact that developmental approach deals with experience in living remains to be considered. The pupil is to live now, intensively, in his educational experience which is to be as far as possible a segment of his real life. The school curriculum is ideally a series of actual experiences. This is akin to the primitive way of learning to do by doing, which is also the modern way in most out-of-school activities. It is the child's way of learning to skate; the older person's way of mastering his work. We have always said that experience is the best teacher. Now we are seeking to realize that proverb in the school.

As a program of experience in actual living, developmental education deals with the living needs of pupils—their inquiries, crises, concerns, and decisions. It helps them meet those situations intelligently with adequate adjustments and effective adaptations. Thus, the teacher can feel the real material of his craft as pulsating and growing life. The pupil, too, can feel that he is living life at its keenest on the very growing edge of history. The whole result is experience that is vital, concrete, practical, energetic, and productive.

This point of view has been described very simply, yet adequately, by Dr. Franklin Bobbitt. He writes:

> The *purpose* of education is to bring each human being to live, as nearly as practicable, in every thing that he does in a way that is best for him. The *method* of education is for each individual to carry on all his activities all the time, as far as possible, in the way that is best for one of his nature, age, and situation. In the education of any person, the good life is both the objective and the process. The basic educational responsibility of the child or youth is to live the good life to the best of his ability; that of his parents and teachers, to help him do so. The educative process is what the child or youth does in living a good life. The teaching process is what parents and teachers do in getting him to live it. . . . To live rightly each day is the best possible way to learn how to live rightly each succeeding day.[2]

---

[2] Franklin Bobbitt, *The Curriculum of Modern Education* (New York: McGraw-Hill, 1941), p. 5.

Summary

The two approaches, traditional and developmental, are summarized and contrasted below. This book proceeds from the point of view that a choice for one or the other is necessary. A leader who examines the diagram will surely conclude that he cannot stand first for the one and then the other. And it is unlikely that anything essentially new will be discovered in the no-man's-land between the two.

Christian educators must come to see clearly, whereas at present there is a tremendous amount of befuddlement. Then they must choose positively, decide firmly, and proceed fearlessly according to their choice. In terms of the diagram, either extreme is to be avoided. Yet leaders must take their orientation toward either the right or the left of center as regards philosophy and procedure. If the orientation is to the right, doubtless many modifications in procedure can be made which recognize some factors of developmental approach. Similarly, if the orientation is to the left, it would be folly not to use some of the features which may typically characterize the transmissive approach. When we want to arrive at a nothwesterly point we sometimes use some of the roads that lead to the northeast. In sailing we have a maneuver known as tacking with the wind. Yet there is never any doubt as to our general bearing.

Use of Developmental Approach

Developmental approach demonstrated long ago that it is a practical and fruitful way of accomplishing the educational task when it is properly viewed and employed. Yet it is not an easy way and it must be used with caution and judgment. It has suffered much not only at the hands of its opponents but also of friends who have not understood it or misused it.

Knowledge

A mistaken attempt at developmental approach may result in too little knowledge and too late. Under any type of education the presentation of knowledge must await some sense of need on the part of the pupil. Yet the leader cannot always wait until the

DIAGRAM I
CONTRASTING EMPHASES OF
MAJOR EDUCATIONAL APPROACHES

On the left: developmental—progressive and creative—constant growth of dynamic personality within developing group life.

On the right: traditional—essentialist and transmissive—preservation, appropriation, application of the heritages.

left of center

	Developmental	*Traditional*	
E	person-centered	content-centered	E
	creative learning	transmissive learning	X
X	teaching as guidance	teaching as telling	
	democracy	authoritarianism	T
T	importance of the how	importance of the what	
	inner control	outer compulsion	R
R	personal insight	thinking others' thoughts	E
	freedom	restraint	
E	social outlook	individualistic interest	M
	stress on present	stress on past	E
M	dynamic personality	static personality	
	activity	passivity	
E	curriculum as life	curriculum as text	C
	inquiry, investigation	acquisition, accumulation	O
	current living	preparation for life	
	transformation	conformity	N
	flexible readiness	encyclopedic mastery	
R	socialized contribution	individualized recitation	S
	inventive production	imitative reproduction	E
A	free convictions and ideals	indoctrination	
	making decisions	accepting decisions	R
D	learning by doing	learning by memorizing	
	flexibility of program	rigidity of program	V
I	dealing with actuality	dealing with symbol	
	psychological order of experience	logical order of presentation	A
	discipline by absorption in task	discipline by rule	T
C	spirit	docility	
	discussion, research, social action	lecture, drill, textbook	I
A	rounded experience	knowledge (and training)	
	knowledge, belief result of action	knowledge, belief produce action	V
L	self-development	passing examinations	E
	education of life	education of the schools	

Note: It is to be understood that the above pairs of educational concepts are contrasting *emphases,* not mutually exclusive sets of principles and procedures. In actual practice there will be and ought to be some interchange of component factors representing the two approaches. Yet a conscious orientation in one direction or the other, avoiding extremes, is essential.

knowledge is needed in the final way. The study of "first aid" provides an excellent example. In such matters, the teacher must kindle the imagination of the pupil to a sense of future need.

Again, the reaction against certain more typical transmissive procedures may swing too far. There is some place for them in developmental approach. Lecture and memorization are not the most favored procedures and will be used only in relation to pupil need, yet they will be employed when they are the most efficient means for a desired result.

Purpose and technique

When developmental approach is misunderstood and wrongly employed, the true goals of education may get lost in the process. There is danger of dallying with superficial or trivial experience just because it appears creative without due consideration for the educational results in terms of standards and values. The doing for learning must be something vital toward an important objective.

Further, it should be done in the best possible way. Yet creative methods are often imitated without full understanding or adequate practice. For example, the discussion techniques by which groups are supposed to arrive at co-operative results in their common inquiries are frequently handled in a way that is simply going through motions. Effective creative discussion presupposes study, observation, and knowledge as a starting point, whereas typical discussion groups are fumbling in a fog of unpreparedness. This is a technique to be used when the problem is clearly defined, adequate preparation has been made, and conclusions are sought in the most reasonably direct manner by persons who know how.

Control

Likely the chief criticism against this type of education arises from error in its use at the point of control. The approach is right in emphasizing intrinsic motivation. The discipline of creative and responsible living is infinitely to be preferred over the imposed discipline of the rod. Yet that does not require complete abandonment of control. Children, even older learners, may be immature, undisciplined, and inexperienced. They cannot possibly see their highest good fully and dare not be humored in their caprice or rebellion. There comes a time when leaders must exercise foresight, direction, and veto. Nothing in the approach, when properly understood, prevents such action. We have a dilemma because, while progress is impossible unless the individual is free, freedom can be misused so as to destroy the conditions which make it possible. Nevertheless we must make the venture of freedom as far as possible because totalitarian control also will lead to ruin. Observing checks and balances, we proceed with caution. This is not a procedure for irresponsibles!

Immediacy

This type of education may be mishandled by clinging too closely to direct experience of immediate worth. Pupils need not be kept always on the lower levels of immediate experience only. They can advance to the place of striving after long-deferred values. They can, too, arrive at the ability to do abstract and symbolic thinking. The procedure can properly intellectualize the educational experience progressively as it proceeds to higher levels.

There are other points at which extreme use of the developmental approach may be wasteful. It may cater too fully to individual experience. It may fail to reverence the past sufficiently, too readily neglecting or rejecting the racial inheritances. It may underrate the importance of discipline and too much accentuate nonconformity. It may not sufficiently appreciate stability in the social order. It may neglect the tragical element. It may become too earth-bound and forget the factor of beyondness in complete experience. All these, however, are only possibilities and not necessities.

Activity Definition

In the light of all that has gone before, another definition of education will be attempted. It aims to comprehend all the proper content of the subject, even the two approaches described above. In due time a statement more descriptive of the developmental approach will be made.

In general, education is the process of accomplishing some change in someone's system of activities. Change may involve (a) the development of a new activity; (b) the elimination of an old activity; (c) the intensification of an old activity; or (d) the diminution of an old activity. *More formally, education is a planned process in which a leader fosters change in a learner's activities to the end of an enlarging abundance of life.* From the learner's point of view, education is a planned learning process through which he achieves such a change in his activities as will result in more abundant living. From the leader's point of view, education is a teaching process in which he assists the learner with his learning process. To teach is to help folks learn (meaning change).

WHAT IS CHRISTIAN EDUCATION?

All this leads to an answer for the question, What is religious education? and ultimately, What is Christian education?

Typical Definitions

Again, there have been many definitions of which several follow:

The aim of religious education becomes this; growth of the young toward and into mature and efficient devotion to the democracy of God, and happy self-realization therein.—George A. Coe

A guided experience in which the meaning of God in Christ is discovered by growing persons.—W. Fallaw

The objective of religious education is the development of Christian personality through guided practice in Christian living.—L. C. Palmer

Our task, then, as Christian educators, is to help our children face the facts of the world of today and master the technique of living on the Christian level.—E. L. Shaver

To minister to growth in Christ is the role of Christian education.—L. J. Sherrill

Christian education is the process by which persons are confronted with and controlled by the Gospel.—P. H. Vieth

The task of Christian education is the task of the Christian religion to bring about the development of Christian persons and a Christian society.—*The International Curriculum Guide: Book Six*

An Activity Definition

In the light of the foregoing definitions of religion and education, it may be said that religious education is the application of the learning-teaching process to those activities which emerge in the God-relationship. *Religious education, then, is that planned process in which learners, assisted by leaders: (a) perform the highest religious activities possible; (b) therewith acquire the corresponding desirable ways of acting; (c) thereby attain a progressively higher measure of abundant living within the relationship to God.*

All this should be concluded by saying that religious education is Christian where God is known in and through Jesus Christ. *Briefly, Christian education is the guided activity by which persons live and grow in the Christian faith-life.*

Performance as technique

For its results modern Christian education looks to the truth of the old slogan, "We learn by doing." It views any form of education as a co-operative learning-teaching process, the fundamental factor in learning being the performance of activities. The pupils learn to believe by believing, to trust by trusting, to serve by serving. It is the teacher's task to assist toward that believing, trusting, and serving.

Christian religious education sees the educational activity of ultimate value to be this: discipleship (including apostlehood) with Jesus, in all that is finest in love to God, self, and others. In that statement, aim, content and method are described in one sentence. Further, they are there unified and integrated as they exist in life and ought to exist in school.

Current living the substance

Modern Christian education deals more largely in current experience. It no longer views itself as altogether or even chiefly a process of preparation for life either here or hereafter. It would have the pupils strive not after deferred values mainly but after immediate ones.

It recognizes that the present moment has its own present values and that personality thrives primarily upon such values. It seeks first, therefore, that pupils shall live richly and successfully day by day and hour by hour having the highest possible self-realization.

Yet this does not declare that no thought whatever is given to the pupil's future. Although the immediate emphasis is placed upon the vertical section of the pupil's moving experience, there is a prime interest in the longitudinal section of his life. Indeed, while Christian education may be busied about the former, it is deeply concerned about the latter, just as the parent who is busy daily with the present needs of a child holds always in the background of his mind his hopes for that child and shapes the present with the future in view.

Christian education holds this attitude because, the present living of the learner being held high, the future tends to take care of itself. The pupil in his intense present experience of wholesome living fits his behavior into patterns which carry him on highly equipped into the future. Actually there is no other way to equip him. So the immediate aim and larger effort of Christian education is located in the pupil's present religious experience while thereby it prepares him for the future.

Abundant life as purpose

The particular goal of modern Christian education is in the abundant life of persons. Recognizing that they desire values having to do with the well-being of themselves and others, it seeks to help them attain those values.

It is not content, however, that persons shall deal with random or low values. Thus, while it permits some normal tendencies to find unhampered expression and requires that others must be curbed or at least redirected, it looks forward, not to maximum frustration but fullness of expression in a life busy with such choice activities as shall be satisfying in the long run and in the highest ways. The by-product of this abundance and the subjective standard of its measurement is happiness. The objective guide and stimulus to its realization are such verities as the Bible, the church, and the inner Spirit of Christ.

Ultimacy of Jesus Christ

Throughout current Christian education the ultimacy of Jesus Christ is recognized. Jesus Christ as God and Saviour is the source and object of the Christian religion. He is recognized as Redeemer and Master. It is he who saves in every sense of the word. Also he is the author of Christian ethical ideals, his precept and example setting the Christian's personality patterns. Thus, the person and work of Jesus Christ constitute the sufficient norms and motives for the outlook and procedure of Christian education. Its fundamental purpose could well be stated in terms of discipleship with him. Its basic subject matter centers in his life and teachings. Its methods are governed by his ways. His indwelling Spirit provides the dynamic. His truth is *the* truth; his way is *the* way; his life is *the* life.

Christian Education and Developmental Approach

Enough has been said to suggest very clearly that the current theory of Christian education is in the spirit of developmental approach. As to the fitness of that approach for such a high purpose, Dr. Bower writes in *Religious Education in the Modern Church:*

> It is little less than astonishing to discover how closely the technique of Jesus anticipated the best theory and practice of modern education. His placing of the supreme emphasis upon the personality, his insistence upon the central position of the growing person in the educative process, his basing his teaching upon the concrete and present experience of the learner, his insistence upon the issue of knowledge in the practical conduct of life, his organization of the school as an informal society of persons sharing a common experience, his basic assumption that we learn by doing, his admission of his disciples to responsible participation in his own work— these are almost precisely the focal points around which modern educational technique is in process of being reconstructed.[3]

[3] W. C. Bower, *Religious Education in the Modern Church* (St. Louis: The Bethany Press, 1929), p. 6.

Chapter III

UNDERTAKING THE TASK

The Sunday Church School has now been viewed in its historical perspective and present relationships, and the theory of Christian education currently shaping its practice has been examined. With that background, there can be more direct answers to the major question for study: What must a pastor, director of Christian education, deaconess, parish worker, or superintendent of a school do, and how can he do it most effectively?

ORGANIZING, ADMINISTERING, AND SUPERVISING

A leader of a Sunday Church School is serving in a threefold capacity. He is organizer, administrator, and supervisor. In organizing, he sets up in orderly fashion and maintains the human machinery of staff and pupils with which the school works. In administering, he keeps the machinery operating efficiently. In supervising, he seeks to improve the processes so that the product of the machinery will be constantly better.

In all organizational, administrative, and supervisory activities, the leader is busy now with one, and then with another, of these ten ways of working:

COUNSELING: he advises workers, pupils, and committees, making suggestions about the solution of their problems.

DELEGATING: he seeks always to extend opportunities for service to others, using his own time and energy for things which others cannot do.

EXECUTING: he does willingly and efficiently the tasks which are his personal duties, and he is ready to do any other needed thing.

HELPING: his whole attitude as a Christian leader is that of the helper—helping boys, girls, men, and women personally through his school.

INSPIRING: he strives toward meeting that perennial need of people to keep loyal and hopeful in their daily living and spiritual effort.

LEADING: he is a leader—in the true sense—going ahead fearlessly as the first to undertake every task for Christian growth through the work of the school.

OBSERVING: he has eyes to see what his own and other workers and pupils are doing, and uses those observations to improve his procedures.

PLANNING: he plans his own work and helps others plan, with long- and short-term policies, for the best realization of the school's purposes.

PROMOTING: he handles the whole enterprise with which he is entrusted so that it grows and expands in effective ministry.

SOCIALIZING: he works to achieve that happy situation found in a school that is unified, co-operative, and loyal to the last member.

PRACTICING CORRECT GENERAL PRINCIPLES

Just as there are principles of good government and of good business, there are principles by which the Sunday Church School leader can organize, administer, and supervise more effectively. Here are six of them.

PURPOSE
GOAL
OBJECTIVE

1. Recognize the Purpose of Organization

Any group of persons can be "organized to death." When too much time and attention go into maintenance of the organization itself; when simple processes are delayed by red tape; when the organization becomes an end in itself instead of a means to a purpose—then organization defeats its purpose and ceases to be useful.

Nevertheless organization is necessary. It is essential to the group action which affords opportunities which cannot be made available by individual effort. It provides the means for pooling resources and using them, distributing labor, arranging for leaders and followers, definitely fixing responsibilities. It masses effort at the necessary times and places and renders a united front possible. It makes for continuity. It gets the right people together in the right way to do the right things.

Then group action, made possible by organization, provides for larger experience and greater service. In Christian education any of the major aspects of the curriculum—study-and-instruction, worship, fellowship or service—demands a group setting for its full operation. People learn together. In all the leadership educational work of the church, furthermore, skilled leadership can be secured, materials and equipment provided, and enterprises undertaken on a group basis which would be impossible for individual members.

As a second reason for organization, there is educational value, —Christian educational value—in organizational experience itself, particularly when the organization makes democratic participation possible. Organization provides for people to fit into a program; to respond to expectations; to carry out responsibilities in and for the group. All those are of high value in the development of Christian personality living abundantly.

These, then, are the two purposes of organization: to render group action more effective in educational results; and to provide in the organization itself an educational medium. Both are to be recognized by the Sunday Church School leader and constantly kept in view because of the great danger that an organization will be stressed for its own sake.

2. Keep the Goal in Sight

A leader is a man or woman who is taking people somewhere. A Sunday Church School leader is taking people somewhere with respect to Christian eduational matters. Such a leader deals with people—especially pupils and their teachers and officers. That requires that he stress personal rather than organizational ends. His concern is for pupils who mean more to him than books, rules, departments, or buildings. He is concerned with workers, too, whose Christian development is more important to him than the mere promotion of his most cherished organizational plan.

A Sunday Church School leader is also a schoolman. His business with persons is educational in character. He seeks first to help the people in his school achieve desirable change in their lives. He does not work merely to perpetuate an institution or to maintain a program. His business is not to build an organization for its own sake, and he was not sent into the world to raise money. He may work at those tasks incidentally but his central mission is the Christian education of the persons under his care.

3. Guide the School by Its Objectives

The purpose just mentioned determines the leader's means, methods, and measurements.

Means

Imagine the church council of St. Paul's Church discussing the building of a gymnasium. Says Mr. A: "Basketball teams would arouse some enthusiasm around here." And Mr. B: "Our boys are going to the _____ Sunday School because they can play on its teams." Mr. C chimes in with the remark that basketball is a good thing, and Mr. D settles the argument by offering to donate $10,000.

Should they build a gymnasium at St. Paul's? Maybe.

Imagine the Sunday School teachers and officers association in session. Somebody proposes the organization of a Girl Scout troop. The girls want it. Some of them already have joined a group in a neighboring church. There's Mrs. E who could be the leader.

Shall St. Paul's have Girl Scouts? Maybe.

Neither of those things should be done unless the gymnasium and the Girl Scout troop would contribute toward the ultimate goals of the church. Objectives should determine means.

Methods

One objective in every Sunday Church School, certainly, is the development of pupils in more effective church membership. But what is meant by effective church membership? Is the ideal member a staid, reasonably loyal, contributing attendant at most of the services of the church? Or, is he a thoughtful and creative student of church affairs, intelligent as well as devoted in worship, and aggressively active in all the enterprises of the church? It requires but little imagination to conceive how the type of materials used and the procedures employed should differ according to the purpose. Objectives properly determine methods.

Measurements

Finally, the measures of effectiveness will vary according to the objectives. What are the more commonly accepted measures of

Sunday Church School success? Judging by the outstanding evidences they are quantitative ones, expressed by numbers—enrollment, attendance, offering. Probably not many Sunday Church School staffs sit down quietly at the end of the year to report the spiritual progress of their pupils. Mary has grown this way, John that way. Spiritual temperature in the school has risen appreciably. The Holy Spirit has been at work, with results in Christian growth. A sound vision of such real objectives should determine the measures of effectiveness.

4. Embody Essential Virtues

In his organizational, administrative, and supervisory work, the Sunday Church School leader will stress such factors as *adaptability, comprehensiveness, democracy, flexibility, simplicity,* and *practicability.*

Every Sunday Church School is necessarily custom-made to fit an individual situation. There are general patterns, to be sure. Yet an effective program must be adapted to the nature and needs of members of a particular group. While a program must take into account the ways in which learning takes place generally, it demands finally a creative adaptation to local concerns. The leader has a general background of understanding plus a knowledge of the school as it is and a vision of what it could be. Then little by little, here and there, directly and through others, he leads it toward that ideal.

In his organization and program the leader will aim to comprehend all types of persons and deal with all essential types of desirable religious activity because the Sunday Church School is the only religious educational agency with which some members will ever have contact. Yet it is not enough that the varied experiences of all age groups shall be dealt with so that there can be Christian growth for all. The program should provide for an integrated experience, not one which is split into segments. Well-rounded Christian growth for all members of the church is the goal.

To have a school in which there is unanimity of favorable

opinion for all the leader's practices is a proper goal. Yet there are times when the leader must be sure he is right and go ahead doing right instead of trying to please all. Everywhere there are those who resist change. The ideal leader tries to overcome such resistance graciously but firmly, even as he expects to accomplish it slowly. Democracy remains his goal—the sharing of plans, purposes, and effort by all parties, not a centralization of authority.

Every leader finds some change in theory, methods, and materials to be desirable with the coming of new situations, new pupils, new assistants. He will preserve maximum flexibility in order to meet those new situations. Also, he will provide maximum freedom for his workers and pupils to exercise individual differences. He will hold rules as guides only, not to be exercised beyond their reason for being. The ideal is flexibility versus fixity on one hand and chaos on the other.

The Sunday Church School leader seeking the largest returns for the least expenditure has no use for purposeless bric-a-brac. He exercises economy in organization with regard to workers, meetings, and the time or energy of his assistants. He uses the most direct and efficient procedures. He does not mistake machinery for production, or mere activity for achievement.

The final test of every organization is its working success. The leader of a successful organization must find the source of his principles in practice and seek always to have a demonstrable reason for what he is doing. He has seen a thing done or has thought it through to its conclusion, until he feels sure it will work. Thus he has a practicable program.

5. Keep the School a Church School

According to Chapter I the Sunday Church School historically grew up outside the church, fostered as a lay movement by lay men and women. Many ecclesiastical leaders, indeed, were hostile in its earlier years. Gradually, however, it was received into the family, although in many places it is still a sort of orphan.

Yet, Chapter I described the Sunday Church School properly as the church at work performing its educational task. The leader is to manage it, therefore, as an integral part of the church's work and organization. It should be under the control of the church council or a committee it appoints. Its officers should be responsible to and report to them. It should have as one of its goals the instruction of members for the congregation. It should be in harmony with and contribute fully toward the entire church program. The pastor of the church is the pastor of the school also. In return, the school can expect that the entire church organization shall contribute to its welfare, recognizing its vital importance, making use of its functions, supporting it with finances, and regarding it with loyalty.

6. Employ Christian Educational Procedures

Every administrator has a major duty in keeping the spirit of his purpose in the details of his processes. For example, an important area is his dealing with his workers who, actually, are not only the assistants of the executive but also in some respects his pupils. Thus it is proper for the leader to proceed in all his dealings with the staff so that desirable religious results are achieved. He selects a candidate with consideration for the religious good of that individual. He enlists a worker by appealing to his religious motives. In training a worker he aims to develop that worker's spirituality as well as his techniques. In appointing, reassigning, or dismissing workers he will consider their highest spiritual welfare. The leader's supervisory dealings with workers' problems will be opportunities for spiritual as well as technical guidance. Committee work and public meetings will be used toward religious growth. Thus every informal or formal contact of leader and worker will advance Christian educational purposes.

TAKING HOLD TO IMPROVE

An earnest leader who reads the current literature on his work and observes outstanding schools will feel, inevitably, that his school needs to be improved at many points. There may be need for little more than a thorough renewal of spirit or the adoption of a clear and resounding emphasis. More likely there is gross need for definite change.

In many cases there will be obstacles. There may be undue conservatism in the congregation. Many people distrust the newer ways in Christian education (although other millions are waiting for leadership in that direction). Again, tradition lays a heavy hand on many an aspiring leader. "We always have done it this way, why change?" In some places the trouble is sheer inertia or even a generally obstructive attitude. In other situations expense may be a real handicap despite the fact that there is much which can be done without financial outlay. Elsewhere discouragement and lack of vision are potent forces. Finally, people so often do not understand and consequently oppose.

What is to be done?

Several of the one hundred leaders who wrote the letters mentioned in the preface were asked: "How would you advise a novice to take hold to improve a Sunday Church School?" Although the writers were thinking largely of a new pastor just coming into a congregation, their views apply widely. So, the replies are mingled in the eight suggestions which follow.

Proceed Slowly

One man wrote: "Do not be in too much hurry to change anything. Unless the situation requires immediate and radical treatment (and I believe such cases are quite rare) it may be that a few months, or a year, carrying on in the old way will injure no one." An older pastor, after a long and effective ministry in a parish, said: "It takes about ten years to make a really good Sunday School, and a lifetime to keep it that way."

Others pointed out the advantages of making haste slowly. It may avoid alienating older leaders. It gives time to study the situation as to the congregation's needs and resources. It provides opportunity to win needed confidence and co-operation. It allows plans to mature so there will be no need for later reversal of judgment.

In modification, not denial, of such statements, a school may be expecting its new leader to remedy some condition at once. There may be a situation which is crying for prompt attention. Then it is wise to proceed immediately. That will give the people some assurance that things are going to be better under the new leader.

Win Confidence

In all matters of improvement, it is necessary "to get everybody interested in making progress" and then to follow the leader. The winning of confidence is essential to that end. As one reply has it, "When the respect and confidence of officers and teachers are won, desired improvements may be effected gradually with their co-operation."

Various means of accomplishing this end are suggested in the following quotations: "Gain the confidence of your colleagues. Be friendly and appreciative of all the good things you see them doing." "Remember that the Sunday Church School has been functioning and doing lots of good. Be appreciative of all that has been done in the past." "The leader's job is to develop an *esprit de corps:* he should conduct himself so that others will catch his spirit and want to improve." "The novice should remember that he is a novice and institute changes tactfully—appreciating the work of all pastoral predecessors and local lay folk to whom he may seem not yet dry behind his ecclesiastical ears."

One fact those writers make particularly clear: it is important for the new leader to avoid voicing negative criticism of former leaders and of older equipment and procedures. There are those who liked them and may have labored valiantly for them. The purpose now is to harness the good will and effort which produced the present situation for co-operation in taking the next steps. Appreciation will serve best to accomplish that purpose.

Work Co-operatively

The leader who wishes to improve a school will need to "be democratic, not autocratic." This involves more than just consulting and securing the approval of those who are responsible. It means taking people along from first to last steps. In the preliminary study, if not earlier, the leader locates officers, teachers, and others who are "anxious for change and improvement." He works with those to the desired ends. Meanwhile, the group will be enlisting other supporters for the cause and all will continue to study and plan together. Always, plans that have arisen spontaneously from the group will have the best chance to succeed. As one writer puts it, "imposed change is not growth."

Study the Situation

This requirement was mentioned by every leader who wrote on the subject. The widely varied suggestions include these four principal ones:

Get acquainted with the school—its officers, teachers, departments, classes, pupils, as well as the equipment. Become thoroughly familiar with the program of the school including all the literature used in it.

Make use of interdenominational workers such as the county or city officers and secretaries; also such journals as *The International Journal of Religious Education*. Similarly, employ the denominational resources in secretaries and publications. "Visit," writes one pastor, "the finest church schools of your denomination and of others in the neighborhood. Pick up all the best points you find and endeavor to use them; see all the bad points and avoid them."

"Study some recommended books on religious education."

Make a survey using International or denominational "standards." Consider thoroughly the community and the constituency in general.

One pastor wrote this precaution: "Be as analytical as the situation requires, but guard against an overdose; watch out for the 'paralysis of analysis.' Better to make one or two improvements on the basis of your findings than to wait until you feel you know all about everything and then do nothing."

Select a Point of Attack

By the time the study of the situation has been finished, the main lines for improvement will be clear. The next step is to select the items which are to have first attention.

Probably there are very few schools which never have tried to increase enrollment and improve attendance. Likewise there are few which never have attempted to improve physical equipment. Those are fairly obvious points of attack and good ones with which to gain favor for advance.

Too seldom, however, do leaders go on to the more important tasks of providing better leadership education; reconstructing the organizational setup; improving the program of instruction and study; providing better services of worship; introducing a larger program of service; offering larger fellowship opportunities; or enlarging the whole program of educational work in the congregation. All those, too, are insistent demands.

Plan in Detail

Certain achievements are impossible except as a culmination of intermediate ones. There are points at which a beginning can be made. After success in the first enterprise, further ones can be completed and the whole goal reached by a succession of smaller steps. This procedure is summarized in the statement: "The most important thing is to know with certainty where we are taking our followers. The second is to have a process or procedure by which our goal will be accomplished. This requires a plan, probably a long-range one with intermediate steps."

There is a negative side to the technique of improvement: caring for the things which stand in the way. The leader must recognize those factors which are likely to impede the program and plan to circumvent or remove them. On the positive side, most improvements will be quite complex in their ramifications with various elements to be foreseen and provided for. Both those things necessitate step-by-step progress in which the leader may keep the over-all plan in abeyance while "first things" are done first.

For more far-reaching improvements, the steps of planning in general are listed in *Book Six*[1] as follows: (1) Work out a tentative plan and submit it to outstanding authorities in church school work. (2) Revise the plan with their suggestions in view. (3) Submit the plan to all groups in the church for study allowing enough time to avoid ill-considered rejection or adoption. (4) Revise the plan to meet all justifiable criticisms. (5) Submit the plan to the congregation or the official body which acts for the congregation.

Secure Support

A plan, once made, must be "sold" to everybody concerned. If there has been democratic procedure in developing the plan, this task is already half completed.

The way of approach in securing support, of course, will be educational. Among the methods of educating and enlisting a constituency toward improvement, a leadership education program is an outstanding means.

If the major Sunday Church School leader is not the pastor, he will make certain that he has the pastor's full co-operation. The pastor can help immensely as he goes about the parish. He, best of all, can bring pupils, parents, and local workers into the program. The leader can reach his constituency favorably, too, through the regular sessions of the school and appropriate special services. He may reinforce his point of view by bringing in a visiting speaker. The proper use of Christian Education Week or its equivalent can have important bearing upon school improvement.

Because of such obstacles as those mentioned earlier, a leader who wants to advance must expect opposition. Of course, if he is on the right track, support will appear even from unexpected quarters. If there are others who cannot and will not go along with him, he will try to disarm them. A favored way is "to show them how the higher interests of themselves, their friends, and their church are in the leader's intentions."

[1] *Book Six: The Organization and Administration of Christian Education in the Local Church* (Chicago: The International Council of Religious Education, 1935), p. 34.

As a culminating step in accomplishing improvements it is ideal to have the people go ahead, so eager about the improvement that they, themselves, take it up and carry it through.

Complete the Enterprise

This is the "proof of the pudding," and the point at which the dish is sometimes spoiled. Careful planning should alleviate many of the common difficulties in finishing. If an improvement is well planned, it should be capable of completion. Closely related is this idea: "Be careful not to tackle too much at one time. It is better to do a thorough job and gain the support of the constituency for further improvement." Sometimes a plan will involve many steps. Then it will be necessary to "work out a time schedule by which the various improvements are to be attained."

A leader should not grow weary in well-doing. Some leaders are constituted so that it is more fun to plan change than see change through to its conclusion. A still more difficult thing is to plod in the prosaic task of employing changed conditions continuously for the effective result which has been planned.

MEETING PERSONAL STANDARDS

As an undergirding for all steps toward improvement, several writers voiced a sentiment which one of them expressed as follows: "Keep your big purpose before you—making the Gospel effective in the lives of those who comprise your constituency. Never forget people; never forget the goals you are seeking in persons." And, it may be added, personal results are strongly affected by personal influence. Thus the first requisite of any Christian leader's work—total work—is to be himself at his best.

There are two principal standards of personal fitness to be met by the Sunday Church School leader. One is educational, the other religious.

The leader of a Sunday Church School is essentially an educator. He ought to possess a profound conviction that the educational method is a possible and desirable means to more abundant Christian living; and he must be growing in his knowledge of its theory and his skill at its techniques. Similarly, he is a Christian. Thus he ought to hold a deep conviction about the superior worth of the Christian way of living and be achieving for himself a balanced and constantly growing Christian experience.

There is but one way to enter effectively into such convictions. "For me to live is Christ," said Paul. That is a majestic motto for the leader in Sunday Church School work with respect to this personal standard—at once the first and last essential in undertaking the task.

Chapter IV

PROVIDING OBJECTIVES

What results are Sunday Church School leaders aiming to accomplish? What ends shall they strive to attain with the schools they organize, administer, and supervise? There are no more important questions than those. Providing for the whole school to understand and serve proper objectives is a major activity.

Education uses many different terms to express the concept of objective—aim, purpose, outcome, goal, results. A combination of all would give some such description as the following: *an objective is an educational aim or purpose, consciously understood and accepted by persons or groups as a desired outcome of endeavor, a goal to be reached, a result to be achieved.*

THE NEED FOR OBJECTIVES

What is the present situation in Christian education with regard to objectives? For example, do workers and pupils understand clearly the purposes of Christian education suggested in the definitions of Chapter II? Observation discloses widespread indefiniteness. Beyond glittering generalities, right enough in their way, the great body of workers and pupils have been "going through the motions" without much consciousness of purpose.

When twelve superintendents in a conference were asked to state the objectives of their work, only one made even a halting effort to respond. In the case of most teachers, someone asked them to take a class and they began to carry on the work in the traditional manner, the way "they" did it. Not seeing the angel in the marble, they just started chiseling away. Unquestionably, too, pupils have been even more vague in their impressions about the purpose for their attendance.

As a result, student reports on objectives in the Sunday Church Schools they observe often include statements like the following:

"They just teach 'the lesson,' that's all."

"An ample statement of purpose should be before all the people, but isn't."

"The program obviously was determined by lack of objectives."

"As I spoke to the pastor about objectives, he generalized."

"Aims are not kept before the teachers or pupils regularly."

Under such conditions, desirable results are achieved largely by chance or an overruling Providence, except where someone who established the tradition had a wise conception of the task. Its aimlessness has been a major weakness of the Sunday Church School.

THE FUNCTIONS OF OBJECTIVES

Knowing the end for which we are doing a thing is one of the most vital phases of doing it. Objectives have five essential contributions to make in the educational process.

"Where there is no vision the people perish," said an ancient sage. Objectives put the essential *vision and foresight* into the process of Christian education for both pupils and leaders. A Sunday Church School where there is no planning is in danger of becoming a sort of merry-go-round. And behind all planning must stand the objectives which supply necessary foresight for the planner. Education is the nurturing of desirable growth, and definite results cannot be expected without a clear vision of the direction which growth is to take. Piles of bricks and lumber and a crowd of workmen mean nothing until there are specifications for the building.

Objectives provide the *standards* for the various components of a school's operations. First, there must be anticipated outcomes for all organizational, administrative, and supervisory procedures. The leader can build his organization carefully and administer it wisely only in relation to the objectives which stand like a plumb line alongside his efforts. His supervisory function must be guided in the same way. He scarcely can devise, direct, or improve the proc-

CO-OPERATION
ECONOMY
INDUSTRY
STANDARDS
VISION

esses until he knows what he is to produce. We cannot use a canning factory to build automobiles or revamp our manufacturing technique unless we know whether we are to build passenger cars or trucks.

Second, the teacher who instructs, the leader of worship, or any person who constructs programs for pupils—from denominational editor to pupil in the school—is similarly dependent upon objectives as standards. Objectives determine the choice of materials and the sequence of their use for a single session of a group or the whole span of a pupil's experience. They govern the pupil's selection of a unit of curricular activity as well as his procedures as he moves forward in completing it. The final evaluation of the work, too, will depend upon objectives as the standards of measurement.

Objectives help to avoid waste and error and make *economy* possible. As a student once put it, they keep you from "working around all day in a bushel." They save the time and energy of pupil and leader who may otherwise be expending effort fruitlessly. More than that, purposeless and aimless working may produce the harmful result of disintegrated personality instead of a unifying wholeness of experience. Some parents have been known to question whether their children are profiting from Sunday Church School attendance. A few have withdrawn their boys and girls because they found certain experiences in the school detrimental. This betrays more clearly than anything else the lack of properly functioning objectives.

Objectives aid the work attitude, provide motivation for the educational enterprise, and so result in *industry*. Consider the man or woman who gets up in the morning, knowing what he is going to do and why. He goes about it with zest. For the athlete, the explorer, the scientist, the true worker in any realm, purpose releases power. That earnest vitality in Sunday Church School work, for which so many have prayed, may await simply the widespread apprehension of the real and important purposes which the work can serve.

A final value of objectives is the *co-operation* they make possible. Two horses, each going his merry way in the pasture, do not get the plowing done. It is when they are hitched to a plow with a furrow to turn that work is accomplished. Likewise, twenty Sunday Church School people each going through some motions will not accomplish anything spectacular. Their separate results may even cancel out each other or worse. Only when they work together at definite objectives with uniformity of aim and unity of purpose can they serve the cause best.

TYPES OF OBJECTIVES

The objectives of Christian education are of many types, take various forms, and represent widely divergent points of view. Some objectives are stated in terms of the *leader;* others in terms of the *learner.* There are *ultimate* objectives dealing with the final issues of the educational process and *proximate* objectives which refer to the intermediary steps to be taken as the pupil moves toward his final attainment. There are *comprehensive* objectives attempting to gather up and express in a single sentence the total result of the entire educational purpose. There are also *specific* objectives which result when the whole complex is described in a more detailed fashion. Lists of specialized objectives may deal with half a dozen or half a thousand aspects of Christian experience.

The most vital variation among objectives in Christian education concerns *organizational* versus *personal* considerations. Objectives of the former type look to some achievement with regard to programs, techniques, finances, or pupil management. Those of the latter type designate some change which is to take place in persons as the result of the educational process.

Organizational objectives

A "Sunday School Standard" formerly promoted by one denomination was largely in terms of organizational objectives. It included the following goals for the school:

1. Open the entire year.
2. Denominational literature used in all departments.
3. Regular teachers' and business meetings.

4. Enrolled teacher training class.
5. The Bible used in all departments above the Primary.
6. The school graded in organization and instruction from the Cradle Roll to the Home Department.
7. Catechetical instruction.
8. An average attendance for the year of 60 per cent of the enrollment, with emphasis on regular church attendance.
9. Regular missionary instruction and offerings for benevolence.
10. Observance of principal festivals of the Church Year.

The following congregational statement of objectives was similarly pointed toward organizational goals: "Nine goals were adopted by the congregation, at the annual business meeting, to focus the efforts of individuals and organizations for the year: (1) stimulating inactive members to helpful participation in the program of the church, (2) winning the unchurched of the community to church membership, (3) giving generously to the building fund, (4) continuing a special ministry to those in military service, (5) forming the new unified program for women and putting into effect certain other features of the church program, (6) organizing Scout troops for boys, (7) increasing enrollment and attendance in the Sunday School, (8) purchasing varoius projectors for use in visual education work, and (9) continuing generous support of benevolent objects."

Personal objectives

While organizational objectives are important and necessary in every school, it is to be understood that they are not ultimate but only proximate goals. The more fundamental objectives are those which consider the outcomes of education basically in terms of persons. Historically, these personal objectives have varied in emphasis from age to age. The several periods of major emphasis overlap, of course, yet they stand out clearly in their more extreme expression. At certain times and in certain quarters the emphasis has been *ecclesiastical*—the purpose of preparing the pupil for complete membership in the church. Again it has been *evangelistic* with the salvation of souls in view, especially their conversion and preparation for the future life. During the nineteenth century and in many schools yet, a primary emphasis has been the *subject matter* aim of pupils well-informed in Bible, creed, and catechism. Still more recently *Christian character* and *social efficiency* have been frequently mentioned. The present-day emphasis is usually in such terms as the concept of *abundant living* developed here.

DETERMINATION OF OBJECTIVES

What shall the objectives of Christian education be? The forces of modern research have been let loose upon their scientific determination. In that effort, research workers have held in view certain factors which should determine the character of them.

Determiners

The church, its nature and work, provides one group of factors in the selection of objectives. Since Christian education is carried on by the church, its purposes should be in total harmony with the historic and present life of the church in its highest expression of the faith. Therein the prominent place of the Bible and the "ultimacy of Jesus Christ" are to be fully recognized.

Society at large is another determiner of objectives. The pupil in Christian education lives in a social setting with a history and a continuity which influences him and which, as a Christian, he will seek to improve. Objectives must recognize that twofold relation of the pupil to society.

The nature of Christian education is a determiner. Only those objectives need be included which are a proper concern of education and they will be those which have to do with spiritual growth. They will also hold in view the various conditions of a Church School staff, equipment, materials, and procedures.

Church School agencies, however, are not alone in the field of education. There is the public school, too, which carries the major share of the American educational load. Christian education does not need to duplicate that work but does need to complement and supplement it.

The home also is a determiner of Christian educational objectives. A pupil lives in a home which will have religious influence

upon him in one way or another. He has responsibilities toward
that home, too. These factors must be recognized as his Christian
educational objectives are established.

Finally, the chief determiner is the learner himself. Objectives
should be selected primarily in the light of his needs, capacities,
interests, and abilities.

General Objectives for Christian Education

Under such general requirements, many statements of the objectives of Christian education have been developed in recent years.
They represent varying educational views and approaches. They
were arrived at by various methods.

A. The most extended contribution to the study of objectives
netted a great body of reports of life situations in which people have
problems with which Christian Education ought to help them. The
work was done under the direction of Dr. W. C. Bower and is reported in a series of papers published by the University of Chicago
Press.[1]

B. A study of vocabulary resulted in a series of "traits" which
should be exemplified in the "finished product" of Christian education.[2]

C. The most frequently quoted and widely used statement of
general objectives was prepared by Dr. Paul Vieth, using consensus
as his major technique. It is promulgated by the International
Council of Religious Education as follows:[3]

1. To make God a reality in human experience; to give individuals a
sense of personal relationship to him.

---

[1] For example, "Behavior Situations of Senior High School Young People."

[2] They include: (1) Co-operation; (2) Courage; (3) Creativeness; (4)
Dependability; (5) Faith; (6) Forgiveness; (7) Good will; (8) Health-
mindedness; (9) Honesty; (10) Humility; (11) Joyousness; (12) Love; (13)
Loyalty; (14) Obedience; (15) Open-mindedness; (16) Penitence; (17) Pur-
ity; (18) Purposefulness; (19) Reverence; (20) Self-control; (21) Self-respect;
(22) Spirituality.
From *The International Curriculum Guide: Book One* (Chicago: The
International Council of Religious Education, 1932), p. 108.

[3] *Yearbook, 1948* (Chicago: International Council of Religious Education)
p. 52.

2. To develop an understanding and appreciation of the personality, life, and teachings of Jesus.

3. To foster Christlike character through progressive and continuous development.

4. To make the fatherhood of God and the brotherhood of man the motivation underlying the social order.

5. To develop in growing persons the disposition and the ability to participate in the organized society of Christians—the Church.

6. To develop in growing persons an appreciation of the meaning and importance of the Christian family, and the ability and disposition to participate in and contribute constructively to the life of this primary social group.

7. To lead all into recognizing God's purpose and plan in life and in the universe, and into appreciating each person's essential part in God's plan.

8. To help man assimilate the best religious experience of the race, pre-eminently that recorded in the Bible, as the guide to present experience.

D. A further research by the International Council of Religious Education formulated a statement of the eleven areas of experience in which the above objectives are to function. Still another step was taken when the relationships sustained by an individual in each of the eleven areas were described.[4]

E. Dr. E. J. Chave[5] of the Divinity School, the University of Chicago, lists ten categories of basic experiences in Christian Education which can be viewed as objectives.

1. Sense of worth
2. Social sensitivity
3. Appreciation of the universe
4. Discrimination in values

---

[4] Both are represented in this outline of "Areas of Human Experience":

I. Specifically Religious	III. Educational
1. Personal relations	IV. Economic
2. Family relations	V. Vocational
3. School relations	VI. Citizenship
4. Church relations	VII. Recreational
5. Other community relations	VIII. Sex, Parenthood, Family Life
6. National relations	IX. General Life in the Group
7. International relations	X. Friendship
II. Health	XI. Aesthetic

(Also from *The International Curriculum Guide: Book One.* P. 97.)

[5] Ernest J. Chave, *A Functional Approach to Religious Education.* (Chicago: The University of Chicago Press, 1947), p. 22.

5. Responsibility and accountability
6. Co-operative fellowship
7. Quest for truth and realization of values
8. Integration of experience into a growing philosophy of life
9. Appreciation of historical continuity
10. Participation in group celebrations

F. A statement which is in accord with the philosophy of education presented in this book grew out of still another body of study, research, and practice in classification.

It is stated in a way which recognizes (1) the learning by doing process in which the objective becomes at the same time the process, and (2) the nature of Christian education as continuous development toward what are expansible or "flying" goals. It should be understood as a listing of component factors in a total Christian experience which finds abundant life in the integrated system of activities they comprise. The list follows with major words arranged alphabetically:

1. Using the *Bible* fruitfully
2. Practicing effective *church* membership
3. Giving supreme loyalty to *God*
4. Maintaining discipleship with *Jesus*
5. Employing processes and products of *nature* beneficently
6. Co-operating in good will with *others*
7. Having personal acquaintance with *religion*
8. Attaining the highest realization of the *self*

It cannot be urged too strongly that the desired results of Christian education never can be stated with absolute exactness; religion is too complex for that. Neither can they be viewed in terms of a completely finished product. No person has ever envisioned, much less attained, full Christian stature. Besides, human personality, society, and the understanding of Christian living all are forever in the process of becoming. Every list of objectives must recognize that incompleteness and fluidity. Nevertheless, these general descriptions of the direction which growth should be taking can serve the purpose in an indispensable manner.

General Objectives for the School

Such statements of objectives as have been cited are in the most general terms only. Since, eventually, they must function in specific communities, churches, schools, and classes involving flesh and blood persons who are candidates for Christian education, the question becomes, What is to be the particular objective with this boy or girl, man or woman, in this situation, now? A beginning at that more immediate and personal adaptation can be made by providing a general statement of objectives for the local school. There are four steps to that process: *formulation, adoption, publication, dedication.*

The leader may arouse sentiment for the creation of such a document but, if possible, will let the demand for it arise from his fellow workers. When once they have begun to sense its desirability, he may lead them to some personal study of the matter and finally to the authorization of a committee which should include older pupils. This group may study the various available documents, adopt one in its entirety or with such revisions as may seem fitting, or draw up its own original statement.

Whatever the method used by the committee on statement of objectives, its findings should be reported back to the entire group of workers. They will consider it, amend it, and revise it if they deem such action advisable. It should then be adopted wholeheartedly by the school as its guiding purpose. The finished product might well be like C or F above.

Every worker in the school should have a copy of its statement of objectives. The copy should not be stored away in a memory book, either, but should be available for frequent reference. It should be at hand, for example, to guide the teacher when preparing a lesson, and the superintendent when planning a public service. Parents and older pupils of the school also should be in possession of copies of the objectives. Wall charts, mimeograph sheets, printed cards, and church bulletins are fruitful means of accomplishing this purpose.

A school with objectives not functioning is little better than a school without objectives. Such a school is fully dressed to go somewhere but it is not yet on the way. When every worker has been provided with his copy of the statement of objectives, it is necessary to secure his constant dedication to their realization. The dedication may begin with the signing of the constitution of the school which presumably will contain the statement, or it may be the signing of the "contract" of the school in a congregation where that procedure is followed. The objectives may and doubtless should be worked into the installation service for the workers. After that initial dedication, too, the leader must periodically by precept and example remind his workers of their purpose to which they have devoted themselves in order that such devotion may not languish.

This plan does not provide for action by a congregational committee on Christian education or a council of all the educational workers of a congregation. A complete study of objectives might be made by such groups. They should proceed upon the assumption that church and school objectives are identical. They should keep the denominational and local church objectives in view. Their work could result in a general statement of objectives for the entire area of educational work and specialized statements for each agency.

Many possible divisions of objectives among the various agencies have been proposed. One writer suggests for the weekday work, the biblical emphasis; for Sunday sessions, churchmanship; and for the vacation school, co-operative Christian living.[6] Doubtless, for a long time to come in most churches, the Sunday Church School will have to carry the basic or fundamental minimum of educational development while all other educational endeavor is viewed in terms of enrichment opportunity.

In succeeding chapters of this book a unified organization and program will be recommended. Churches which adopt that procedure will require general statements of objectives for the total program only. Specific objectives would pertain only to the individual curricular units in which the pupils engage.

---

[6] Frank Otis Erb, "A New Orientation for Religious Education," *The Colgate-Rochester Divinity School Bulletin*, October 1941.

Specific Objectives for the School

Returning to the more typical Sunday Church School situation, the school will need to have specific objectives selected in the light of its general and comprehensive statement. A particular community or church situation may arise to suggest a special objective of some sort: reducing juvenile delinquency in the community; providing a recreational program; resolving theological difficulties among the youth; introducing new forms and materials of worship; ameliorating economic dislocations; developing racial brotherhood. Congregations sometimes have annual meetings in which they outline their special objectives for the year and that suggests at least one annual meeting of educational workers to consider their special objectives for the year. Pupils, as far as possible, should have a determining voice.

At this point mention must be made again of organizational objectives. The Church School needs, first of all, clear-cut objectives in personal terms. It also needs to face the problem, what are to be the organizational goals by which we develop the setting in which our personal goals may be attained most effectively? Local communities, churches, groups, officers, teachers, and pupils will have to work at determining those objectives, too, in the light of the personal objectives of Christian education.

Specific Objectives for Units and Sessions

The vital need for general and for more specific objectives for the school as a whole has been made clear. Those objectives will have to be "broken down" for the various departments of the school. Still more important, perhaps, is the need of objectives for each curricular unit and for each session of the school.

Units are properly selected and planned in the light of problems, interests, or needs of the group. Objectives can readily be fashioned out of their personal and social situations. They can be determined in the planning sessions. They may be flexible and subject to change, yet they should be kept clearly in view by all members of the group as they proceed with the unit.

The issue finally stands or falls with the objectives of the individual sessions of the school. To say that pupils must always be lucidly conscious of their objectives as they engage, for example, in a service of worship would be absurd. Nevertheless, it is just as absurd to say that they need have no knowledge of the purpose of the service. As for leaders, every session pattern, whether written or prepared mentally, may well be headed with a statement of the aim for the day. Perhaps it is a worship service for which the statement may read, "My aim is to lead these worshipers in the kindling and expressing of their trust in God." Likewise, a teacher of a class may state, "My aim is to help my pupils emulate Joseph's forgiving spirit more fully."

The Pupils' Part in Determining Objectives

Throughout, it has been emphasized that objectives must ultimately be conceived in terms of helping pupils. They should be related to pupils' wants and needs as well as graded to their capacities. Furthermore, they should be planned as far as possible by the pupils themselves or the pupils in lively co-operation with the leaders. Those facts deserve reiteration. What a shock many a Sunday Church School leader would receive if he were to know how far away from his pupils' interests his program has drifted! Furthermore, pupil participation in determining objectives would not only keep the program vital, it would also enlist co-operation in achieving the objectives. The total effect might be educational effectiveness beyond anything yet attained.

An Intermediate was discussing his Sunday Church School experience with his father. "We're having lessons about Moses and the plagues again," he said complainingly. "I think Moses was a great leader of people, but we never go into that. I'd like to have some lessons on how to live. Instead we just study those things that never happen anymore anyhow. Why don't they let you study what you're interested in?"

There is a lad who is ready to sit in a planning session to determine objectives for a unit of study! The school might profit from having him sit with a committee on determination of objectives for the whole school. At least his point of view should move the teacher in the planning for each class session and the superintendent in arranging the services of worship.

CRITERIA OF OBJECTIVES

In selecting an objective, such criteria as those in the list below should be applied. While it would be impossible to secure a perfect score for many important objectives, the score should be high or the objective should be omitted.

Is it *attainable:* within the capacity of individual or group?

Is it *Christian:* in harmony with the Christian way of living?

Is it *correlated:* pertinent to past and present experience in home, school, community, and church?

Is it *fertile:* rich in leading on-and-out value?

Is it *forward looking:* does it anticipate future experience: is it constant in time?

Is it *graded:* difficult enough to challenge; easy enough for success?

Is it *important:* significant; related to larger aspects of life?

Is it *necessary:* not adequately provided for elsewhere?

Is it *practicable:* feasible under school conditions of time, equipment, and leadership?

Is it *progressive:* valuable in relation to changing civilization?

Is it *social:* of general interest?

Is it *spiritual:* having religious value?

Is it *timely:* related to situations in present living?

Is it *valuable:* productive of growth in relation to method as well as content?

Is it *vital:* considered worth while by students?

Clearly there is much yet to be done in this field of objectives. To equip one of the giant new aircraft with the latest engines of propulsion, load it with cargo and passengers, then send it out without charts or flying orders would offend all ordinary intelligence. So, in the Sunday Church School, it is not enough to be going at it blindly and leaving the place of arrival to chance. Objectives need to be located and defined for each group, leader, and pupil, determined repeatedly and kept constantly in view.

Chapter V

DEVELOPING THE EDUCATIONAL ORGANIZATION

This chapter is concerned with the Sunday Church School leader's efforts at building the human machinery of pupils and staff for the educational work of a congregation. The problems of such persons as the following are in view: a pastor who is setting up an educational program in a new congregation; a pastor, director, parish worker, deaconess, or superintendent revamping an organizational setup because it has outgrown its present form; any Sunday Church School leader who believes he can improve his school at this point.

STANDARDS

The standards for organization arise out of the purposes mentioned in Chapter III. We organize so that persons may have benefits which are otherwise impossible. First, organization is required for the group action by which we provide larger educational opportunities. Second, participation in organizational activity provides in itself learning opportunities which develop the type of Christian personality that can function effectively in a democratic society.

The present practice in most congregations can be described as a multiplicity of educational organizations which are operated from more or less remote control by the officers of the church and which exist as almost entirely separate agencies. As Hartshorne and Ehrhart point out,[1] many a Sunday Church School, organizationally speaking, is more separate from the related church than if it were a mission in another part of town. The chief thing which unites

[1] Hugh Hartshorne and Earle V. Ehrhart, *Church Schools of Today*, (New Haven: Yale University Press, 1933).

such churches and their various educational agencies is the fact that the same persons meet in the same building. Meanwhile, too, the separate agencies have no correlation with each other. The situation is represented in Diagram II which resembles a series of disjointed box cars. Imagine a public school enterprise which would have no more connection with local and state government than these educational units have with the congregation; and no more relationship between its units—grade schools, high schools, and colleges!

DIAGRAM II

EDUCATIONAL AGENCIES EXISTING AS SEPARATE UNITS

The Congregation	Sunday Church School	Women's Missionary Society	Young People's Society	Vacation Church School

Some measure of relationship to the congregation and correlation between the agencies has been attained in certain other churches. Even so, the situation is often as confused as Diagram III suggests.

DIAGRAM III

EDUCATIONAL AGENCIES PARTIALLY INTEGRATED
AND CORRELATED

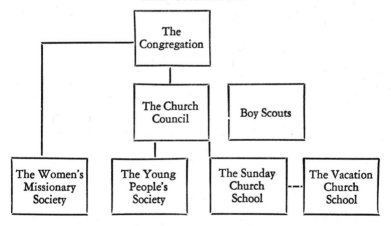

Does such organizational practice serve the purposes of organization as fully as possible? Hardly, especially when we bring into view these principles which apply to the entire organizational, administrative, and supervisory work of the leader according to Chapter III: embodying the essential virtues of adaptability, comprehensiveness, democracy, flexibility, practicability, and simplicity; and keeping the school a Church School.

Thus, in regard to the problem of developing a congregational unit, two clear-cut requirements arise:

Standard I: *The educational organization should be integral with the basic organization of the congregation, not separate from it.*

Standard II: *The educational work of the congregation should be unified in organization, not divided.*

INTEGRATING THE ORGANIZATION

The typical separateness of the church and school is the result of history on the one hand and theory on the other. Because the Sunday Church School arose as a lay movement outside the church proper, it is not yet everywhere fully adopted into the church. Further, the actual identity of church and school purposes has not always been recognized. Many have viewed the church as an evangelistic agency whose primary purpose is to save souls, while the purpose of the school is to build up souls in knowledge, character, and conduct. As some have seen it, the latter purpose is not nearly so important as the former. Thus the school is allowed to be a more or less detached appendage.

The truth is that since we are total personalities salvation and sanctification are not actually as separate in a Christian's experience as some would make them. Evangelism and education are correlative functions for there is educational evangelism and there is evangelistic education; they have been well likened to Siamese twins.

Thus the time has arrived for recognition of the inseparable relations of church and school in the common task of winning persons and developing them for Christian purposes and blessings. Let education be recognized as a function of the entire church program. Let the school be viewed as the congregation at work educating itself. Let the pastor be seen as the leader of an educational enterprise. Then, let there be organizational arrangements to achieve the already integrated purpose. What we seek is not some loose federation of services, schools, and clubs but a cell of the body of Christ.

In order to achieve that goal, the organization may well take the form represented in Diagram IV below or V on page 83. The latter represents a relatively complete and therefore a somewhat elaborate situation. Yet there can be all the simplification necessary for a small church without destroying the purpose of eliminating the separateness of educational organizations. An example follows.

DIAGRAM IV

FURTHER INTEGRATION AND CORRELATION OF
EDUCATIONAL AGENCIES

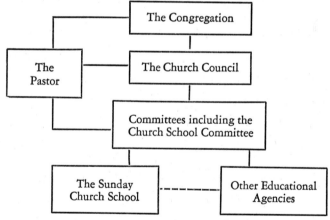

Overhead Administration

Diagram IV, and especially V to follow, show how the goal of educational organization integral with the basic organization of the congregation is to be realized through a properly devised and functioning overhead administration.

The church council

The overhead administration of the educational work of a congregation—that which is above the level of the immediate operation of the school—should begin with the official representative body. The constitution and by-laws for congregations in one major denomination lists among the duties of the church council: "To provide for and show interest in the Christian instruction of the young and all requiring it." That is a pitifully incomplete statement. Yet it does manage to suggest, if no more, that the church council is to assume intelligent general oversight of the Sunday Church School to the point of taking necessary steps to insure its maintenance at an efficient level. The church council will operate largely by delegating its powers to the pastor and others working under its direction. Beyond that, though, it ought to consider major policies or problems, hear reports at appropriate intervals, give attention to adequate financing, and make appointments or nominations of principal officers.

The pastor

What is the proper relationship of the pastor to the Sunday Church School? As duly constituted head of the parish, he should be viewed certainly as its head. This does not mean that he shall be general superintendent, although he may be. It should mean first that, as he is the pastor of the congregation, he is the pastor of the school in spiritually guiding and inspiring it.

In addition, he will at least help to shape its major policies, coordinate its activities with other agencies of the church, introduce ideas which come to his attention for its improvement, and seek to build an educational consciousness in the parish. In some situations he will serve the functions which might be described as the work of a director or supervisor. In the smaller and newer congregation he will do many of the actual tasks themselves—enlisting pupils, recruiting workers, choosing literature, teaching classes, being superintendent for a period, even tending the stove to heat the room. A more complete statement of the outstanding activities of the pastor follows. Clearly, the pastor is "it."

1. Recognizing the importance of "the teaching office" in his ministry; kindling enthusiasm for education throughout his church; promoting the Church School in every possible way.

2. Accepting responsibility as pastor of the school and chief educational worker in the congregation.

3. Studying and evaluating the local situation in the light of his training and experience and laying out plans for its work.

4. Initiating progress toward the plans devised, proceeding by educational means.

5. Keeping intimate contact with all phases of educational work; attending as many educational group sessions as feasible.

6. Establishing helpful personal relations with all members of the staff, with all pupils, and with all homes through pastoral visits and the like.

7. Assisting with the construction of the pupil program; helping workers to select and plan activities, particularly courses of study and special services.

8. Helping to establish new organizational and administrative forms when needed.

9. Teaching confirmation class and other classes when necessary; assisting in services of worship.

10. Helping to enlist pupils and workers.

11. Working at the preparation and improvement of the staff, teaching the leadership classes in many cases.

12. Acting as supervisor, helping to improve worship and instruction.

13. Assisting in unusual situations, such as disciplinary problems.

14. Looking constantly to the improvement of the physical conditions.

15. Advising with respect to budgetary matters.

16. Cultivating the fellowship of the school.

17. Being the chief counselor of the superintendents.

18. Acting as an integrating and unifying agent in the local church and promoting co-operative relationships with Christian educational work outside.

19. Serving as ex officio member of all committees; delegating tasks in all possible matters; stepping aside for other competent leaders.

20. Seeking continuous personal improvement in this area of study and helping all others to get a common understanding of the task.

The Church School Committee

Moving down the scale in the administrative setup, the next unit is variously called Church School Committee, Board of Religious Education, or Committee on Parish Education. This is a standing committee which should be provided for in every congregational constitution. Just why in the typical church there should be committees to look after the purchase of coal, maintain the property, care for the finances, and oversee the music, while there is none to supervise the large and vastly important educational work of the congregation, is quite past comprehension.

Such a committee affords many *advantages*. It recognizes that Christian education is a method for the total work of the church. It dignifies the work of Christian education advantageously in the minds of all concerned—council, parish, workers, parents, pupils. It provides a group outside routine duties to consider policies broadly. It gives workers the support of a responsible body authorizing their work and hearing reports upon it. It helps to secure more active co-operation and otherwise lends support to new ventures. It makes effective action easier because it is less personal for the pastor and the superintendent. It provides for continuity in policies beyond change of elective officers. It furnishes an agency through which the congregation can express itself in co-operative programs.

The committee's *functions* include: Giving general oversight to entire educational program of congregation. Promoting general understanding of educational work and creating educational consciousness in congregation. Laying out general objectives and policies. Studying whole pupil program and arranging for it to be carried out with maximum effectiveness. Determining desirable enterprises (new or old) and approving or initiating new enterprises. Helping provide administrative and teaching personnel and arranging for leadership education and supervisory attention. Looking after improvement of working conditions; endorsing provision of new equipment. Promoting financial support of the school; assisting in drafting and raising budget; considering major expenditures. Fostering use of standards, surveys, measurement. Giving special attention to relations with the home and providing for co-operation with agencies of community service. Handling relations between various educational agencies in congregation and working toward unification of educational program. Serving as the linkage between congregation, church council and school.

The following paragraphs will answer major questions about the *personnel* and *work* of a Church School Committee.

Who? Five to seven members representing the interests suggested below. (In many cases one individual will qualify in two or more ways.) The pastor, ex officio, as responsible educational head of congregation and the one best informed in general on Christian education and in particular concerning the parish and its needs. One or more from the church council as such. One from the missions or social service area. One parent. One or more with special knowledge of education through public school experience. One or more with administrative experience in Christian education. One or more teachers. A leadership education graduate. At least one pupil from the young people's division.

How? Elected by the congregation; appointed by the church council; or appointed by various educational agencies. Designated for three years, the various terms of office expiring at different times to avoid radical change of personnel and so allow carefully considered programs to be concluded.

What? The operation of the committee will include: organizing itself with chairman (not pastor), receiving delegated responsibility, meeting regularly, studying its work, hearing reports, making reports, keeping itself subject to congregational direction. It is essential that regularly established meeting times be observed and definite work undertaken and kept going. Such a group can quickly decline into uselessness unless it has vital work to do and meets regularly to do it.

Director of Christian Education

The executive officer of the Church School Committee is properly a director of Christian education, an officer for whom relatively few congregations have yet provided. Among the young people of the churches there are thousands with college, and many with graduate, degrees who would like an opportunity to serve some church in the capacity of educational director. Yet many church leaders have been able only to point out what a pity it is that these young men and women cannot be used for this ministry.

Here and there the situation has been met in a partial way. Two or more congregations support a worker co-operatively or a worker serves on a part-time or volunteer basis. Much commendation is due both congregations and workers who are meeting the issue as best they can. Yet the limited educational vision which permits this waste of needed, dedicated, and trained talent is no less a scandal. Likely, the need will never be fully met until we have and use a male educational ministry.

Such workers could be, next to the pastor, the official heads of the educational work in their congregations. They could organize all the teaching work save that of the pulpit. They could plan and supervise the entire curriculum of worship, instruction, service, and fellowship. They could enlist and train workers. They could be the confidential conferees of officers, teachers, and pupils. They could themselves carry out many of the educational enterprises of the church.

In order that the educational organization may be integrated with the total congregational organization it must work under some such overhead administration or modification of it. Even the smallest church can have its Church School Committee or, at the very least, operate in close contact with the church council serving as such a committee. Only by such means can the school be actually the congregation at work educating itself.

The School Itself

The ideal form of Christian education might consist in having the immature members of the Christian community living and working with the more mature; ready to help one another in real experiences, especially at times of crisis. Yet Christian education is usually conceived as taking place more or less exclusively in groups of pupils organized as schools.

Pupils

The typical groupings provide for classes, departments, and divisions. These are usually organized according to the ages of the pupils. There are certain names for the groups which ought to be used uniformly so that all workers can understand each other.

In a school of 500 pupils with appropriate equipment, the pupils might be grouped as follows:

Divisions	*Departments*[2]	*Ages*	*Classes*
Children's	Nursery[3]	1, 2, 3,	(as
	Kindergarten[4]	4, 5	
	Primary	6, 7, 8	
	Junior	9, 10, 11	
Young People's	Intermediate	12, 13, 14	*need-*
	Senior	15, 16, 17	
	Young People	18-24	
Adult[5]	Adult	from 25	*ed)*

A typical school of 100 pupils meeting in one room might be grouped in this manner:

Kindergarten Class	(ages through 5)	
Primary Class	6, 7, 8,	

---

[2] This book will not make further reference to the Home Department. That department typically cuts across all lines of age to serve the various types of person needing its ministry. In general, its work could be done best by the regular teachers and officers of the appropriate age groups working, possibly, under a special secretary or superintendent for this area. A separate department is not advised. In addition, as Chapter VI will show, there should be home relations for all departments.

[3] Whenever Nursery Department is mentioned, it includes Nursery or Cradle Roll. Ages 1, 2, 3 means birth through three. The Church Nursery, maintained to care for children while parents attend services is not being considered.

[4] Kindergarten is used because it would be manifestly out of order to call the members of this department "beginners" in a school where there is a Nursery Department.

[5] This includes work in Young Adult groups.

Junior Class	9, 10, 11
Intermediate Class	12, 13, 14
Senior Class	15, 16, 17
Young People's Class	18-24
Adult Class	from 25

Adaptations of the pupil groupings to local conditions should be made with the maximum of common sense. On principle, the program should be the ruling consideration. Other determining conditions are: numbers, building, available staff, and tradition. It will be advantageous, always, to keep the usual framework and terminology in mind and approximate it as fully as possible.

The International Council of Religious Education is studying and a number of congregations are experimenting with a 2-2-2 system of three departments for the elementary school age.

The staff

Many pastors and other leaders will enter situations where the staff has been established. They do not face any problems in this respect save when some reorganization must take place. By those who are starting a new school or reorganizing an old one, two general principles should be followed. The first principle is *adaptation*. As a major requirement the staff must be adapted to the achievement of the school's objectives. Beyond that, it must be adapted to such local conditions as size of the school, nature of the building facilities, leaders available in the congregation, and the traditions of the community. A second principle is *economy*. While the leader will plan to have an adequate staff, he will include no more members than necessary to do the work effectively.

The following outline suggests the possible staff members from which choice can be made according to those principles (no school will have all):

Essential Adult Staff (depending on size of school)
    General Officers: Superintendent; Assistant or Associate; Secretary; Treasurer
    Divisional Officers (usually as above)
    Departmental Officers (usually as above)

Music Leaders: Pianist; Orchestra Leader; General Director
Teachers (with associated workers)
Optional Adult Staff (depending on available leaders and program)
Supervisors: Divisional; Departmental; Activity (possibly recreation, service, missions, or drama)
Absentee Secretary
Enrollment Secretary
Librarians
Ushers
Staff Committees (in larger schools; their functions in small schools will be carried out by entire group excepting special committees)
Executive (for routine business)
Pupil Program
Membership
Leadership Enlistment and Education
Special
Pupil Officers (general, division, departmental, and class, depending on local conditions)

Relation to program

Only the organizational problem is under discussion here. Matters pertaining to program are to be considered later. However, a school's organization may be ever so fully integrated and yet fail to attain full integration with the congregation. When church and school have identity of purpose raised to full integration in program as well as in organization they have attained their goal. Such integration in program includes items such as winning members for each other, fostering attendance for each other, developing a mutual program of worship and promoting related study.

UNIFYING THE ORGANIZATION

For some time, educational leaders have been saying that there are too many educational agencies with all their officers, committees, and memberships. No one is to blame for the present situation; it just grew up like Topsy. Each agency arose because of a felt need. When, almost a century ago, it was seen that the Sunday School alone was not adequate to meet the educational needs in the church, leaders began to develop various allies for the cause. Each has made its contribution and is continuing to do so. Nevertheless, there is much overlapping of objectives, duplication of programs, over-stimulation of pupils and workers, neglect of certain areas and groups, fragmentariness and disunity of experience and, at times, conflicts in and rivalry for loyalty. Thus, the various agencies are getting in the way of one another administratively while their multiplicity hampers the effectiveness of their various programs.

Unified organizations have been effected (and unified programs are in operation) in certain centers. Many local experiments have been undertaken and some overhead combinations have taken place. All these are steps in the right direction and more of them will be undertaken. A chief deterrent is the normal resistance to change. There remains, too, a certain amount of organization for its own sake due to the personal loyalties which institutions command, due also to the outcomes of promotional drives and perhaps to the competitive spirit.

A Unified Church School

There is but one ideal way to accomplish unification although there are many possibilities of temporary expedients while working toward the ideal. The ideal way is the development of a Unified Church School.

In the various experiments in this direction no one pattern has yet been accepted as the customary type. An ideal form will be presented for consideration here with the understanding that local churches are only to keep the picture in mind as they develop something of the sort to fit their local needs. It is represented in Diagram V, page 83, which repeats the overhead administration previously discussed.

Pupils and staff

The pupil groups should be noticed first in Diagram V. It is proposed that there be only that one sequence of pupil groupings for the whole educational organization of the congregation, no more of any sort. Similarly, there is to be only one educational staff, the administrative and teaching leadership, organized into a Church School Council which operates under the overhead administration.

Diagram V

An Integrated and Unified Church School

The Congregation

The Church Council

The Pastor

The Church School Committee

The Director

The Church School Council
(General, Divisional, Departmental, Class Officers; Supervisors,
Teachers; Committees)

THE PUPILS				
(grouped to meet local situations such as size of school)				
Divisions	*Departments*	*Ages*	*Grades*	*Classes*
Children's	Nursery	1, 2, 3		
	Kindergarten	4, 5	Year 1, 2	
	Primary	6, 7, 8	I, II, III	*(as*
	Junior	9, 10, 11	IV, V, VI	
Young People's	Intermediate	12, 13, 14	VII, VIII, IX	
	Senior	15, 16, 17	X, XI, XII	*needed)*
	Young People	18-24		
Adult	Adult	from 25		

Relation to program

Although a unified organization is receiving primary consideration, it will be necessary to consider a unified program briefly in order to evaluate or perhaps even to understand the unified organ-

DIAGRAM VI

PROGRAM OF A UNIFIED CHURCH SCHOOL

Dept.	Sessions[6]			
	Sunday	*Weekday*	*Vacation*	*Home*
Nur.	Nursery	Clinic	As weekday	Program carried on by home fostered and supervised by Church School to include: Literature, Visitation Parent and Pupil Meetings and Enterprises
Kdg. Pri. Jun. Int.[7]	A.M. Church School session	Local Church School or community Weekday Church School sessions	Local Church School sessions or Community Vacation Church School sessions	
Sen. Y. P.	A.M. Church School session P.M. Church School session	Local Church School sessions: Business Enterprise Social Study	Camps Conferences	
Adult	A.M. as above	Church School sessions Study Groups Enterprise Groups Conferences Assemblies	As above	

----

[6] The integration of this program with that of the total congregation is discussed on page 86.

[7] A division in the Intermediate Department to provide for confirmation classes to attend the chief service is possible.

ization. It is presented in Diagram VI. There is to be but one educational program in the congregation. It may meet in Sunday morning sessions, Sunday evening sessions, weekday sessions, vacation sessions, and home sessions. Yet it would be but one program. To make the plan complete, the program should, like the organization, be integrated with the total congregational program. That would meet the ideal of the church as a school.

The basic idea of the Unified Church School, then, is to have one staff, one school, one set of pupils, with sessions enough to provide for all present activities and more if possible. The meeting of pupils in the same organized group at all times with the same staff of leaders is meant to center instead of dividing their loyalties. It permits them to complete larger units of study without any interference and with diversification. It should eliminate some of the present strain upon money, time, energy, and talent while producing results which cannot be achieved in the present way, despite the objection that we cannot find personnel who could give the time. The point is to avoid the enormous waste in our present overlapping agencies which consume time so voraciously by useless repetitions and duplications.

Steps toward Unification

Correlation

The first major step which many churches might take toward unification is to correlate their Sunday Church School work with that of other educational agencies. This correlation might be accomplished by the Church School Committee working with the various staff members of the several agencies, and by those staff members themselves co-operating in mutual planning. Still more effective correlation likely would result from the services of a director, a Church School Council, and a special committee or what some have called an educational cabinet consisting of leading representatives of these agencies.

The relationship between the Sunday Church School and the Weekday Church School of the same congregation may be taken as an example to show some points at which correlation is needful and possible. Shall the two schools have the same objective or different ones? If different ones, how shall they be distributed between the two? Shall they use similar or different materials and which school shall use each? Shall the same teachers work in both? If so, with the same pupils? Shall their enterprises be different, similar, related? What shall each foster?

Consideration of such matters makes still more clear the likelihood of confusion in a congregation where no correlation has been undertaken and highlights the need for a Unified Church School. But, if such a school is not possible, then the Sunday Church School which develops the basic experience must be given first place and all others be subordinated to it.

Mergers

In many situations a beginning at unification could be made by merging two or more organizations. For example, there was a city church which had a junior choir and a junior missionary society. Then the director of Christian education was asked to start a weekday school, and it was suggested that a junior young people's society would be a good thing. Instead of trying to work with four organizations, he developed a Weekday Church School which had missionary programs at least once a month, used forty-five minutes weekly for junior choir rehearsal and did additional weekday work to a total of two hours on Saturday mornings.

Relationship to common services

This chapter has been looking toward a double-double ideal. The first goal mentioned was an educational organization integrated with the total congregational organization and unified in itself. But, in the study of that goal another became apparent, namely, a program that is unified and also integrated with the total congregational program. It is possible now to take the last step in considering that total complex.

It concerns a possible relationship of the Sunday sessions of the Church School to the common services which would bring about the final unification of the whole congregational endeavor. While this is not the province of the Sunday Church School leader specifically, he might advantageously promote some such arrangement. The basic idea is a unified Sunday morning program in which the teaching-preaching activity would be combined in one two-hour program. For example, members of the congregation through the intermediate years would have a two-hour school session while their elders have one hour of school and one of common worship.

There are those who see some such unification of present teaching and preaching services as a crying need of the church. It would, indeed, bring about true unification and integration of the whole church enterprise. It would realize the ideal of the church's using education as one of the methods of pursuing its total task.

Additional problems would be solved. One example suggests many others. A few weeks ago a visiting pastor arrived at his preaching appointment ten minutes before the announced time of the service. The walk leading to the building was crowded with two streams of traffic, one "going to church," the other "going home from Sunday School." Speaking to one of the members of the church council, the pastor said, "Why doesn't the church plan a two-hour program for its people each Sunday morning; then train them to think of their Sunday morning attendance in those terms instead of attendance at one or the other of two services?" "I never thought of that," was the reply. The combined teaching and preaching service is discussed further in Chapter XX.

Not a few congregations have planned for a children's service to be conducted parallel with the main common service. Proponents of the idea believe that it is fruitful in educational value. It can be seen, however, to have the fault of prolonging the unfortunate idea of separation of church and school. In addition, it has often been guilty of seeking to initiate children into practices more suited to adults. Such an extended session of the Church School as that described in Chapter XX seems preferable.

The most extreme plan for accomplishing the unification of the congregational program has been employed by those who have adopted the Graded Church idea. Essentially it means that the congregation would meet of a Sunday morning in at least three divisions. Each division would have a two-hour program combining what is now done in the various separate services of the typical congregation. While the idea has many items of merit to be commended, great care will have to be exercised lest the idea of the unity of the congregation be lost.

Chapter VI

MAINTAINING RELATIONSHIPS

No small factor in making a Sunday Church School effective is the maintenance of mutually helpful relationships with the congregation as a whole and particularly with the other educational agencies of the congregation. Furthermore, there are denominational and interdenominational agencies working at the same task: community character-building institutions like the Young Men's and Young Women's Christian Associations and the Boy and Girl Scout movements; welfare organizations such as the American Red Cross; the exceedingly significant public school and other public agencies; and last but not least, the home. With each of those neighbors, the Sunday Church School leader will need to foster co-operative relationships so that all may accomplish their objectives in the most united and, therefore, most effective ways.

WITH THE CONGREGATION

Happy relationships between the Sunday Church School and its mother congregation do not exist everywhere. One pastor wrote a searching article in which he presented some complaints which have been lodged against the Sunday Church School as an institution. He quoted the charge that it is figuratively a wild branch drawing sap from the production of proper congregational fruit. He reported the observation that there is a widening gap between Sunday Church School and the church, with people increasingly giving their attendance and service to the former and not to the latter. He showed how some believe that the resulting division of loyalty hinders spiritual awareness, religious realization, worshipful emotion, doctrinal conviction, and moral purpose.

But the picture has another side. Certain Sunday Church School leaders deplore the church's lack of support for the school. Indeed, some churches depend upon the school financially while the school goes without equipment and supplies needed to make its program effective. Even the ugly word "jealousy" has been used to describe the attitude of the church toward the growth of the school and the enthusiasm it engenders. "Why," asks the Sunday Church School proponent with a thinly veiled meaning, "do the people come to the school and not remain for church? Is it our fault?"

To proceed so that the Sunday Church School is the congregation educating itself in one organizational form has been stated already as the proper relation between the two. Using a somewhat inappropriate but useful figure of speech, the Sunday Church School is not to be either a side show of the circus or the whole show, but one of the rings under the big tent. The previous chapter showed how to accomplish that purpose.

Congregation and school being not separate and distinct as to their purpose, but essentially identical, they ought then to proceed accordingly. Yet, whether the Sunday Church School exists alongside other congregational endeavors, correlates itself fully with them, or loses its identity in a Unified Church School it can somehow serve the ideal of reciprocal relations with the other elements of congregational life. At least the ideal for the entire complex can be: united as to ends and co-operative as to function, with the understanding that there will be a minimum of separateness and maximum of reciprocity.

A pastor testifies on this matter: "Successful congregations are developed not only by strong preaching and faithful pastoral service but also by good organization. . . . There can be successful organization only when there is a worthy program moving toward definite goals with recognized leadership and delegated responsibility. . . . The whole work of the church including services, school, prayer meeting, young people's groups, finances . . . should be brought under one program and administration to avoid overlapping, waste, and division. The program of religious education should extend to all of those branches so as to correlate them into harmony."

General Relations

There are many things which the church should do for the Sunday Church School in maintaining a reciprocal relationship. While, in general, it should provide for a unified educational organization and program fully identified with the congregational organization and program, one writer on the subject enumerates several necessary prerequisites to such an organization and program.[1] He says first, that the congregation must understand that its purpose is not to be ministered unto but to be a servant of all. Next, says the writer, the congregation must view itself as a group of children as well as adults, whereas most people envisage the adult portion only.

Another point is to think of the church as something besides a pulpit-centered institution. While, of course, the preaching of the Word is always to be exalted, that is but one means through which the purpose of the church is achieved. A final suggestion is that the church should understand its educational task, a goal which demands that both ministry and laity be educated with respect to the educational work of the church.

Church for school

Given a congregation with the prerequisites suggested, what shall it do for its Sunday Church School? Here are a few general suggestions in addition to the proposition that it should organize itself properly to carry on its educational work and set up a definite educational program:

Let the congregation hold itself responsible for the maintenance and effective operation of the school.

Let the congregation provide for the adequate financing and equipping of the program.

Let the congregation furnish a strong leadership.

Let the congregation provide for all the people, including the children, to share in all the church's work all the time.

---

[1] Henry F. Cope, *Organizing the Church School* (New York: George H. Doran Company, 1923).

Let the congregation exalt the educational work for what it truly is, a major enterprise of the church.

The whole requirement is met by the congregation that has educational interest, vision, goals, and sense of responsibility; all made effective in and through the school.

School for church

What of the Sunday Church School and its responsibility toward the church in maintaining a proper reciprocal relationship?

Let the school educate the members of the congregation, not only for "initiation" into the fellowship but also for increasingly effective service in it. A proper program will include units involving church history, work, doctrines, programs, and enterprises.

Let the school work at the development of a trained church leadership.

Let the school help the congregation recruit members. This recruiting may be among the pupils themselves or parents and other adult relatives. The school may properly have the motto "Every Church School Member a Church Member."

Let the school encourage attendance upon congregational services of worship. As stated above, there are laments that this is not now working. The basic solution of the problem lies not in the elimination of the Sunday Church School or in using various devices to exhort, encourage, or draft its members into church attendance, but in the merging of the school program with the other services of the church. Experiments with something like a two-hour "teaching-preaching" program for every member of the congregation every Sunday morning are bringing hopeful reports.

Let the school help the church with regard to finances. The ideal is a unitary budget for the entire congregation with all persons contributing to all expenses. Otherwise the church should make itself financially responsible for the educational program, with the school contributing to this as well as other expenses of the church. Certainly, also, through lessons on stewardship, the school should build the giving spirit and habits of the congregation.

Evangelism

It will be seen that the Sunday Church School's relationship with the congregation brings it into the field of evangelism. As the new movement in religious education developed, evangelism and education were unfortunately placed in opposition. That arose from the fact that certain leaders of the new movement conceived evangelism largely in terms of revivalism. Happily, the trend now is to recognize the validity of evangelistic education as well as educational evangelism.

Evangelism is sometimes broadly understood as confronting persons with the gospel and eliciting their daily response to it. From that viewpoint, education becomes the basic means or method of evangelism, or vice versa, to the point that the two are the same in essence. Thus the educational movement sees its general objective as being identical with evangelism broadly understood, namely, cultivating a saving relationship with Jesus Christ.

For many people, though, evangelism has a more narrow meaning. It refers to the efforts which the church and its workers make to secure personal confessions of Jesus Christ as God and Saviour and professions of commitment to discipleship with him. It is more or less identical with winning church members. Viewing evangelism in that more narrow way, the educational movement aims to bring its personnel into the beginnings of church membership, and promote their active continuance in it.

Similarly the evangelistic forces are recognizing education as a means of promoting their purpose. There is a definite trend away from professional revivalism in some of the churches which hitherto relied upon it. An increasing number are employing the equivalent of the confirmation class which other churches have long used. Interestingly, too, the last mentioned are beginning to make their confirmation classes a part of the regular Church School program, for example, the seventh and eighth grades of a Weekday Church School.

Other Christian Educational Agencies

A Sunday Church School, as so often observed, is not the sole educational agency in the congregational field. Instead, a typical congregation has a half dozen, a condition which is producing unfortunate results. Thus, while the Sunday Church School leader will rejoice at every manifestation of interest in education and foster an ever-expanding program of educational opportunity for the constituency, he will not favor the multiplication of educational agencies. If a new agency is proposed he will be ready with certain questions. Do we need a new organization for that? Can we not serve that objective within our present framework? He will be ready, too, for mergers of other agencies outside of the Sunday Church School, or absorption within it of any agencies whose work his school can do as well or better by some modification of its program. These would be steps toward the Unified Church School which is the ideal goal.

Throughout, he will recognize that his is the largest and most influential of all educational agencies and will see that it keeps its proper place in the sun. The program of the Sunday Church School is, of necessity, the educational program of the church. As it rises or falls, so does the parish. This is in accord with that finding of the Madras World Missionary Conference of December, 1938: "The Sunday School has had a primary place in the development of religious education. It is still central in that task."

WITH THE HOME

Recent sociological studies have shown that the home is the most important agent of all in character development. If the Sunday Church School's work is to be effective, it must be conducted in lively co-operation with the home. Indeed, this matter is so important that one Christian educator has said he would like to be the pastor of the first congregation which would give the home a central place in its whole work. Another has published a most significant book in which the major chapter is entitled "Unifying Home and Church." [2]

A "Home-centered" Viewpoint

It is possible that there should be careful study to determine whether the church or the home has the primary responsibility for seeing that the children are religiously educated. Perhaps the home should be made the primary agency of Christian education while

---

[2] Wesner Fallaw, *The Modern Parent and the Teaching Church* (New York: The Macmillan Company, 1946).

the Sunday Church School serves only a complementary and supplementary function.

If we were to take the home-centered view of Christian education, we would begin turning our congregational effort less exclusively to the development of a Sunday Church School program. Instead, we would have our church first foster the home program of Christian education through the provision of literature, home visitation, parent conferences, and the like. Then we would use the Sunday Church School in its supplementary capacity to provide larger social experiences of Christianity, and in a complementary way to reinforce the teaching of the home. It would enrich and underscore the all-week-long Christian development which is taking place in the family circle of younger and older fellow learners in Christ.

Interrelated Effort

Whatever the conclusion on that matter, there can be no doubt of need for a joint attack upon mutual problems. There follow, therefore, ten suggestions about things which the home can do for the school and the school can do for the home as partners in a common task. Underlying them is the assumption that the leaders of the school view themselves as servants of the home, while the parents look to these leaders for valued assistance.

1. Let the home send (better, bring) the pupil regularly, on time, with the right attitude, and properly prepared. Preparation will demand that the home provide time, place, equipment, and example. It can include general and specific preparation. General preparation involves conversation and reading about the church, its work, and all it stands for. Specific preparation will vary with the curricular program of a particular school or department. While there is a trend away from home study of the older type, even new type approaches provide for homework of one kind or another in the form of special assignments or enterprises in advance of the class session or after it. One author suggests that the time should come when there are three curricular manuals—one for teacher, one for pupil, and one for parents. Indeed, beginnings have been made.

2. Let the home strive to understand the school's needs, procedures, and purposes thoroughly enough to respond as intelligently as in the case of public school matters.

3. Let the heads of the home visit the school, get acquainted with the

workers and work, and consult the leaders about the progress of their members.

4. Let the home plan to carry on with the work of the school. Daily prayer and Bible reading with regular habits of helping and giving, for example, can be cultivated only with such assistance. There is, too, the whole realm of Christian character and conduct, and especially service to be fostered by the home. The Christian life needs to be under guidance in the home, too.

5. Let the home express itself in the councils of the school to a degree that will keep the workers informed of its needs, problems, and desires.

6. Let the school leaders recognize the paramount importance of the home and adjust the school work to that recognition. Units on the home, discussions about conduct in the home, literature for the home, and planning for family worship, are suggestions.

7. Let the leaders visit the home to get acquainted with the pupils, build a co-operative attitude, know the home conditions, and relate the program to it. The teachers in one children's division, it is reported, are visiting each home every two months.

8. Let the leaders report to the home regularly concerning the typical items of attendance and the like; also, concerning the progress of the pupils.

9. Let the leaders inform the home concerning their objectives and plans. This matter can be cared for in parent conferences and letters. Further, the school can plan to welcome the parents at the school frequently. Special programs of special days, promotion services, and exhibits are profitable opportunities. A parent-leader meeting at the beginning of each unit is recommended regularly by one denomination.

10. Let the school provide for parents to study, in and through the school, the home religious training of their children. Such enterprises as providing letters and literature, classes, conferences, forums, reading circles, parent-child relationship and guidance meetings or courses are indicated. Mutual celebration of National Family Week is a possible opening wedge to a larger program of this type.

WITH THE PUBLIC SCHOOL

No Sunday Church School leader can afford to overlook the place which the public school holds in the life of the typical young American, and the esteem with which his parents regard it. There are boundless latent resources in the relationship which might be maintained between the Sunday Church School and the public school.

While we are committed in the United States of America to a separation of church and state with regard to the organization of the two types of schools, we could profit immensely by recognizing that they are mutual in their basic purposes. The public schools, like the church schools, are working toward more abundant living on the part of their pupils. The former emphasize abundant living in the more material realm, the latter in the spiritual. There should be many points where the two could co-operate.

The task of religiously educating the great populace in America will never be accomplished completely of course, until one of two things has been done. One possibility is to work out a complete system of church schools paralleling and co-operating with the public schools, extending from cradle to grave and reaching all the people of the country for an adequate amount of time each week. Another possibility, very much in the limelight at present, is to teach religion once more, directly or indirectly, in public schools. Promising beginnings have been made along both lines, although the recent Supreme Court decision has forced a re-examination of the whole approach. In any case, however, we have only scratched the surface of a mere corner of the field. Perhaps we should regard our experience as only experimental. The final issue awaits great educational and ecclesiastical statesmen to lead movements.

Meanwhile, the Sunday Church School leader may do what he can in his own situation. He can lead his pupils toward the practice of Christian principles in the public schools. He can aim to co-operate with the public school in certain items of the extra-curricular activities which are carried on. He can relate his program to the progress of the pupil in the public school, for example, in history. It will be well, too, for Sunday Church School workers to attend some of the programs of the public schools and see the children at work there.

It is particularly useful for the Sunday teacher to know the weekday teacher. Sometimes these two can solve a problem mutually. There was, for example, a primary boy who required at least one departmental worker to look after him each Sunday morning in order that he might not disrupt the entire department. The problem was solved when the primary superintendent got acquainted with his weekday teacher. She disclosed to the superintendent some characteristics of the boy which she had discovered and told her some of the plans which she had used in controlling him. The result was a boy saved for the Sunday Church School.

If civilization is a race between education and catastrophe, and we are to win the race, a chief point of effort will be the maintenance of right relationships between religious and general education, between the Church School and the public school.

WITH DENOMINATIONAL AGENCIES

Every Sunday Church School leader should be thoroughly acquainted with the denominational program of his church and make full use of it. He should have some knowledge of the nature and extent of its total educational enterprise. He needs particularly to know its administrative, secretarial, and editorial personnel and the services of its national headquarters. He should, generally speaking, use its lesson books and hymnals, read its magazines, consult its secretaries, and send his workers to its camps and conventions. He should also give appropriate support to its synodical, conference, and local programs of promotion and training and employ them intelligently.

It can be an eye-opening, even a heart-warming, experience to learn what one's denomination is doing for Christian education. One denomination operates through two overhead educational boards, one dealing with higher education and the other with the work of the local congregation. The former directs and supports the program of many seminaries, colleges, and training schools. The latter fosters Sunday, Weekday, and Vacation Church Schools, special children's work and young people's work, and leadership education. It has an executive secretary, associate secretaries who work in distinctive areas, traveling secretaries, editors, and writers. It produces great quantities of literature of many kinds for use by pupils and makes every effort to help leaders improve themselves, their equipment, and their programs. In that effort, it not only fosters a fully rounded and comprehensive leadership education program but also publishes a monthly periodical for local church workers. Throughout, its services are designed for local Church School leaders who solicit them.

WITH INTERDENOMINATIONAL AGENCIES

Co-operation has characterized the Sunday Church School movement from the beginning and, increasingly, the local leaders of the country are co-operating with interdenominational agencies of Christian education. That is proper for at least three reasons. For one thing, this co-operation is contributing to the breakdown of sectarianism. When the history of the ecumenical development in this era has been written, co-operative work in Christian education will be adjudged a major factor in bringing about whatever measure of unified action is ultimately attained. In many areas of educational activity there has long been neither race nor clan. Sunday Church School workers and pupils have long worshiped, studied, served, and fellowshiped without consciousness of denominational barriers.

Second, every Sunday Church School worker is profoundly indebted to co-operative endeavor. Such items as uniform lessons, the gradation of pupils, and the leadership education curriculum are interdenominational fruitage. The best things we have in principles and methods have been freely shared by those who, of whatever denomination, discovered and developed them. The major leaders in every denomination have been trained in the same schools. through the same writings, and in fraternal study with persons of many denominations. Now they work together in co-operative publication of lesson helps, journals, and books; promotion of weekday and vacation schools; as well as sharing of interdenominational editors, secretaries, and directors.

Third, Sunday Church School workers can profit from and help through interdenominational relationships. All the agencies are devoted to the improvement of the results attained by their constituents. They seek to elevate standards, foster better management and teaching, provide better materials, disseminate information, assist with problems; in short, to be practically helpful at every possible point.

At present, the International Council of Religious Education with its various state, county, and district units is the outstanding interdenominational agency in the field. More than forty denominations, representing nearly twenty-five million Protestants in the United States and Canada, have joined efforts to realize their objectives more fully through that organization. It is entirely a voluntary co-operation with no policies binding upon the constituent denominations. Each is free to use or discard the products of the co-operative effort. Yet its contribution to the whole cause has been and continues to be a well-nigh indispensable one. It is expected that the council will become an educational division of the National Council of the Churches of Christ in the U. S. A.

The significance of the council's work will become clear through the enumeration of a few of its departments: educational administration and research, children's work, adult work and family education, vacation religious education, weekday religious education, lesson studies, leadership education and church school administration, *International Journal of Religious Education,* radio and visual education. From that group of departments, the Sunday Church School leader can find some help for almost any problem in any area of his work. Mention could be made also of the United Christian Youth Movement and a similar adult enterprise. Also, it is not to be forgotten that the International Council is sponsoring the Revised Standard Version of the Bible.

There is, too, a World Council of Christian Education. It was once the World's Sunday School Association which federated the co-operative Sunday School movements of some fifty nations from the Argentine through the alphabet to Uruguay. Its recovery after the disruption of World War II was marked by a world convention in Toronto, 1950.

The American Sunday School Union is the oldest interdenominational educational agency in the United States. It can be dated from 1817 and in addition to an extensive publication program, operates in the support of some one hundred and fifty missionaries. Those workers establish and conduct Sunday and Vacation Church Schools and summer camps in areas removed from the beaten path of evangelical endeavor with the understanding that the schools they establish will grow into congregations with a denominational affiliation. The Union cherishes its chartered purpose: "to organize and maintain Sunday Schools, and to publish and circulate moral and religious literature."

A Religious Education Association which was founded in 1903 holds national and regional conferences and publishes a journal, *Religious Education*. It fosters more particularly the theoretical studies of religious education and operates more broadly on an interfaith level.

The Federal Council of Churches of Christ in America with its state and municipal branches serves educational interests, too. Its various executive secretaries and, in some cities, its full-time educational secretaries have been particularly active in promoting Weekday and Vacation Church Schools. Its educational commissions have done research along practical lines and its various conventions have featured educational reports, addresses, panels, and discussion groups.

The World Council of Churches now embracing more than one hundred church bodies in more than thirty countries will have increasingly important educational relationships. A recent bulletin mentions some of its activities as follows: relief action on behalf of the war-stricken churches, upholding the Christian standard of conduct toward friend and foe, organizing interchurch aid looking toward rehabilitation of church life, co-ordinating services for refugees and displaced persons, enlisting youth in the Christian world community, building a world fellowship in Christ of men of good will, giving Protestant Christendom a united voice and a center of united action.

To round out the picture of co-operative educational effort, the work of the various overhead missionary councils is noteworthy. More locally, too, community young people's councils are accomplishing commendable results and local ministerial associations often provide active leadership in educational affairs. Recently also, as newcomers in the field of co-operative endeavor we have the Protestant Film Commission and the Protestant Radio Commission.

WITH OTHER COMMUNITY AGENCIES

There are useful community agencies not specifically denominational or interdenominational in character. Indeed, some of them are not specifically religious in their purpose. Yet the Sunday Church School leader can co-operate with them advantageously at certain points.

There are, for example, the Young Men's and the Young Women's Christian Associations, Boy Scouts, Girl Scouts, and various playground associations. In those movements the leader will discover men and women with ideals much like his own. They, too, are seeking to achieve a better Christian life for the people of the community. It is often possible to work out certain mutual problems and common objectives in helpful co-operation with them.

The welfare agencies of the community, too, are not unrelated to the interests of Sunday Church School leaders. The school will co-operate with proper relief organizations and institutions. The Red Cross and the W.C.T.U., likewise, deserve appropriate consideration. More recently the child-guidance clinic and social-group and case-work developments have provided new areas for co-operation. The list might be extended to include governmental agencies like the departments of agriculture and labor, as well as United Nations.

Local libraries and moving picture theaters are powerful forces for weal or woe in the community. Many communities have found ways of raising the tone of the movie offerings. Means of guiding and training people in the choice of the movies they attend are available everywhere. Almost any librarian will co-operate in purchasing and featuring religious books and magazines. Sunday Church School leaders should give some attention to these matters.

Finally, radio stations are important community agencies. Congregations do well to guide their people in selecting the best programs. Many, too, can provide programs which make the local station a truly Christian educational agency. Closely related, the local newspapers deserve much more consideration than they receive. They can do more harm than the church can readily overcome by even herculean efforts. On the other hand, many papers are responsive to intelligent use of their columns for religious advancement in the community. At least the older members of a school should study the Christian's duty in this regard and have an opportunity to discover Christian standards of evaluating newsprint and ways to use it for the church.

Throughout the whole range of its educational program the church needs to recognize that it has community responsibility near and far. The community does not exist merely to provide the setting for a church and it is not merely to be used as a learning laboratory for the members of the school. It is, also, a place of need for Christian social action.

Chapter VII

ADMINISTERING THE STAFF

Some years ago, in a book entitled *How To Teach Religion,* Dr. George H. Betts used this dedication: "To those who have in their keeping the religious destiny of America—the two million teachers in our Church Schools." The author was rightly paying his respects to Sunday Church School workers because of their strategic importance from the social point of view. And they are equally significant for the school itself. Every leader knows that his school rises or falls with the type of workers he can enlist and the quality of work they do. A wholehearted, intelligent, and skilled leadership with vision is the paramount need throughout the program of Christian education.

ALLOTTING DUTIES

The Sunday Church School leader who is charged with the major organizational, administrative, and supervisory functions will be responsible for distributing the tasks of the school among the several types of workers. What duties fall usually to each?

General and Associate Superintendents

In most congregations, the chief educational responsibility belongs to a general superintendent of the Sunday Church School working under the pastor and church council or other official group. In a few cases there will be a director of Christian education, paid or volunteer, full or part time; or there may be a deaconess, parish worker, or assistant pastor by one of whom many of the duties will be discharged. In that case the superintendent will look to that worker for help and direction. Yet superintendents are a most important class of lay church workers who deserve a special salute for faithful service that is scarcely understood and appreciated by those whom they serve and by the church at large.

The office is not a mere tradition; it is the complex task of managing a school so that its pupils grow in the Christian way of living. The duties basically are two: planning for the school when it is out of session; and governing it when in session.

A general superintendent's task, properly conceived, is not primarily the conducting of services of worship. That may be important and necessary where there are no divisional or departmental superintendents and where pupils have not been developed for the purpose. Yet, the general superintendent is an educational executive, a school superintendent in charge of a school system, the leader of a group of principals, teachers, and pupils.

As a school executive, the general superintendent deals primarily in human engineering. That fact determines certain more personal requirements and duties to be mentioned here while the more technical aspects of his task are being considered throughout these chapters.

Ideally, the general superintendent would be the outstanding person of the congregation. He must be particularly strong in his Christian character and conduct. Above all else, he must take the attitude of a servant of servants. Friendliness, sympathy, earnestness, and forcefulness are necessary. An unusual amount of initiative and resourcefulness is required along with an equal amount of self-effacement. The incumbent cannot be one who will despair when a cherished plan goes awry or show visibly the hurt when his toes are stepped upon. He will need to remember that his Master was misunderstood, even abused.

The kind of general superintendent needed will display aptness at working with people. This is personnel management—the fine art of getting others to share visions and work for their realization. He distributes responsibility but does his own share of work; he never does anything, however, which another can do almost as well or better. He keeps inconspicuously in the background while he allows others to make suggestions and encourages them to carry out their own ideas, letting them know that he depends upon them and believes that they cannot fail. With many visions of larger and better things he patiently develops the talent of those who can accomplish those things and generously gives them full praise for what they have done. Not the least of the superintendent's qualifications is the capacity for entirely co-operative service under the director or pastor.

The ideal general superintendent shows an unusual personal interest in pupils and staff members alike. He is particularly thoughtful of his fellow officers and teachers. He has time always for a needed personal conference. He sends appropriate letters of cheer, good wishes, or congratulations and calls on sick colleagues. He provides the best possible working conditions. He never trespasses upon other workers' fields of labor. He is also thoughtful of the entire school. He is not absent or late, barring the most serious reasons. He avoids ruts and hobbies in his leadership. He is planning always for the finer school he sees in imagination and is doing constantly the things big or little that count toward that improvement. Throughout, it is "our school" and not "my school."

With such important responsibilities and requirements involved, what tragedy is revealed in an observation report which states: "The superintendent holds his position merely because no one else will accept it!"

A general superintendent who has assistant, divisional, departmental, and activity superintendents, will delegate as many of his labors as possible to those colleagues. In most cases, he will have at least one assistant superintendent. Often that office has been merely an honorary position. The general superintendent, instead, should let the assistant be a true helper and officer of the school. At least, anticipating the time when the assistant may need to step into his chief's shoes in order to carry on the work of the school, he will help the assistant to get experience and be in readiness.

A better title for this officer would be "associate superintendent." That would suggest that the superintendent and the associate are in a real partnership. The two might divide the duties both in planning and in operating the school. Sometimes the associate will be on the platform serving there with or instead of the general superintendent. At other times he will be handling other tasks and so enabling the superintendent to concentrate upon his special responsibility. Together they would provide for the leadership of the sessions; look after the welcoming of pupils; have oversight of latecomers; provide for substitute teaching; maintain good order; and achieve smooth progress of the program. Each would care for the other's work in case of absence. The two would co-operate in planning on both short- and long-range levels.

Divisional and Department Superintendents

The nature of the building as well as the size of the school may determine the duties which belong to a divisional or departmental superintendent. As schools grow larger, the work of the general superintendent and associates becomes chiefly that of directing and co-ordinating the efforts of these officers who do for a division or department what the general superintendent does for the entire school when it is small.

In certain schools of moderate size, the divisional or departmental superintendents may have a less prominent position. In those circumstances, they do not lead services of worship, keep records, or supervise a special teaching program. They represent in a general way the interests of a particular age group; look after their promotion; suggest plans for their progress; and lead them in special enterprises. Meanwhile, the general superintendent leads their worship, provides for their teaching, and generally manages their work. In many respects such officers are really associate superintendents with particular age group responsibilities. Nursery and home department superintendents may not fit this pattern because their departments are more personal in their functioning and have corresponding requirements.

While divisional or departmental superintendents need attitudes and have duties similar to those of general superintendents, they need the additional quality of co-operativeness with those under whom they work. They will be special students, too, of the psychology of an age group and of an effective program on that level.

Activity Superintendents

These officers care for particular fields of work. Typical examples are missionary superintendents who provide special forms of missionary instruction and service. Other possibilities are superintendents of dramatics, stewardship, handwork, music, special day programs, or recreation.

One author mentions supervisors of study, worship, fellowship, and service. According to the newer concept of curriculum all aspects of educational work are included in integrated units of activity, great care being exercised to avoid fragmentation of the program. Under that restriction, such leaders as the following may be used: superintendents of worship who seek to lift the level of worship experience in all departments; recreational leaders who develop well-rounded programs of fellowship development; persons skilled in community enterprises who can be superintendents of service. A closely related work is done by resource leaders secured for special enterprises especially in the instruction and study area. Sunday Church Schools have employed all these types of workers scarcely at all in proportion to their possibilities.

Secretaries and Treasurers

A secretary, general or departmental, can be a most useful officer in building up the school and helping all other workers carry forward their tasks with greater effectiveness. Usually the secretary contents himself with collecting records of the session, making oral reports, taking minutes, and caring for correspondence. How much more the general secretary with his possible associates in larger schools, such as membership secretary, statistical secretary, enrollment secretary, recording secretary or the like might do, is discussed in Chapter XVI, "Securing, Reporting, and Using Data." The treasurer of school or department can render an important service in addition to the collecting and disbursing of the pupils' offerings. His work is described more completely in Chapter XV on *Financing the School*.

Music Leaders

The importance of music in the school can scarcely be over-emphasized. The need for excellent leadership in that field is correspondingly significant. A pianist should be the best available. This is not the place to give young music students a chance to play in public. The contract of the employed church organist if there is one should be extended to cover playing for the Sunday Church School. In fact, the church organ, if it is located suitably, may well be used for the school services.

Pianists should prepare themselves for each session. This was recognized in the report of an observation which reads, "It would be better if the pianist would familiarize herself with the music before she begins." There may, of course, have been the difficulty described in another report which states: "The music could be improved if the pianist were co-operative. She is a pillar of the church who will not be ordered around—which is her interpretation of any suggestion for improvement." A closely related need is emphasized by a report which says that the pianist's preparation in advance would "make it necessary, of course, for the superintendent to select the hymns in advance."

Choristers or leaders of hymn-singing, likewise, should be the best available persons. That does not necessarily mean that they be highly trained musicians. The basic requirement is an understanding of their real function as leaders in the pupils' growth of ability to express religious feeling through music. In Chapter XIII, a period of departmental instruction will be suggested in which there can be study of music and preparation for worship. In that period the leader of singing will interpret and teach new hymns and provide for other development in music. During the worship services themselves he will efface himself except to carry the singers along by his voice. Beating time in conspicuous fashion, exhorting people to "sing out," announcing various ways of singing, humming, whistling, and the like are out of place.

A later chapter will mention the desirability of using special forms of music like solos, duets, quartettes, or instrumental numbers. A particularly fine development is the introduction of Church School choirs and choruses. These have such manifest values that it is to be hoped that the movement will grow rapidly. Leaders of these groups should not only be competent in their technical ability but also alive to their teaching aim in terms of rounded Christian growth for all the participants. Orchestras cannot be recommended unless more skilfully handled than they usually are.

The phonograph and the wire and tape recorders provide striking new opportunities for music leaders. The possibilities should be studied and the instruments employed widely. We are equipped now, certainly, to cultivate this educationally neglected aspect of the church program.

Every music leader is to be essentially a minister of music. His task is to help the members of the school develop the capacity of worship and other religious experience through music. In addition he may discover musical talent, assist in planning budgets for music, and otherwise cultivate this area as another aid to Christian growth.

Ushers and Librarians

The smooth management of a school of considerable size requires the help of ushers and aides. Depending upon the nature of the building and size of the school, the following are duties which might be allotted to them: greeting workers and pupils as they enter; welcoming visitors and guiding them to their proper places; introducing newcomers to the enrollment officers; keeping doors closed during worship or otherwise caring for latecomers; distributing programs; arranging chairs and other equipment; seeing that all persons have hymnals or other materials needed; caring for announcement boards and bulletin boards; ringing signals; distributing communications from the officers to other workers.

Many Sunday Church Schools have had libraries for a long

time. Some have been of a general nature similar to public libraries. In other cases they have provided inspirational literature of a religious character. Some libraries have included commentaries and similar reference works for Bible study. More recently they have stressed books for the educational and other workers in the church. The importance of the library is increased under newer trends in curriculum where reading as a technique in Christian education is being recognized for its true value.

The librarian of the future, therefore, will not merely keep records of books. He will co-operate with the teachers and other workers to build intelligently and promote the use of a body of reading and reference materials serving all the members of the school. Books on the Bible, theology, ethics, the church and its enterprises; materials for worship services and fellowship events, as well as books on the theory of these activities; a file of materials pertaining to social trends in which Christians are interested—the librarian will be building a collection of those things and fostering their use. Essentially he will be a minister of reading for the school.

Teachers and Supervisors

Teachers are the front rank members of the staff. With them lies finally the issue as to the effectiveness of the school. Among their many duties preparing for and conducting the Sunday sessions of their groups are paramount. Chapter XI will suggest the nature of that task in more detail. Also, it will emphasize the fact that under modern Christian education, the work of a teacher is a much broader concept than is commonly supposed. Even under the traditional approach, teachers dare not feel that their responsibilities are ended with preparation and the conducting of a class session.

A general superintendent arranged for an address to his teachers concerning some things that would make them more efficient. The speaker asked him to propose the topics for discussion. He responded with a list of five. "Ask them," said he, "either to be present when the time comes for them to do their work or else get a substitute—at least advise the superintendent if they must be absent.

Ask them to manifest the attitude of hearty willingness, not going to their work in an unhappy martyr's spirit. Ask them to be punctual, always a little ahead of time for the session so that they can help the pupils to get situated and prepared for worship. Ask them to be workers all the week long, calling, phoning, or writing to their pupils, taking hikes with them, providing parties for them, and seeking new members with their assistance. Ask them, finally, to be present for all meetings, in particular those in which we are trying to advance their improvement in the work."

Many plans have been tried in the effort to make sure that there will be a fully prepared teacher present every Sunday to lead each class. The best means is to have workers called "associate," not "substitute," teachers. Their names should be printed or otherwise mentioned along with those of the regular teachers. They should be regularly supplied with all the same materials. They should be invited to all the regular meetings and affairs. They should have opportunities not only to substitute in the event of an absence but also to assist regularly and to have practice in full leadership.

The meaning and techniques of supervision will be described in the following chapter. Pastors and directors most often serve in this capacity, yet special officers of the general type are being introduced in an increasing number of schools. Persons trained and experienced in public school supervision who also have Church School experience are the most promising candidates.

Churches are using still other workers. "Counselors" are made available to help persons of all ages with their more crucial problems. "Church visitors" call on the constituency to win members for the congregation or cultivate the fellowship spirit of the group. "Youth workers" have special responsibilities with the high school age and older young people.

SELECTING STAFF MEMBERS

Many Sunday Church School leaders have very little opportunity to select workers. When a new staff member is needed, they ask the one person available. Assuming, though, that they might select their workers for the various duties, what types of persons should they choose?

General Qualifications

Shall the workers preferably be men or women and what is the most desirable age for people to start serving in the various capacities?

When the Indiana Survey[1] was made, approximately 2000 workers in 250 schools in that typical state and in typical counties and towns of the state were visted. It was found that 27 per cent of them were men and 73 per cent were women. The average age was about 37 years, one-fourth being under 27 years and one-fourth above 47 years. One-half had begun their work between 25 and 45 years of age and one-fourth were on either side of that group when they began.

Clearly, as things stood then, the majority of workers were women. Also, many had started working either when quite young or after they entered middle life. Are those practices desirable? The tendency in public school education is to introduce more men into the ranks; and greater maturity is becoming requisite for teaching there. It seems desirable that Sunday Church Schools, too, move in similar directions.

It would be better for pupils to have now a woman teacher and then a man teacher in somewhat regular succession. In those schools where boys' and girls' classes are separated—an unwholesome practice in itself—it is neither necessary nor desirable that there be always women teachers for girls and men teachers for boys. It is more normal to have boys and girls together with men teachers at one time and women at another. In that way religious education will be more balanced and richly varied.

As to age, there is a question whether the youngsters who sometimes become teachers have had sufficient life experience to fit them

---

[1] Walter S. Athearn, *The Indiana Survey of Religious Education* (New York: George H. Doran, 1923).

for such serious work. Many struggle with inadequate experience and training to meet well-nigh impossible situations. The results are unfortunate in the discouragement of the young workers and the loss of their pupils. While it is impossible to set exact age qualifications, the worker should be able to handle the situation with a degree of satisfaction to himself and his pupils. This demands that he be mature enough to command their respect and young enough to share their spirit.

Personal Qualifications

Deep, broad, and vital Christian experience is demanded in Sunday Church School workers. As one student observes: "A step in advance would be to secure teachers devoted to Christian principles in daily living." Those who hope to lead others preferably have gone themselves through the experience into which they are trying to lead their pupils. Only religious knowledge, assent, and confidence gained through a vital experience of Christian living will meet the need.

Among all desirable characteristics there is one which stands out most prominently. Several hundreds of college students have been asked to describe the best Sunday Church School teacher they ever had by naming the outstanding characteristics of that person. Many things have been mentioned, among them: enthusiasm, sympathy, broad-mindedness, optimism, sense of humor, friendliness, conservative spirit, earnestness, honesty, conviction, and faith. There is another, however, which appears always, and usually first. It is Christian sincerity. Learners do demand of their leaders a hearty effort to practice the things they urge. Needless to say, they will be members of some church, preferably of the one in which they serve.

The qualifications already mentioned are the major constituents of that ineffable something called "personality." It is faith, sincerity, friendliness, and all the others. Yet it involves emotional stability and poise, high ideals, understanding, and love. From another angle, an outstanding need is a zeal for improvement with a willingness to study without stint. The current educational approach requires, too, a special measure of creativeness.

Educational Qualifications and Experience

Regarding general education in the secular schools, the Indiana Survey found that the average worker had had eleven years of schooling with 39 per cent having had less than ten years. Unless the statistics have changed markedly, the average Sunday Church School worker has scarcely completed high school.

It has been assumed always, and rightly, that the more education workers have, the better qualified they are. In applying that standard, however, it should be recognized that there is a difference between schooling and education. Ordinarily the two go together, but it is possible for education to go on when schooling is ended for there is education in life, reading, study, and travel. That sort of education plus the largest possible amount of schooling would seem to be the ideal.

The most desirable worker has, also, the best possible religious education. Above all things else, he will know the Bible. A great change has taken place during the last century in moving from a Bible-centered curriculum of Bible only to a person-centered curriculum with extra-biblical materials. Yet the Bible remains, and will remain, the heart of subject matter; workers should know it, not only as to content but also as to origin, development, and interpretation. A close second is knowledge of the church in its history, program, and enterprises. After that might come theology and ethics. Indeed, there is little information of which one can think which does not have place in the preparation of a Sunday Church School worker.

Another factor in cultural qualifications is professional education. Many Sunday Church School workers are public school people. These have had various courses in general education and usually some study of psychology, principles and philosophy of education, and general methods of teaching. Thus by study as well as experience they have gained knowledge of pupils and skill in leading them in the most fruitful kind of learning experience.

The most highly qualified Sunday Church School worker, other things being equal, is the one who has had professional training in Christian education. This person, in addition to knowing his Bible, church, pupils, and teaching will know religious education. Let it be repeated, although religious education has been always an activity of mankind from the days of the tribes down to this era of the nations, the last few decades have brought greater advances in the field than have perhaps taken place in any quarter millenium preceding. There is now a new literature, a new vocabulary, and new techniques, materials, and agencies. Really to understand those and employ them to the highest degree of effectiveness requires professional study.

We should choose ordinarily the worker who has had the broadest possible experience in Sunday Church School work itself, both as pupil and leader. Second place might be given to one with public school teaching experience. Another type of experience which fits people for successful and efficient Church School work is parenthood. Many of the finest Church School workers have been recruited among the parents who have been sincerely interested in having their boys and girls undergo the best possible Christian development.

Executive and Teaching Ability

As a summary of the desirable qualifications for workers, the following section is quoted from *International Standard A for the Sunday Church School:*[2]

The final test of a worker is the degree of success with which he performs the tasks which he undertakes. In the following list of questions the first group is to be asked concerning teachers only and the second group is to be asked concerning officers only.

For Teachers:
1) Does he consciously seek to meet the moral and spiritual needs of his pupils?
2) Does he attempt to acquaint himself with the interests of the mem-

---

[2] Chicago: The International Council of Religious Education, 1929, p. 17.

bers of his class and adapt his teaching procedure to their individual interests and needs?

3) Does he familiarize himself with the course of study as a whole before the first session of the class, and regularly prepare for each session?

4) Does he consistently secure and hold interest and attention?

5) Is he skillful in the choice and use of appropriate teaching methods, such as the use of suitable questions, leading discussion, telling a story, leading pupils into fruitful activities?

6) Does he successfully secure the co-operation of the pupils and their homes in the preparation of assignments?

7) Does he show initiative and ability in planning his work and in meeting the various situations that arise in the conduct of it?

8) Does he stimulate and effectively guide co-operative study and discussion instead of doing most of the talking?

9) Does good order prevail in his class?

10) Is he open-minded and fair in bringing out the different aspects and points of view regarding disputed questions?

11) Does his leadership contribute to the continuous growth of the members of his group in Christian character?

For Officers:

12) Does he hold the respect and confidence of the workers who serve under his direction?

13) Does he secure the co-operation of teachers, officers, and pupils with whom he works?

14) Is he regular in his work, faithful to promises, and does he get things done?

15) Does he show initiative and resourcefulness in planning his work and in meeting emergencies and new situations?

16) If responsible for the conduct of worship programs, does he do this with dignity, reverence, and appreciation?

DISCOVERING AND ENLISTING STAFF MEMBERS

Here the Sunday Church School leader has a twofold goal: a continuous and adequate supply of capable workers first, for immediate needs and second, for future needs. The immediate needs again are twofold. A school needs both regular workers and associate, assistant, or substitute workers. How to secure them all is a perennial problem which is becoming more acute with the mobility of population and increase of enrollments. Also, someone has said that there is the equivalent of a complete turnover in Sunday Church School staffs every five years. An article recently was entitled, "More Than a Half Million New Workers Needed Annually."

Such observation reports as the following indicate that most leaders have not solved the problem: "There is no set plan for recruiting teachers." "The pastor is forever on the lookout for new talent." "New workers are discovered only by observations of the superintendent or pastor. Naturally, anyone offering his services is accepted."

On the other hand, one pastor describes a program which includes the following points:

1) "At least once a year the executive committee and I go through the entire church roll and make up a list of potential workers, keeping all departments in mind as we do."

2) "We try to get as many of the present teachers and potential teachers to attend leadership school as we can."

3) "Pupil participation beginning in the lowest grades brings out ability and the desire to teach."

4) "Liberal use of helpers in the Cradle Roll, Nursery, Beginners, and Primary Departments produces a surplus of teachers."

5) "We give assistant teachers a chance to work."

6) "Vacation Church School is a fine opportunity to train teachers. Some will start there who will not begin in the Sunday Church School."

7) "Leadership camp has been a big help. We stress it and our school sends those who cannot otherwise afford to go."

8) "Much depends upon the way in which the challenge is given to the prospective worker. We stress the stewardship of talent. Once the acceptance is given and the work starts, the joy of work does the rest."

9) "An annual election of officers and teachers provides a partial rotation of workers."

Sources of Workers

Five sources of worker supply are the congregation in general, the community, various adult classes and groups, the young people's group, and the parents of the younger pupils. The congregation is first. As Dr. Philip Jones says: "Our religion, if vital, ought to reproduce itself. A church should be able to develop members capable of propagating the gospel and who feel its compulsion urgently enough to want to share its redemptive power." [3]

Adult classes, presumably having the best trained persons in their numbers, should be fruitful sources although one may have hard work convincing them that they ought to give up the comfortable listening to their teacher's lectures. New members of the congregation, not already laden with other responsibilities, may wish to undertake this task as their regular form of service. Women's societies and men's clubs should be considered, also, and certain young adult groups are taking up study for leadership as one of their major enterprises. Parents sometimes accept responsibilities for the sake of their children or because they have an interest in Christian education generally as a result of their parenthood. There may be those who served once and may return. Camp graduates are particularly valuable.

These sources should yield the necessary supply of workers present or future. If not, there are possibilities in the community where persons not engaged in their own congregational programs will help in an emergency. Sometimes persons away from their home church can be enlisted, such as students in a college town. In these cases, though, it should be recognized that this is not the final answer to the problem.

Securing Workers

A beginning in securing workers is made by surveying the above sources to discover those who (a) meet the desirable qualifications most fully and (b) are willing. This may be accomplished by studying the class roll, congregational register, or telephone directory. Better, a mimeographed or printed questionnaire to be used with present members and friends of the congregation may be employed. It should contain questions on such subjects as the following: How long a church member? Types of church work and num-

---

[3] *The Church School Superintendent* (New York: The Abingdon Press, 1939), p. 54.

ber of years engaged in it? Experience in Sunday Church School
work? Types of service preferred? Special training? Opportunities
for training desired?

The most valuable suggestion possible is a leadership committee
charged with the permanent task of discovering, enlisting, and
training workers. Ordinarily it is unwise to ask for volunteers, except for a leadership class. Likewise, difficulties may arise when a
teacherless class is asked to suggest someone.

When prospective workers have been discovered, they must be
asked intelligently and invited persuasively. Dr. Leach, in a book
called *Putting It Across,* says that some administrators seem to lack
the ability to understand the desire of others to serve. If it be true
that people really desire to serve, we wonder why it is so difficult to
enlist them for this work. The possible reasons are several. They
may not realize the importance of the work or it may appear uninteresting to them. Some are not actually qualified and know it;
others have not yet discovered their abilities and may lack confidence. Many do not know how to start and so, properly, fear
failure. Not a few remain untrained in the service ideal.

With such an array of possible obstacles, a careful technique
is needed to enlist a prospective worker. Suggestions follow.

1. Lay sound foundations. The pastor teaches and preaches the
service ideal, setting forth the needs for service and showing the
joy in it. Teachers can present the same ideal to classes where
prospective workers are studying. Case reports of boys and girls
needing guidance and accounts of lives saved through the work are
valuable material for the purpose.

2. Make the proper approach. While it may be desirable to
issue a general call, personal solicitation usually is necessary. Let
a convincing leader confront a qualified prospect with a specific
need. And not on the telephone; it is worth a personal call if it is
worth anything. The enlistment should be serious, not casual. The
request will be made not in a way that minimizes the task saying,
for example, that it will not take much time. It should take time,
and people want a real challenge.

3. *Appeal to the proper motives.* Why are people willing to serve in a Church School? According to the Indiana Survey, the leading motives are church loyalty, love of children, joy of teaching, and service to society. One might mention also duty, service to God, richer personality, and the evangelistic attitude. As an ideal we should like to assume that the prospective Christian worker is so filled with the spirit of Christ, is so enamored of the Christian way, is himself so surely growing in that way that he overflows with the desire that others may live abundantly.

4. *Train future workers.* There are Sunday Church Schools which have more prospective workers than they can use. In these churches this particular suggestion probably has been effective for years. The subject will receive more adequate treatment in the next chapter.

5. *Provide the best possible working conditions.* Sunday Church School workers are without salary and a majority would not wish to accept remuneration. The least to be done for them is to provide the best equipment and helps possible. They should be able to expect guidance when needed and full opportunity to learn on the job. In addition, there ought to be freedom to work with spontaneity.

6. *Exalt the work as it deserves.* This can be done formally, for example, in a consecration service where the various appointees are brought before the congregation, properly introduced, and properly consecrated to their task. Publicity of the right sort is helpful. More informally, this is a matter of everlasting recognition of the importance of educational work in general and appreciation of the efforts of each worker.

7. *Have a reputation for doing good work in your school.* Then the prospect can be challenged to share in a worth-while task. Besides, he is honored by the connection.

8. *Protect members of the staff from excessive demands.* Teaching or other educational work is a task large enough for anyone's full measure of service.

APPOINTING STAFF MEMBERS

When workers who meet all standards as fully as possible have been selected and enlisted, they should be officially appointed. Another series of problems arises. Who should appoint the workers to their places?

In many schools the answer will be the church council, the pastor, or the general superintendent. In other cases, the situation is more complex or the school wishes to proceed more democratically. Then this is a good rule: let the next person or group in authority above the staff member under consideration make the nomination; let the group to be served elect the member. This would mean that the church council or Church School Committee would make nominations for the general superintendent; the workers of the school would elect. Also, the superintendent would nominate prospective teachers for the older classes and the members would vote on the nominations. Another way is to have a special committee which will nominate, while the class members elect. Proper maturity is required, of course, before students vote for their leaders.

Whatever the technique of appointment, the candidate's willingness to be nominated should be ascertained in preliminary conference. Then his election should be followed by proper introduction to his work and induction into office by the congregation. The annual change of officers and teachers occurs usually the first Sunday of October. That requires all elections to be held prior to that date. All appointments should be for a definite period, preferably one year. It will be understood that thereafter the worker can withdraw or the school can elect another worker if either party is so disposed.

Closely related to appointment of staff members is the problem of reassignment or dismissal. Not infrequently a worker might render better service in some other line of church work. A worker might fit into another department more advantageously, too. For the good of themselves and the cause, these persons should be reassigned. The purpose should be fully shared between the person responsible for reassignment and the person receiving it.

The dismissal of a member of the staff is particularly difficult. It should be made only when the worker is quite incompatible or incompetent, and the rarest of ingenuity should be used. A most important possibility is the substitution of another job, changing the "release" into a reassignment. In view of such difficulties, constitutions should provide orderly procedures for regular change of officers.

INDUCTING WORKERS

To select, enlist, and appoint a worker ought not be the end of the matter if the leader wishes to build for permanency and efficiency in his staff. Only a real task should be given any prospective worker. If the work looks and proves trivial, much harm will result. For a work that is really worth while, the worker needs every possible inspiration and help. He is likely to be young, inexperienced, and untrained. Besides, the teaching of religion is one of life's most difficult tasks.

A good beginning is made by an installation, induction, dedication, or consecration service. It should be a public one in which the members of the congregation, parents, and pupils of the school are present. The pastor leads the service. All present are made conscious of the importance of the educational work of the church. Each worker declares his purpose to give faithful service. Those to be served, including all the members of the congregation, should proclaim their intention to support earnest effort. The order for such a service can be procured from most denominational offices.

The worker's induction should be followed by a helpful introduction to the work which he undertakes. His superior officers should give him plenty of time to examine related books or materials. He should be presented to his group under the most favorable circumstances. There should be many and frequent contacts with the new worker during early days. If necessary, "first aid" should be administered promptly.

A teacher who is plunged into his job abruptly and then allowed to work without guidance or assistance will do one of three things. He may get discouraged and quit. He may, and likely will, hark back to the methods used with himself. Least likely, he may work his way through to effective ways of dealing with the job. Following up on new teachers with inquiries into their problems might save many a one and develop all for greater efficiency.

SECURING WORKERS' RESPONSES

The ultimate goal of every Sunday Church School leader with his workers is to secure on their part the most desirable responses to the demands of their work. Ten words will name the outstanding responses to be sought. Five of these words carry their own meaning sufficiently: *co-operation, attendance, example, preparation,* and *responsibility.* Five other will be elaborated.

The Responses Desired

Constancy

The word is used as Paul used it when he urged the Galatians, "Let us not grow weary in well-doing." The ideal worker is a seven-day worker for the increasing effectiveness of his school. Each day brings the teacher some suggestion for his group lessons or it provides an opportunity to do something for some member of his group. The superintendent always has plans to be made, pupils to be followed up, or fellow workers to be helped.

Creativity

Co-operation, mentioned above, need not mean servile response to minute directions. Every worker should have opportunity to exercise initiative within his own sphere. Building one's own plans or adapting wisely the designated ones; showing resourcefulness in meeting special situations; and being ready with original ideas are desirable responses, indeed.

Promotion

Most Sunday Church Schools grow slowly if at all. They need a continuous program of educational recruiting to boost their membership. Back of this must lie, though, the missionary spirit deeply imbedded and keenly vital in every worker of the school. The missionary spirit must be, too, the kind which sees the local as well as the distant field white unto harvest.

Purposefulness

How often thoughtful leaders in Christian education find themselves emphasizing this need! Workers need clear-cut objectives, an advance picture of their outcomes, visions of their goals. Sunday Church School work is not merely an effort to carry on a tradition, maintain an institution, and keep certain activities alive. It is an enterprise to meet the moral and spiritual demands upon needy pupils and foster their corresponding growth.

Spirit

Workers differ widely in this regard. Some are scarcely willing to do the minimum demanded of them to avoid utter failure. Others bring to their work a fresh enthusiasm that lifts it out of dullness into brilliancy. Ready to lend a hand wherever it is needed, they make the effort a marked success not only by ability but also by consecrated spirit.

Eliciting the Responses

How may the leader secure such responses? What are the stimuli which will produce them? To have the worker properly selected, enlisted, appointed, and inducted is half the battle. Beyond that there are seven important suggestions to be considered.

Leadership principles

The science of personnel management, as well as psychological study and common-sense experience, provide a number of maxims having practical value for managing a Sunday Church School staff. For example, in the manner of giving instructions, they propose that indirect suggestion be used if it is definite and not too subtle. In cases of direct suggestion the leader must ask, not boss; suggest, not order; win, not dictate.

Contracts or covenants

In reports on observations of schools this statement is frequently made: "There is no contract or covenant for the worker; they do have an annual service for consecration." Yet there is a growing custom in which each member of the staff signs an instrument of this type upon entering service. Such a procedure cannot be forced upon a school but there are many staffs which would voluntarily adopt it if brought to their attention. It makes for understanding of the workers' responsibilities and provides a stimulus where enthusiasm might lag.

Program for improvement

A mother told about her visit to the Sunday Church School department attended by her six-year-old boy: "The room was uncomfortably cold. No program for the day had been planned in advance. A gum-chewing individual called a teacher helped the children color some papers, tried to get them to say the memory verse after her, talked a bit about 'all things bright and beautiful,' and passed wisecracks with the superintendent. The session closed with the superintendent and pianist 'teaching' the children a new song which they had not themselves learned, while the boys beat each other over the head with the Sunday Church School papers."

To put it mildly, that church owes its workers an opportunity to participate in a program of improvement. It should provide them a supervisor who could go into that department and begin with its workers to clear up their deficiencies one by one. The superintendent should be provided with helpful books and urged to attend the leadership classes available in the community. The younger workers should have had a course of study before they began. Lacking that, they should have a leadership class in the local church now. A good beginning would be made by dismissing the department for a Sunday while the whole staff would visit some good, well-conducted school.

Remuneration

With most Sunday Church Schools the question of paying the staff is only an academic one for there is no money available. In other schools the workers, especially superintendents and supervisors, sometimes teachers, are paid or might be.

Could better work be secured if there were financial remuneration? Undoubtedly, in some schools and at certain points. A beginning in the whole matter might be made in some denominational and ecumenical situations by employing full-time regional, state, county, and city secretaries. Then, thousands of congregations should be employing full- or part-time directors and supervisors. Only a lack of vision concerning the importance of educational work and lack of understanding of possible improvements are hampering this development.

As for paying local superintendents and teachers, there has been considerable experimentation in Sunday as well as Weekday and Vacation Church Schools. While it is hoped that properly prepared persons may always find a place in voluntary service, results show that no opportunity ought to be overlooked to provide for the work to be done on the highest level possible. Many who have established remuneration as the policy believe that it does raise the level of work. To be sure, professional leadership is not enough in itself. We need a way for lay men and women to come to fruitful expression of their Christian faith-life in mutual interaction with their fellow members of the church working at Christian tasks. They need the kind of experiences they have while working in the Sunday Church School. Similarly, the learners need these uplifting contacts with leaders who as typical lay Christians are freely sharing their Christianity.

Yet the principle of remunerating pastors, sextons, organists, secretaries, and treasurers of the church in order to have more expert service has long been firmly establshed. It is difficult to find reason for hesitating to apply the principle in this area, too. For the present, many schools can do no more than provide excellent working facilities, good libraries, registration, and other fees for attending conferences, tuition for study at camps and the like and these all should be made freely available. Many schools, though, are capable of doing something more if they would set their budgets to do so, and they should.

Recognition versus criticism

One writer has said that the Sunday Church School leader should have two eyes to see much, but only one mouth to say little, and that little, commendation. More often than realized, commendation is needed to lift a weary spirit out of apathy or error. Yet, people often must be directed and sometimes curbed. Tact is required especially since the workers are volunteers. Patience is the first necessity. After that, one may solicit the help of friends who can give advice. Finally, the leader may need to face the issue forthrightly with the worker, on the level of mutual devotion to the best interests of the cause.

Some years ago a cartoon featured a demure lady of uncertain years with the comment: "Few people know that little Miss Wiley has been teaching a class of girls for six years without missing a Sunday." Yes, "few people know." Doubtless, too, many a "little Miss Wiley" does not much care. Yet, the roll of the school staff can be published in the church bulletin; the annual induction can take the form of a recognition service; outstanding achievements can be brought before the school, the parents, the entire congregation. At least, the superintendent can appreciate his workers' efforts and let them know that he does.

Worker determination

We want worker intelligence, initiative, interest, responsibility, and co-operation. Allowing for determination of the program on the part of the workers themselves will go far toward accomplishing those things. Letting them decide upon policies will enable them to understand them better. Workers cannot show initiative unless they have opportunity. When they do, the enterprise becomes peculiarly their own responsibility. Then they are interested and their co-operation results.

Co-operative fellowship

Every successful worker needs to feel that his "boss" is with him. An outstanding principle of personnel management, therefore, deals with making the work a co-operative enterprise. Perennially we are reminded that the workers in the plant where Lindbergh's engine was built put up a poster with the legend, "We put Lindbergh across."

The workers' conference can be handled to provide solidarity in the group with every worker taking pride in the school and working wholeheartedly for the pupils. Other ideas for group integration are an annual retreat, an appreciation day, a service in recognition for leadership courses completed, the sending of delegations to conventions or camps. Always, the leader will say "we," not "I" and make it so.

Chapter VIII

IMPROVING THE LEADERSHIP

The Indiana Survey considered the preparation of the approximately two thousand workers in the two hundred fifty typical Sunday Church Schools visited in that typical state. Findings showed that a great majority of the workers were not specifically trained for their task in any way. While one-fourth held public school teaching certificates, next to none of those or any others had taken professional courses in religious education. Very few had ever read a professional book. Less than half went to conventions with any regularity, while very few ever attended community teachers' meetings. Only one hundred twenty-five of the total number had graduated from leadership schools in twenty-one years; only eighty-three were enrolled then; and only twenty-eight were studying in the leadership classes of the churches surveyed.

To what extent the situation has improved in the intervening years no one knows. Unquestionably the problem remains acute. Indeed, it may be all the more so in view of progress in the theory of Christian education and improvement of practice in outstanding schools.

Christian education may need to take a leaf from the history of public school education. The first state normal schools were launched more than a hundred years ago. Already by the end of the last century good beginnings toward adequate preparation of administrators and teachers had been made. Since that time, there has been rapid progress. Now, throughout major areas of the United States, no child studies in any field or on any level under a teacher who has had less than a college education or its equivalent. As a result, the public school system of most American communities is a source of pride in which the pupils show interest in their work and have confidence in their leaders.

Incidentally, a special problem is emerging at that point. It results from the disparity between the outlook, preparation, and practice of leaders in the Sunday Church School compared with those in the public school. Many Church School workers who are also public school teachers find a great gulf between the respective approaches in the two types of school. Many pupils find themselves in a rather unfamiliar world when they leave the public school room and go to Church School. Everyone involved, including parents, experiences increasing tension. People with one foot in an airplane cannot proceed well with the other in an oxcart.

Yet there has been excellent progress in leadership education during recent decades and there is large promise in the programs now under way. The greatest obstacle is that of general lethargy. Perhaps when all parties to the situation realize that the teaching of religion is infinitely more subtle and complex than the teaching of arithmetic, they will insist that teachers of the former be at least as well trained as teachers of the latter.

NEEDS AND MEANS

Two kinds of effort at the improvement of leadership are needed: (a) programs of preparation for those who have not yet begun their work; (b) means for workers already in service to develop themselves.

Before considering the possible agencies for meeting those needs, it must be noted that leadership education is being conceived more broadly now. This larger outlook takes into view the whole scope of church work and every type of church worker, for example, the church councilman. Yet the majority of church workers are those engaged in educational tasks; so leadership education programs continue to deal rather largely with preparation for and improvement in that work.

Here, of course, the subject is not primarily leadership education in general but the improvement of the Sunday Church School staff.

Fortunately, many agencies are available. Some are of a group nature; others are more personal. Certain forms serve better for in-service training; others for pre-service preparation. Many appear either interdenominationally or denominationally while some can be conducted in one or the other of those forms only. Some are co-operative; some local church; and others more personal.

The General Curriculum

Those agencies are all in addition to the important leadership development which takes place in the general curriculum of the school. A major work of preparing leaders is done there although the fact is rarely recognized. From the earliest age, candidates for the staff are learning the basic facts they will need in their later service—Bible, Church, and Christian conduct. Each small task performed for the school at any point is a step in developing leadership responsibility and skill. In every Sunday Church School relationship pupils are gaining some sort of educational outlook and learning some type of educational procedure. Those are the foundations upon which the various special forms of later leadership education must depend.

Group Agencies: Wider Community

Among wider community agencies of leadership education there are conferences, conventions, institutes, summer assemblies, summer camps, and summer schools. Most colleges, seminaries, training schools, and universities provide courses in Christian education, too, and a variety of home study or correspondence courses is available. Finally, there are laboratory schools and workshops.

Conferences, conventions, and institutes on Sunday Church School work have been held for more than a hundred years and continue still to be one of the most popular forms of leadership improvement. Outstanding examples are the quadrennial conventions of The International Council of Religious Education. From those major efforts stems a long series of interdenominational and denominational gatherings which serve the churches of regions, states, counties, cities, general church bodies, and smaller areas. Often the meetings concern a special field such as children's work.

Programs of conferences, conventions, and institutes still lean toward general themes and inspirational speeches. More recently, however, the practical is being stressed, particularly in specialized group meetings such as departmental conferences within the convention program. There the workers have opportunity to ask questions and share experiences concerning their immediate situations. Another promising development is the introduction of newer procedures into the program itself—film presentations, panels, forums, and the like.

Speaking generally, all such forms of leadership education require little effort on the part of those who attend and, therefore, have less value than other forms which stimulate more active study. Yet Sunday Church School leaders can profitably take colleagues or send representatives. They will hear worth-while speakers, meet new ideas, and have an apportunity to talk with leaders as well as fellow workers in their special areas of effort. The book displays usually available at larger meetings can be of utmost value. Those who attend will be inspired with a consciousness of the importance of their work, if no more.

The basic problem of the leader is to make sure that something gets done as a result of attendance. At this point a convention speaker of twenty years' experience made an important suggestion. It grew out of the candid remarks of a woman who has been attending conventions for the same number of years. She said that she always comes home from a convention with enough good resolutions to revolutionize her department. But, alas, those resolutions evaporate one by one.

That woman's pastor or general superintendent could help by calling pre- and post-convention meetings of the delegation. Before the convention they would go over the program and plan what they are to look for and do. They will take notebooks and pencils with them. Then, back home, they will decide upon one or more things they will undertake and carry through to completion.

The *summer assembly, camp, or school* is most widely represented in numerous interdenominational or denominational camps. There local workers go for one or two weeks to live in out-of-door surroundings while studying under the guidance of outstanding leaders. The typical program is varied. The classes usually are in the First or Second Series of the Standard Leadership Curriculum. There are worship, dramatic, and recreational activities under expert guidance.

Unquestionably, much of the improvement in local church educational programs during the last decade or two is due to the camp leadership education movement. Camp experience is singularly well adapted to meeting the needs of those who can and will study for a short period under ideal circumstances. The leaders are usually of high rank. There is uninterrupted and concentrated work free from distraction. There is rich fellowship with choice spirits in both faculty and student membership.

One problem concerning this training is the considerable cost. To meet that issue many congregations provide "scholarships," through the regular budget, for a given number of promising and faithful leaders. The best available persons should be chosen; full reports should be expected; and new ideas should be put into effect at once unless there is good reason to do otherwise. Pastors often speak of accomplishing revolutionary improvements in their educational programs by this means.

Colleges, seminaries, training schools, and *universities* are contributing especially to the development of higher leadership for Christian education. This work is largely a product of the present generation, paralleling the development of the so-called "modern movement" and in no small sense responsible for its continuation.

Colleges have sought to provide courses in which prospective lay leaders, both men and women may prepare themselves for service in this area. Seminaries are helping the oncoming pastors gain an advanced educational outlook and be equipped to carry forward the educational work in the parish which they are called to serve. Denominational and interdenominational training schools have provided directors of Christian education, deaconesses, and parish workers who can give expert guidance to the educational work of a congregation. The universities have developed means by which teachers of teachers may do advanced study and others may prepare for such highly specialized tasks as planning curricula, organizing denominational forces, and serving as general secretaries. In addition they have fostered research which has worked back into the guidance of the new movement. The contribution which can be made by all these agencies is restricted only by the unreadiness of churches to provide opportunities for their graduates to serve.

Home study and correspondence courses are promoted by nearly all major denominations. They make it possible to engage in leadership education wherever mail is delivered. One typical announcement of such work offers a choice of fifteen different Second Series courses including *Jesus and His Teachings; Ways of Teaching;* and the *Growth of Christian Personality during Childhood.* Two or more hours are required to be spent on the study and preparation of each of the ten lessons in a course. Ordinarily the student would prepare and send in one report each week but he may make any schedule which will fit his needs. The papers are returned with corrections and suggestions. If satisfactory work is done, a Course Card is issued which may be counted toward a Second Certificate of Progress. Several persons in a congregation may enroll for the same course and engage in group discussion along with their individual study. In any case the student has the advantage of taking as much time as he wishes for the lessons and having the reports of expert teachers upon the papers he submits.

Laboratory schools and workshops are the most recent newcomers in this area. They are operated as separate units or as features within, for example, a summer camp. Well done, they are leadership education at its best. Here people learn to do by doing. That is particularly important in view of the current philosophy of Christian education. Workers need to learn how to lead others in learning to do by doing, through personal experience in the same procedure.

Group Agencies: Nearer Community

Among nearer community agencies of leadership education there are numerous local conferences, conventions, and institutes, and denominational or interdenominational leadership education schools and classes.

Local conferences, conventions and institutes may be of more brief duration than those of wider community character. A day or an afternoon and evening are customary, although some city "institutes" have been planned to extend over several weeks. In all cases, greater permanent value results from the small group study where local workers can discuss among themselves and with an experienced leader the specific problems which confront them. Workers should participate fully with a willingness to share as well and an open-mindedness to learn. They should take notes and talk personally with the leaders. Reports to their fellow workers should follow in a local church meeting where new procedures are discussed and instituted promptly if they appear desirable.

The term "leadership education" properly suggests first of all *The Standard Leadership Curriculum* promoted interdenominationally by The International Council of Religious Education as well as by the various denominations. It is provided through classes or schools of many types. Here the interdenominational program will be described with the understanding that the denominations have adopted widely and are promoting vigorously the same type of work with similar standards and procedures.

There are three levels of courses—First, Second, and Third Series—in order of advancing requirements.

First Series courses are meant for beginning students and young workers. At least ten hours of work are to be done for each course, usually five hours in group sessions and five in out-of-class work. Recommended texts are to be used wherever possible. The class should be enrolled with an accrediting agency, either The International Council or the denomination. Course Cards will then be issued to each student who completes the course, and a First Certificate of Progress can be secured when requirements have been met in the areas indicated below:

1. Religious Development: participation in the work of the church and reading of a religious journal; the adoption of a plan of religious growth including systematic use of such means as prayer, Bible study, and other reading.

2. Leadership experience: at least one year.

3. Educational growth: reading of an educational magazine and books, and attendance at conferences.

4. Completion of four First Series courses, at least one being in the area of the worker's special responsibilities in the church.

Such First Series courses as the following are listed: *Personal Religious Living; The Life and Work of Paul; The Program of My Church; The Children We Teach; Youth at Worship; Teaching Juniors.* They may be taken by individual study or informal group work; in an institute or camp; or through a workers' conference which uses a course as a part of its program. Usually, however, there is a special "leadership class" for the purpose in the local church or a community denominational or interdenominational school.

The larger part of nearer community leadership education is done in schools or classes working on the level of *Second Series* courses. These courses must continue for at least ten fifty-minute periods. The sessions can be arranged so as to be completed in five days, two weeks, six weeks, or twelve weeks, a great variety of schedules being possible. Many communities have fall and spring semesters of six weeks each. In all cases it is expected that there will be two hours of outside work for each hour in class.

A Second Series class for which a Course Card is to be issued must have an instructor who is accredited by International or denominational leadership headquarters, and a school which offers several such courses must have an accredited dean. Approved texts or equivalent materials are specified.

The Second Series curriculum looks forward to the completion of work for which a Second Certificate of Progress can be issued. The requirements include again: (1) religious development; (2) churchmanship; and (3) educational growth.

The last mentioned requirement involves the completion of six Second Series courses (or twelve First Series courses) distributed among general courses (4), and specialization courses (2), in some area such as Young People's Division courses. General courses include the fields of Personal Religion, Bible, the Church, Psychology, Method, and the like.

Standard leadership education on the Second Series level is done usually in community schools, although there are possibilities for individual study, group study in a Sunday Church School class or local workers' group, and similar enterprises. Leaders may go beyond it to a Third Certificate of Progress and The Certificate of Achievement.

The maintenance and operation of a community school of leadership education, whether denominational or interdenominational, becomes an academic enterprise of considerable complexity. Those who contemplate establishing such a school and those who teach in one will need to secure the International or denominational bulletins for their guidance and consult the appropriate offices of national or state secretaries of leadership education.

The great value of such work comes through the variety and quality of its courses, the caliber of the instruction, and the academic character of the procedures. A leader who wishes to have its advantages reflected in his school will either provide for his workers to attend available schools or work with his pastor, ministerial association, or a community council of Christian education to establish one.

Local Church Agencies

The agencies thus far discussed are all meant to influence the local church situation. They are to be attended and used directly or indirectly by the local church workers, although they are planned and administered as larger group enterprises. However, there are additional agencies for leadership education which are distinctly of local church origin and meant to be managed exclusively in the local church. In many respects they are most important of all.

While the previously mentioned agencies fit leaders of leaders particularly well, these agencies fit the rank and file more closely.

The most formal local church agency is a *leadership class for present workers.* Something of the sort should be available at least once each year for every worker in every church. Already it has been made clear that a class of this sort may be done on the Standard Leadership Curriculum basis with interdenominational or denominational standards, approval, and credit. In many respects that is the preferred policy.

However, a course planned and conducted locally, if done with similar or higher standards, has advantages. It enables workers to meet their precise interests and needs in accordance with their particular equipment, leadership, and pupils. The planning and conducting are of high educational value in themselves. The pastor should be the leader if no other is available. Indeed, it provides him a unique opportunity to guide the development of his church. Under any circumstances he should be an active participant. The list of courses presented in the interdenominational or denominational leadership bulletins will offer suggested units of work. Printed resource materials such as leaders' guides and textbooks are listed there, also. Abundant flexibility in schedule and program for a progressive approach which deals with real problems is desirable.

Another local church agency which deserves more attention than it is receiving is *Sunday Church School class or department work for future educational workers.* There are a few pastors who report more trained workers available than they can use and inevitably one finds that they have employed this means.

In such cases there may be a leadership education division parallel to the young people's division. In one instance, a general invitation is given for enrollment and selected persons are urged to enter. Thereafter, they have two years of study, observation, and practice. At the end of that time they graduate and are placed if possible in a position of leadership. Then another class is started.

More simple procedures are possible. In one case a young people's class is started each autumn to continue through the year. The members study appropriate resources, then observe and assist under guidance for just one year. In a small town setting, three churches pooled their resources for such a class. This work, too, may be done in terms of First or Second Series Standard Leadership Curriculum courses.

Somewhat related to the above, there are various types of volunteer and informal *study groups,* which can promote leadership education in the local church. A small group of people can gather periodically to study some of the available material on current problems or hear an outside speaker on some vital topic. Also somewhat related is a *coaching conference* on lesson preparation. Once a month, if not more often, certainly once a quarter, the staff of a department or school could go over forthcoming lessons or units.

Another form of local leadership development is available to congregations through *visits by professional or semiprofessional leaders.* Major denominations have field secretaries of Christian education who regularly survey and observe in local congregations, then hold conferences and make recommendations. They may study the whole program or some feature only, such as children's or young people's work.

One form of leadership education which is available for every congregation is *guided reading.* A church school workers' library, however small to begin, can be established. Lists of recommended books can be secured from denominational houses which keep revising their lists to include new publications. A librarian may be needed to promote the reading, although that work can well be done by the pastor and superintendent. Some schools maintain a reading program like that in which a Kindergarten Department superintendent led all the workers and mothers in reading a series of books on the religious training of small children. A book table is a regular feature in some Church Schools. Public librarians will gladly co-operate where intelligent use of books is made. Every school should place *The International Journal of Religious Education* on its budget for the superintendents and similar leaders and the denominational educational periodical for every worker.

Of all local church agencies, the *monthly workers' conference* can be the most pertinent unit in the improvement program. Properly a workers' conference would be a meeting of all the workers of the church for inspiration and study to the end of larger effectiveness in the total program of the church. A simple organization with a chairman, secretary, and program committee might be effected. Objectives would be clearly determined and regular meeting times would be appointed. Plans would be laid for general programs and for specialized ones to serve the various group interests such as those of the Sunday Church School workers.

In what is to be presented here, however, the appropriate successor to the typical "Teachers' and Officers' Meeting" is in mind. Those meetings have been given over usually to routine business with a discussion of problems relating to the Christmas program, the annual picnic, attendance, reward systems, and the like. The workers' conference will necessarily take care of those items, but will never be devoted solely to them. It will attempt to lift vision to true goals and increase effectiveness in attaining those goals. It will be a time in which the workers consciously and co-operatively strive to improve their capacity to carry on the Christian educational work of their church.

The program will be fourfold. It will include devotions, not perfunctory, but planned in such a way as to employ and indirectly demonstrate improved procedures in planning and conducting worship. There will be business, conducted along parliamentary lines and limited to important issues, the routine having been cared for by the proper officers or the executive committee. Nothing will kill the whole idea more than an undue waste of time on business. Fellowship is just as important here as anywhere else. There may be a simple meal together or refreshments. Sometimes the meeting may be held at a home where it may conclude with games or visiting.

The study program is to be the heart of the meeting. The most strenuous effort will be made to deal with topics of immediate and practical interest although an adequate treatment may take the group into so-called theoretical considerations. The term "conference" should govern the procedure. That is to say that there should be abundant opportunity for all to participate fully. In many cases a general presentation or study may be followed by age-group conferences or interest-group meetings for the workers concerned with particular areas.

The topics for consideration should be chosen by the group under wise guidance which will help them to get a balanced and rounded program. Much aid will come from the denominational and interdenominational journals and various books which publish suggested programs. Topics like the following may be fruitful: What shall we do about homework? What is the proper way of viewing and handling memory work? Are we holding our young people and what can be done about it? What are our real objectives? How can we help our pupils appreciate the true meaning of Christmas? What does teaching really mean?

The ways of handling the topics will vary with the resources at hand and with variety in view. They may include discussions, lectures, outside speakers, research and reports, book reviews, and studies of textbooks in the Standard Leadership Curriculum.

The new leadership education items in filmslides, filmstrips, sound filmstrips and recordings may be the greatest boon yet. They enable the leader to present pertinent items in ways he could not duplicate in any other manner. They provoke discussion and all in all provide an unexcelled launching platform for progressive action.

A regular meeting time should be established and rigidly adhered to. The most important means of securing attendance is to provide a program which makes every worker feel a sense of opportunity. In addition there should be abundant publicity so that no one can possibly forget. Each should feel, too, that he is expected, and missed if he is not there.

Individual Agencies

Among other and effective ways of training and improving the Sunday Church School staff are several more personal agencies.

Here as elsewhere there is no better way to learn than by doing —*apprenticeship*. We have long recognized the value of "training on the job." Many present workers have begun that way. Quite young people, intermediates for example, have been called in to help with younger children. By that means they get acquainted with pupils of a given age and see the program in operation. Beginning with rather simple tasks like handling chairs, greeting pupils, assisting with coats and hats, gradually they assume tasks of more difficult nature such as telling the story, leading discussion, and guiding handwork. Incidentally, this is not, if properly handled, taking them away from their "lesson." Likely, though, they should have opportunity to maintain relations with their classes and after a time go back to regular work with the class.

Properly, an apprenticeship should involve some pre-training and should be coupled with careful coaching and guided study. The coaching can be quite informal but real. Simple suggestions can be given in advance, and the worker can be cautioned or commended after the work is finished. The reading, too, can be related to specific problems that have arisen although in time it is broadened to cover more background.

Apprenticeship may be part of a specific leadership education course. Then it takes on the character of the "practice teaching" by which public school teachers have been prepared. *Practice teaching-leading* is regularly a part of the program in some churches which maintain a leadership education division, department, or class. After preliminary study, members of the group are assigned to experienced leaders who give them opportunities to teach or lead in other ways. Meanwhile they are under the guidance of their leadership education teacher who confers with them personally and conducts sessions in which the members of the group may share their experiences and arrive co-operatively at solutions for their problems.

Under this general heading, personal *reading* must have a large place. A magnificent number of books and journals are now to be had. They must be made readily available and their reading encouraged by pastor, superintendents, librarian, and other interested persons. Somehow we need to help workers understand that this is not only a part of their responsibility but also a splendid part of their privilege. When one begins to be more intelligent about his task it becomes more meaningful and interesting.

Doubtless *weekly preparation* should be included as a form of leadership development. One study showed that teachers spend an average of two and a half hours preparing for each Sunday session. That is not enough time, yet it has educational value in content terms if no more. It can be made more valuable if the school will provide commentaries and other helps, also if teachers are trained to prepare written session patterns.

The word *observation* covers a considerable variety of means to carry on personal improvement. Workers may visit other schools to see the equipment and observe the work being done. Recently an interdenominational committee made a list of schools in which good organization and administration, curriculum, worship, and the like could be observed. The idea is to encourage people to see and carry home the fruits of their observation to make it effective in the home school.

Only good situations should be observed, or the observer should be helped to recognize that which is not good. Arrangements should be made in advance for persons who will guide the visitors and help them avoid disturbing the work. Observers should have previous direction concerning definite things to look for, and should have an opportunity to discuss their visit on their return. Visits to public schools as well as to Church Schools can be of service.

Demonstrations are sometimes arranged in conferences and conventions. They have the disadvantage of staging so that the situation is unreal and leaders as well as pupils are under strain. Nevertheless those who observe, if wisely guided, may receive much benefit. The demonstration should be preceded by a discussion of the prospective session and followed by a conference to consider its procedure and results.

Finally, earnest workers, too, may profitably employ *personal rating scales and survey schedules* now available for discovering their strengths and weaknesses.

In relation to all these matters a valuable suggestion, particularly for small churches, was made recently. Let the Sunday Church School select one very enthusiastic, promising, and popular member of the staff to become its specially trained worker. He could be provided with a magazine or two, furnished a few books, and sent to conventions, camps, and training classes. He would then become the one to whom the various members of the staff might look for suggestions in meeting their problems and he would tell his workers from time to time about his interesting discoveries.

Supervision

There is much misunderstanding about the meaning of supervision. Besides, the definition of the term has changed as the function has clarified itself. Once the supervisor was the teacher of a special subject or a person who correlated the activities of various departments. Now the supervisor is a master technician available to help those who are less mature in their experience. Supervision more broadly has the purpose of improving the acts which occur when a learner meets a leader. More narrowly, it is personal guidance of workers, on the job, for the improvement of their work and results. Somewhere it has been popularly defined as "two or more people tackling a problem that otherwise one would have to face alone." Elsewhere certain names for the supervisor have been used which help to describe the task—"teaching consultant"; "helping teacher"; and "worker counselor."

The Sunday Church School leader, as Chapter III defined his work, is supervisor as well as organizer and administrator. Likewise, pastors are constantly serving as supervisors. In the broader sense they supervise when they consciously take hold of the local situation at any point to effect improvement in the learning-teaching process.

In the more narrow sense they supervise when a worker comes to them with a specific problem and they together study the various solutions of that problem until some improvement is effected. One director of Christian education is meeting his supervisory responsibility by visiting each worker in his school once a month for a two-hour conference.

Such work is needed for many specific reasons in addition to the general fact that Church School work is subject to improvement. Superior workers can be encouraged and other workers can be lifted out of a rut. The timid who are conscious of their shortcomings can get help without undue embarrassment. The self-complacent can be shown the need for change. Beginners can have help and first aid. Very important, too, all these can work together to provide external conditions for more effective work.

Supervision will succeed most surely when it is provided as the result of a demand from the workers themselves. Otherwise a pastor, director, deaconess, or superintendent may foster it. It should be supported and directed by a responsible body such as the Church School Committee. The whole congregation should understand the work of the supervisor. Special care must be exercised in establishing right relations between the supervisor and those supervised. All supervisory processes should be conducted on a democratic, co-operative basis for this is not something which can be forced upon people.

The fundamental approach of a supervisor is through the learning-teaching act. Of course, teaching in this case is more broadly viewed as guidance in any area, session, or circumstance, not simply classroom instruction. The supervisor is interested in what takes place when leaders meet their pupils in a unit of activity. How do they study, worship, serve, or conduct fellowship? How do they work at a unit of activity? How could their performance and consequent results be improved? In particular the supervisor seeks to work with problem situations. There he observes symptoms, diagnoses causes, and suggests remedies.

The characteristic technique of supervision is threefold; including, (1) a preliminary conference with the worker involved; (2) a visit at the session in which the worker leads; (3) a conference with the worker after that visitation.

The preliminary conference is meant to enable the worker and the supervisor to arrive at mutual understanding about the goals and plans for the session and the purpose of the supervisor's visit. The visit itself should be conducted in an unobtrusive manner so that all the conditions are kept as normal as possible. Always the visit should continue throughout the session. In the post-conference meeting, the good features of the session receive paramount consideration with mutual agreement upon the steps of improvement to be undertaken. Follow-up is essential until satisfactory results are evident.

In effecting remedies for a situation, the program of improvement may extend far beyond the supervisor's immediate range of effort. Here he meets his broader task. It may include working for improvement in such areas and through such methods as the following:

Fostering the many forms of leadership education
Establishing better leadership selections
Using standards and goals for the schools and tests and measures for pupils
Improving the equipment and its management
Securing better use of records, reports, and surveys
Reorganizing
Suggesting better administrative management
Providing more adequate financial support
Educating the entire constituency of the congregation about its school
Cultivating morale
Building for better relations with the home
Developing co-operatively an improved curriculum

Out of the many forms of leadership education listed and discussed above each Sunday Church School leader faces the task of planning a complete program for the improvement of the staff in his school. It will vary with the size of the school and many other conditions. It should include every present and prospective worker and provide the maximum opportunity which can be made available and which will be used by the workers.

A minimum standard would seem to be: *some definite leadership education experience for every present worker each year and some definite preparatory possibility for prospective workers each year.* If possible, these enterprises should include regular credit courses in addition to the more informal means of improvement. The emphasis can well be placed upon growth " on the job."

MOTIVATION

Providing various means for the improvement of Sunday Church School staff members is one thing; their use of those means is another. Statistics show only a relatively small number of workers profiting by the vast efforts to help them grow in their capacity to do increasingly effective work. The suggestions which follow are meant to help the Sunday Church School leader motivate his colleagues for active participation in the available opportunities for their leadership education.

1. Set an example. Here is another place where the leader must lead. His reading, study, and attendance at conferences, camps, schools, classes, and the like will be contagious.

2. Convince workers of their need. This may well begin with a conviction of the importance of educational work in the church. It passes then to a recognition of need for progress in that work. This suggests the need for leadership education in general. Finally the individual worker should see a definite point at which he feels the need of help.

3. Convince them that they can grow. This means not only that some may think they have already attained their maximum capacity, but it also recognizes the fact that some may humbly doubt their capacity to be helped by leadership education.

4. Show them they will not be embarrassed. They will not have to take an examination, make long talks in public, give answers that may be wrong; and their written work will be seen only by themselves and the instructor.

5. Help them see the real interest in the work. Leadership education is not necessarily dull. Many people love to sharpen their wits in a study experience. Here is a challenging field.

6. *Help them develop a hunger for such study.* An outstanding camp is an ideal place to catch the spirit. Perhaps the more hesitant can be taken to visit a camp or at any rate meet an enthusiastic camper.

7. *Make the means practicable, readily within reach.* Place, amount of work required, and time schedules are important considerations. In some cases, too, financial problems must be eliminated.

8. *Make sure that the experience will contribute.* It should add to the worker's larger satisfaction in his work. This requires that he have opportunity to deal with practical problems on specific points of felt need.

9. *Plan for appropriate marking of progress.* The course cards and certificates of progress of the International Curriculum have this purpose in view.

10. *Build workers into the fellowship of the cause.* Association with important leaders will have value in this direction. Each one should see himself as part of an important movement in which honored persons are working.

Chapter IX

ADMINISTERING PUPILS

The major items in the management of pupils have to do with what is typically called the curriculum. They are discussed in chapters X through XIII. Here only those topics which concern the administrative handling of pupils are to be considered.

Less than three-tenths of the total population of the United States is enrolled in Sunday Church Schools. They attend on the average only about 60 or 65 per cent of the Sundays in each year, and no one knows how small is the percentage of punctuality.

It is proper, therefore, that three of the questions arising constantly in Sunday Church School conferences are these: How increase enrollment? How secure more regular attendance? How promote punctuality? The first of those questions will be answered in Chapter XVII; the others here.

SECURING ATTENDANCE

A member has been won for the school. He has come at least one Sunday or has been in attendance the required number of Sundays to be considered a regular member. How can his regular attendance be secured so that he will be present more than the customary eight Sundays out of each quarter?

1. Have the best possible school. This is the most important suggestion of all. Until each child, young person, and adult, along with every officer and teacher, views the Sunday Church School as the most worth-while activity in which he can engage at that hour, there is grave doubt whether any outstanding improvement in attendance records can be achieved. There is a world of suggestion in the report of a pastor who asked certain pupils to write on,

"Why Children Do Not Go to Sunday School." One answered, "Because those who go are not any different from those who do not."

It is not enough to depend upon institutional loyalty. A sense of social obligation to attend the school and support it is wholesome in its way. A concern for the "record of our class" and the "good name of our school" is not to be deprecated. Nevertheless, the proper percentage of attendance cannot be attained without primary attention upon the development of a school in which every member will find that his expenditure of effort is notably worth it for himself and others.

2. Have a common attendance goal. This is to recommend a definite organizational objective for attendance. When devising a goal for attendance effort, the school's secretary may first compute the average attendance for the past year. Then all members of the school may consider and decide upon some percentage of attendance which they will strive to achieve. It is reasonable to begin at 75 per cent, then run up to 80, 85, or even 90 per cent. The goal should be accepted by or announced to the congregation as well as the school so that everybody concerned may be working toward it. It should be visualized, progress toward its attainment being represented in charts and graphs to be placed on blackboards and bulletin boards and printed in the congregational bulletins.

3. Care for the absentees. The secretary of the school, in cooperation with the teachers, should keep careful records of attendance so that lists of absentees can be prepared each Sunday. These should be followed up, preferably by the teacher, perhaps by an absentee secretary or, if necessary, by the superintendent. Cards or letters may be sent after the first absence. Telephone calls may follow continued absence, and a personal or committee call be made if the absentee does not return promptly. Whatever the exact procedure, some definite system is necessary.

The reason for an absence is perhaps more significant than the fact of it. If there has been minor illness or similar reason, showing an interest and encouraging the absentee to return is enough. Often, however, a more basic cause is involved and a persistent study should be undertaken so that the school may counteract it. Is the pupil disinterested? Is he not fitting comfortably into his group? Is the school displeasing to him at some other point? Is his work not meeting his needs? Does the leader fail to understand him and minister to him effectively? Are there home conditions which could be changed? Does he need help with a transportation problem? Such an analysis of reasons for absences may reveal important problems which the school can solve.

4. *Surround the pupils with friendship.* Not long ago a young woman made a glowing report of her reception when she went to visit a neighboring school. She was greeted at the door, ushered to the proper place, guided through the service, and welcomed in a class. She says that she will always be interested in that school although she has no intention of becoming a member of it.

Contrast that reception with the coldness with which a newcomer is sometimes received. No effort is made to remove the sense of strangeness. He enters the room, looks around for the most inconspicuous place to sit, feels unwelcome stares of curiosity, makes inquiries about the proper thing to do and the proper class to join, then awaits the close of the hour in order to escape.

One objective of the Sunday Church School is that of fostering fellowship. People learn to practice fellowship by experiencing its worth to themselves and being led by their teachers and officers to shed its grace upon one another in the school. That same activity will advance the school toward its attendance goal.

5. *Avoid eliminations.* The high rate of elimination of pupils from our schools appalls every leader who knows the statistics. According to one study, the peak of attendance comes at about the age of twelve. From that time the exit sign is up. Of twelve boys in Sunday Church School at eleven years of age, six will have gone by the time they are sixteen and eleven by the time they are twenty-two, leaving but one member. Of eight girls attending at twelve years of age, one will be gone at fourteen, five will be gone at eighteen and seven at twenty-two, leaving only one.

What shall be done about that situation? Certainly it is not enough to lament it. Careful study of the reasons why the young people of a particular school are leaving that school should be made. Then the conclusions which arise out of an analysis of those reasons should be acted upon.

Two of the most important considerations in avoiding the typical elimination of pupils will be maintaining a program and providing a type of leadership that will continue to interest the pupils as they advance in age. Sunday Church School pupils must have, always, a growing experience which is adapted to life's changing interests and avoids the monotonous repetitions which too often characterize the program. A third essential is to secure the participation of the pupils in the development of policies, the determination of programs, and the control of organization. The pupils must be worked into the school as integral parts of its ongoing societal functions. Special attention to this matter should be given to the pupils on junior and senior high school levels.

6. *Secure home co-operation.* Through the Indiana Survey, already quoted several times, it was found that "the chief factor in regularity of attendance in the Sunday School is the religious sentiment of the various homes." That suggests that the development of more regular attendance is to be accomplished in part by building religious educational sentiment in the home.

There are, however, additional considerations with respect to the home's relationship to Sunday Church School attendance. Have provisions been made for the parents and older persons in the home to have an ongoing program in the Sunday Church School, so that they will wish to attend and in doing so bring the younger members of the family? Does the school meet at times and under other conditions which are favorable for home co-operation in attendance? Has the home been kept fully informed of the work of the school so that it is interested in that work and co-operative in carrying it on? Does the school aim to help the parents with certain problems of the children so that parents welcome this opportunity for assistance? This is to say that home co-operation is not necessarily something which the home alone must give to the school. It suggests that the school, even more fundamentally, be co-operating with the home.

7. *Send quarterly reports.* Reports to the pupils and through the pupils to the parents are chiefly in mind. Needless to say, though, there should be reports upon the parents as well as the pupils. Such reports might open the eyes of everybody concerned regarding the facts and so challenge and promote more regular attendance.

8. *Recognize achievement in this respect.* Artificial incentives are to be avoided in all Sunday Church School work. Regularity of attendance depends primarily upon the program's ministry to the interests of the pupils and to the values realized in the lives of the pupils. Even the Christian life, however, leaves room for some recognition of genuine achievement. Any person who exercises his Christian responsibilities with vitality deserves the commendation "good and faithful steward." In the Sunday Church School commendation may be given through a kindly word by teacher, school executive, or pastor. There can be an honor roll or perhaps an honor day. The church publicity can carry the names of those who have been regular in attendance.

9. *Avoid contests.* The various publishers of Sunday Church School equipment have well-nigh exhausted human ingenuity to discover new forms of Sunday School contests. There is more than one fault about them all. They concentrate attention upon winning the contest and that is not the proper motive for religious work. They set group against group in competition whereas the only rivalry appropriate in Christian institutions is that of a group against its own previous record. Thus, in contests, time and effort are expended in ways which are not fruitful for Christian growth. Then, too, there are always the losers as well as the winners of the contest!

10. *Educate all concerned.* It ought to be unnecessary, yet it needs to be said—the procedures of a school should be educational. Consequently in matters of attendance it is desirable to share the

facts among pupils, parents, teachers, officers and all others involved
so that they may understand the situation and respond to it appropriately. Certainly a Sunday Church School service held weekly
for one hour, at intervals of seven days, is a meager enough educational program to care for such high interests. Then, when people
waste that inadequate provision by attending only 60 per cent of
the time (and usually late), they multiply the difficulties in doing
a thorough educational job.

The whole membership should know the facts. They should
understand the difficulties which they create by irregularity. They
should acknowledge in their own spirits what they are missing.
They should realize the privileges which they may have and the
advantages which they may enjoy by regular and prompt attendance. These matters must be brought before them constantly and
kept before them.

The use of the congregational bulletin is suggested as a primary means for this purpose. In addition, the special programs
which the school provides from time to time can be utilized, and it
is well in periodic calls upon parents to bring out these facts.

SECURING PUNCTUALITY

Who would venture even a guess concerning the number of
people on time for Sunday Church School sessions? Would it be
75 per cent? Would it be 50 per cent? Would it be only 25 per
cent? More important, what shall be done about this matter? There
is at best only an hour. When five, ten, or fifteen minutes are lost,
a good portion of the golden opportunity is wasted.

1. *Make the opening moments worth while.* This is the most
vital suggestion of all. Fundamentally nothing can secure permanently the goal of punctuality save a program that is vital. The
opening of the school begins essentially when the pupil arrives.
His leaders should be on hand to greet him. Preparation should
have been made for pre-session conversation, fellowship, and work.
If possible, the pupil should be given some task to help with the
work of the school, or he may start some piece of work on the

unit of activity in which the class is engaged.

More formally, of course, the school session will begin with worship. Some years ago a pastor reported that his Junior Department superintendent was conducting the finest services of worship he had ever known. When asked whether the pupils were coming on time, he replied that they were. Similarly, in a large institute, three hundred leaders were asked to tell how many of their pupils come on time. The leaders of only one school replied in terms above 80 per cent. When asked to give the reasons for that high attainment, they mentioned first the fine services of worship conducted by the superintendents in that school. To feel that you will miss something worth while if you are not on time is the highest incentive to be there punctually.

2. Have a mutual goal. As in the matter of attendance, the school should study the problem of punctuality and set a goal. It might begin, for example, at 50 per cent of the people on time. The point is to start at a figure which can be reached in a reasonably brief period of time and then move forward step by step toward the highest ideal. That probably is represented in the public schools which maintain a punctuality record approximately 98 per cent. Progress toward the goal should be made concrete by interesting charts or graphs presented and discussed in the school.

3. Have the staff on time. One cannot blame Jimmie and Mary for coming late every Sunday when the teachers and officers are late. The attainment of a punctuality goal depends first upon the earnestness with which the workers themselves accept the responsibility. One school recently published a bulletin which set forth in unmistakable terms each worker's duty to arrive ten minutes early. It states that 93 per cent of the cases of being late are inexcusable. Every officer and teacher is to be at his post of duty at nine-twenty. Anyone coming at nine-thirty, the regular Sunday School hour, is considered ten minutes late. The bulletin presents a long list of reasons for being early in terms of what it will do for the school in contrast with the results of being late. A major consideration is the sense of sincerity which is created by those who are on time as over against the lack of confidence which is cultivated by those who seem not to be taking their work seriously.

4. Start promptly. When we know that a certain program will start on time unfailingly, we aim to be there promptly. Contrariwise, if past experience teaches us that we shall waste our time by punctuality, we wait until we know that the business will start. So does the Sunday Church School membership. The superintendent who is beginning to work for punctuality should start on time if there is nobody present but himself.

5. Close the doors. This is not to be carried out in a spirit of bitterness toward the dilatory but in a spirit of fairness toward the people who have come on time. More fundamentally it is proper education for proper church membership. The typical Sunday Church School opening service is a time of confusion and chaos caused by people arriving late. They swish their clothing, drop their caps or gloves, step over other people's feet as they get into their places, and distract attention generally. Thus it is impossible for the members who have come on time to enter into a hearty experience of reverent worship. Meanwhile, too, all are learning bad habits.

Depending upon the arrangement of the doors, the late people may be ushered to a position at the back of the room where they can be given books and so enter into the service from that point. Or, it may be necessary to have ushers in the hall who keep people quiet until an opportune moment has arrived for them to enter the doors and take their places. At any cost, the punctual should be protected in their right of undisturbed meeting with God.

Under the preceding topic, "Securing More Regular Attendance," five additional suggestions were made which pertain equally to this matter of securing punctuality. They are: (6) *secure home co-operation;* (7) *send quarterly reports;* (8) *recognize achievement;* (9) *avoid contests;* (10) *educate all concerned.*

GROUPING, GRADING, AND CLASSIFYING

In even the smallest of schools, the pupils must be grouped.

The standard setup includes children's, young people's, and adult divisions, and in larger schools, nursery, kindergarten, primary, junior, intermediate, senior, young people's, and adult departments divided into various classes.

The purpose in grouping pupils is not merely to meet some prescribed standards of organization. It is to get homogeneous units. Education requires that people of like experience and of similar purposes and interests—the people who can and will work together—meet in groups of their own kind. In schools which recognize that point of view fully, the typical Sunday Church School organization of divisions, departments, and classes is not sufficiently flexible. Consequently, in presenting this treatment of the subject which will fit the usual situation, but scarcely the more progressive school, it is understood that additional flexibility will be allowed where necessary.

In all situations we organize for the sake of purposeful, democratic activity. Therefore persons are put into the groups where they can do what they rightly want to do and where they can work effectively to accomplish their objectives. There is, too, the fact that pupils need to develop the capacity to work in and with groups. Therefore they must be put into a group where they will fit properly to have that experience.

The usual bases of differentiation for grouping are age and sex. Ordinarily, for example, the children nine, ten, and eleven years of age are put together in the junior department. Usually, too, boys are separated from girls. Sex segregation is unwise. Fallacious psychological reasons are often used to explain it, but in all probability the practice grew out of the ancient tradition by which men sat on one side of the church and women on the other. That custom, the vogue when Sunday Church Schools originated, simply carried over into the school but now should be discarded as outmoded.

Boys and girls work together in public schools. They do now and will continue to live together in homes. Their religious experiences are not particularly dissimilar. So they need not be

separated in Sunday School; indeed, it is better to put them together. That minimizes their differences instead of emphasizing
them. It gets the boys and girls of the congregation acquainted
with one another. Sex does not make much difference in the ability
to get good ideas, and both men and women are broadened by
sharing their ideas.

Regarding other differences, calendar age is not the ideal basis
of classification although it is perhaps the most practical one.
There is a physical age, a social age, a mental age, and theoretically,
a religious age which we may sometime be able to determine.
Meanwhile, there is reason to believe that the religious age will
normally correlate rather well with the mental age. Consequently,
some Sunday Church Schools are using the public school grade,
based in part on mental age, as the basis for grouping the younger
pupils. Among older pupils, their interests in particular subjects
or their general social situation may provide the best basis of dif-
ferentiating. Something must be said in favor of recognizing the
interests of those who form spontaneous groups outside of school.
Practically, though, most schools cannot do much better than to
follow chronological age grouping.

The proper sizes for the various groups is an important consideration. There was a time when exact specifications had been
worked out. Now it is recognized that the proper size of a group,
particularly a class, depends upon objectives, equipment, methods,
discipline, and conditions of leadership. The trend is toward larger
groups if conditions are favorable. A good teacher in an adequate
setting can accomplish more with a large group than two or three
less qualified teachers with parts of the group. Yet the class must
not be so large that the teacher cannot give careful guidance to
each member. Large classes are not to be undertaken as an escape
to something easier. They demand appropriate types of teaching,
careful planning, and special efforts at keeping personal contacts.
The final question is, does this plan provide the best way of developing the Christian life of the pupils involved?

PROMOTING

If the Sunday Church School has a definite system of grouping it must provide for the regular progression of the pupils from one group to another. The progression of a pupil through the school is accomplished by promotion.

In larger schools pupils are promoted from one class or one department to another. In the smallest schools there should be a promotion about every three years or as often as a pupil is ready for another department. To remain throughout the larger part of one's Sunday Church School experience with one teacher or in a particular class, even to be kept too long in one department is no less than a calamity for any pupil. There should be a sense of progress in a church school just as there is in public school. Further, there should be variety of experiences with different groups and leaders.

In developmental Christian education there could be more flexibility about such matters than in the typical school. A student might be permitted to shift from class to class, even department to department, in relation to the unit of activity in which he is most interested or in which his growth can be fostered best. Even so, a time should come when the various units of activity are brought to a place where there can be what is usually called promotion day.

Promotion Day

Promotion day gives significance to the beginning of work under new conditions; it provides a degree of recognition for work completed; it develops in pupils and leaders in the school a feeling of attainment; it furnishes the school an opportunity to look back over its work with satisfaction. Its basic importance may be in the fact that the school is compelled to reclassify its pupils and start them anew upon activities which are appropriate to their progress.

In most cases promotion day is the last Sunday in September or the first Sunday in October. Then the pupils are all back from summer vacation and the school is ready to take up the work more seriously for the oncoming year. It is also the beginning of a new quarter, in many schools the beginning of the first quarter of the new Sunday Church School year when the pupils start their work with new lesson materials.

The day ought to be celebrated with a service of definitely religious character. It is not to be what one harrassed worker referred to as "commotion day." Parents may be invited and it may be a Sunday Church School day in the congregation. There should be some concrete and visible evidence of promotion if possible. Diplomas can be used and classes can be moved actually up to their new positions. There they should be thoughtfully introduced so that they can begin to feel at home. Such standards as the following may be applied: Is it worth while educationally, memorable? Does it recognize accomplishment? Does it produce school spirit? Is it orderly? Does it provide for a true religious experience?

Shall the teacher be promoted with the class? In many cases the answer has been affirmative with the result that teachers have remained with a group for many years, perhaps through their entire Sunday Church School experience. The disadvantage of that procedure lies in the fact that those pupils have had but one interpretation of Christianity and one Christian personality influencing their lives. It is considered preferable to have a teacher remain with a pupil through the three years of a typical department. This avoids the difficulty just mentioned and the further one which arises when the pupils change teachers every year so that neither they get well acquainted with their teacher, nor their teacher with them.

Standards

Many Sunday Church Schools require certain standards for promotion. These are put usually in terms of requirements. The following is a typical example:

Junior Department Requirements

1. Know the Ten Commandments.
2. Be able to recite the Christmas and Easter stories.
3. Know the Apostles' Creed and Lord's Prayer.
4. Be able to name the books of the Bible in order.

Are such requirements desirable? It was Promotion Day in a mid-western city. Members of the junior department were brought before the congregation to recite the memory requirements for advancement to the intermediate department. More than half of them did not know the requirements, yet they were being promoted. That was no less than immoral and irreligious. There is some question whether we can ever have real standards for promotion in the Sunday Church School even if it were agreed that we should. Meanwhile, it is better to have honor work in each department and let pupils who complete it be promoted with special diplomas.

Special Problems

Unfortunately, every school has its quota of subnormal pupils. What shall be done about promoting them? In some cases, special provision should be made for these unfortunates in the school itself, in a special school which might be arranged in larger cities, or in the home. They do create certain social problems for both teacher and pupils in the typical school. On the other hand, it may be argued that they provide a special opportunity for the members of the school to exercise the right sort of Christian democracy. As a general rule it is best, if possible, to let them go along with their class, keeping somewhat within the same age range as those with whom they would normally be associated.

At the other end of the scale, there are superior pupils who are out of step with their age group because of their greater advancement. These pupils too, create problems. Again, the general principle is to keep them on their own age level or in their own school grade. There, though, they should be given special work to do. In some cases they can be made officers or assistants for some type of work in the school.

HAVING "DISCIPLINE"

A university student of Christian education, observing a teacher at work, heard the teacher scold the pupils twenty-three times in nineteen minutes. A pastor whose Sunday Church School building was just across the street from a public school building asked the question, "Why do they behave so well on the other side of the street in the public school, but so badly in our church school?" Yes, why is there so much disorder, irreverence, and misbehavior in the typical school?

Concern about this problem is proper for two reasons. First, order creates the conditions under which good work can be done while disorder makes it impossible to accomplish the school's objectives. Second, a matter so often overlooked, disorder provides bad character training whereas good character training is the purpose.

Before discipline can be discussed to the highest advantage, it needs to be defined. The ideal school is not that in which pupils are regimented into military discipline and where the proverbial pin can be heard to drop. On the other hand, it is a school in which there is no confusion save that which is a normal part of work going on busily for the achievement of proper objectives. The highest discipline is present where the members of the school are proceeding by inner control which grows principally out of their assurance that values are being achieved. We have gone beyond those thirteen "Rules of This Sunday-school" reported in *The Teacher Taught* of 1839 where this one was printed in capital letters: "I MUST ALWAYS BE STILL."

Reasons for Disorder

Bad order in a Sunday Church School may arise from many different sources. One of these is *the general condition of the school*. The school's traditions may be involved. Many a boy has come into the school (let us say at twelve years of age) and entered a class where the other boys did not behave. It is hardly to be expected that he ever will behave. Contagion often works to this same end. Some one person in the class or the school starts something and disorder spreads throughout the room. Very often misbehavior grows out of a desire for attention.

Much disorder arises from inadequate equipment. To have a

large number of classes in one room at one time; to have unsuited chairs, no blackboards, inadequate quantities of material—these make pupils restive and subject to disorder. The prevalence of distraction needs attention too. Pupils moving restlessly about, workers flitting hither and yon, the scraping and moving of chairs, the confused buzzing of voices make bedlam for sensitive nerves. Finally, there is the matter of low ideals on the part of the Sunday Church School workers. Many workers have themselves grown up in schools where poor discipline prevailed. They do not realize that they should insist upon a greater degree of reverence and secure a finer spirit of co-operation in real work toward the objectives of the school.

Another source of disorder is in *matters for which teachers and officers are largely responsible.* Tardy leaders are an occasion for the beginning of trouble. The very fact of their late arrival suggests their lack of seriousness about the matter. Besides, leaders who arrive late cannot exercise their influence to keep order from the beginning. Unprepared workers are another major cause of disorder. If a teacher does not have a general background of understanding of his work, if he does not know what he is going to say or do, he probably will neither do nor say much that is worth while. The pupils consequently find something more interesting to do. Particularly distressing is the habit of irregularity on the part of the leaders. When somebody from the adult Bible class who is unprepared for the task, unacquainted with the pupils, and not particularly skilled in teaching is called unexpectedly to act as a substitute teacher, good order can scarcely be expected.

The first place to look for causes of disorder should be, of course, *in connection with the pupil program.* Bad discipline is inevitable if there is lack of pupil purpose. When pupils have neither a definite purpose in their minds nor any assurance that the purpose, if they have one, could be realized, order is not to be expected. Unsuited programs may be the difficulty. If the pupil finds that the program is uninteresting, beneath his dignity, above his understanding, in short if it does not wholly absorb him in co-operative participation for the meeting of his needs and interests, he will turn his attention elsewhere. Finally, there is the lack of pupil determination which is so prevalent in many schools. Pupils do better if they feel that the school is in some measure their own school, for whose good name and effectiveness they are personally responsible.

Securing Order

In proceeding from the typical Sunday Church School conditions to more ideal ones there are certain standards which should be applied. Any effort at discipline should be tested by these questions:

Does it harmonize with social ideals being taught in the school; is it Christian?

Does it represent a positive and constructive approach rather than a negative and repressive one?

Does it proceed by indirect rather than by direct means?

Does it appeal to the highest values which the pupil can understand?

With those standards in view, ten positive suggestions for improvement follow:

1. *Eliminate the cause of disorder.* Manifestly the first effort at discipline should be the correction of those predisposing conditions described above.

2. *Depend upon the co-operation of the pupils.* This suggests letting the whole school assume responsibility for its good order. It is everybody's school; let there be as much self-government as possible. Get the pupils to work at the increase of order. Let them control the other members of the group.

It is a good plan to permit all classes to set aside the regular lessons for one Sunday in order to discuss and arrive at some conclusions on the question of proper school etiquette. Out of this might grow a council to be chosen and charged with responsibility in this field or a series of regulations growing out of the situation itself. There could be a program of stories, poems, songs, dramatizations related to the matter. Self-rating charts or records could be devised.

3. Develop morale and esprit de corps. In all efforts for discipline, the pupil's self-respect is not to be sacrificed or his good will destroyed. On the contrary, every effort will be made to build up morale on the part of all. Let the teacher set the pace for work, interest, and good will. The pupils will catch the spirit. Let the superintendent be a person of genuine, wholesome, and stable enthusiasm. The resulting contagion will work out eventually in some of the most unpromising pupils.

4. Insist on good deportment. Some years ago a school psychologist, talking on problems of discipline, emphasized this point of firmness. "A firm hand is to be kept upon the throttle when necessary and no foolishness is to be tolerated," she said. When plans have been made and regulations established, then they should be carried out. There is to be no backing down unless it be discovered that wrong has been done. At the same time the leader must keep his self-respect and self-control.

5. Don't whine, plead, beg, or scold. Always the pupil is to be approached with the ideal of helpfulness to him and with the expectation that he will co-operate. The opposite approach may only increase the difficulty. Human nature is sometimes so perverse that persons like to go away from the class boasting about the trouble they caused. Good humor is important.

6. Let the facts be understood. As suggested above, it would be wise from time to time to set aside all other lessons while the pupils discuss proper etiquette in their school: What is proper to do and what is improper? What shall we approve and what shall we frown upon? Reprimands, ridicule, sarcasm have been found to give chiefly negative results. Friendly conference has been found to give good results. The best approach is to recognize the importance of dealing with the real thing, the life itself, and the rewards which inevitably accompany it.

7. Be reasonable, not officious or fussy. Under the conditions existing in most Sunday Church Schools, some distraction and confusion cannot be avoided. The typical equipment, for example, breeds a degree of excitability and consequent disorder. Although ideals ought to be high, they ought not be unreasonable.

Conditions can be improved if workers arrive early, make sure that everything is ready, and have something for the early arriving pupils to do. Teachers and officers themselves should reduce to a minimum the noise and confusion they make. Sessions should not be interrupted by persons who drop in for casual visits. As one particular, the so-called "Sunday School story-papers" should be distributed in a manner which will not cause disorder. Then, too, there should be proper transition from one part of the Sunday morning schedule to the other.

8. *Suggest, expect, ask, discuss, instead of commanding.* While, of course, the time may come when definite instructions must be given, it will be better to practice democratic procedures. The final showdown, the fight-it-out attitude, should be avoided except as a last alternative. The leader can do much by a good-natured and tactful spirit, exemplified with a great deal of mental alertness in handling a situation at the beginning before it develops into something serious.

9. *Let regulations grow out of situations.* It is best when the need for rules is discovered by the pupils themselves. Then they will be ready to set up their own rules and obey them.

10. *Make the social approval and disapproval of the members work for order.* Too often those who misbehave get the attention and interest of the group. They may feel that they are being admired for the "courage and manliness" which they are showing. Leaders must switch that stimulus of group approval to those who do the real work in the group.

Handling Individual Adjustments

When all such efforts have been made, there may yet remain some problems of individual adjustment in certain cases of special difficulty. Here are a few suggestions for the handling of these persons. Get acquainted with them. Give them a big brother or sister. Arrange so that, perhaps, they recognize their foolishness. Get persons to help the individuals to find their places socially and forget their independence. Have the pupils avoid laughing at them. The best suggestion of all for helping with individual problems is to *make the school wrecker a school builder.*

SECURING FAVORABLE RESPONSES

Essentially, this chapter has been dealing throughout with matters of securing favorable responses on the part of the pupils. The following in particular, have been considered: attendance, punctuality, interest in progress, and good order. There are many other responses which are desired. They include such things as general enthusiasm, readiness to serve, co-operation, interest, and support.

Just as the responses which are desired from the members of the school are many and complex, likewise the methods of securing those responses are not simple. Two major suggestions will be made beyond the inevitable one of providing a program which the pupil finds worth while.

Providing for Determination

Provision for determination deals with arrangements by which the pupil will have full opportunity to participate in the selection of the objective he is to serve and the procedure by which he attempts to attain that objective. It thinks of the pupils as persons who are directing their own education while teachers and officers of the school are their helpers. The smallest child can begin to have his part in the work of the school by doing some small task in the nursery department; perhaps he is asked what he might like to do and given the opportunity to choose between two alternatives as to work which he will undertake. The teacher, too, may yield to his request for something that he would like. A little later the same child may take some small part in the program of the morning session, doing something for the entire group.

As the pupil makes progress he has an opportunity to discuss some topic, decide upon more important policies, control expenditure of money, vote upon some conclusion, conduct some program such as a service of worship. Meanwhile, too, he has been taking his full part in guiding the unit of activity which is the present work of the class, and selecting that which is to follow as the next unit in the sequence. All the time his leaders have been the directors, the responsible heads of the program. They have shaped the situation so that the program will not drift off into wastefulness, yet they have taken their position essentially as coaches, guides, and helpers who provide the setting for profitable educational experience to take place.

The pupil's first step of a more formal sort in the determination of the work of the school may be service on some committee. Another step in pupil determination would be membership on a departmental board, such as representative on a young people's council or the Church School Council. In time he might become a member of the administrative staff.

Organized classes foster self-government, develop individual initiative and personal responsibility, satisfy social tendencies, enhance class spirit, general esprit de corps, and school loyalty. However, it must be asked whether the school is being overorganized, whether the class is really contributing to morale, whether the attitude toward the whole school is a desirable one. Classes certainly should not be organized unless there are definite objectives for them.

Knowing Pupils

In all these procedures the Sunday Church School leader will need to know his pupils. He will need to know pupils in general, that is, the characteristics which are common to the various age groups. He will need to know them specifically, with regard to their situations at home, at school, and the like. And finally, the leader will need to know the individuals so that he can mention them by name and work with them in the spirit of true fellowship.

There should be cards or letters of congratulations and good wishes at appropriate times. Members of the school should be cordially invited not only to its various affairs, but also to all the activities of the church. Books should be shared. Young people should be helped with their lifework. New pupils in the school should receive special attention. All in all there should be an abundance of fellowship between all youth and all adults in the school so that there is indeed a social, intellectual, and religious sharing of personality which is appropriate to democratic and Christian living.

Chapter X

PROVIDING A PUPIL PROGRAM

Chapters X through XIII are to deal with the leader and what is usually called the curriculum. That word is not used in the chapter titles, however, because of the wrong meaning sometimes attached to it. "Curriculum" is taken often to mean the lesson books used in the school. The meaning here is much broader, indeed, different. Lesson books are only curricular texts, resource materials, or pupil and leader guides. The curriculum is all that the pupil does under the guidance and with the help of his leaders, especially his teachers. Properly, it includes activities of study-and-instruction, worship, fellowship, and service undertaken in units which develop as a program unified in itself and integrated with the total program of the congregation.

These matters which pertain to curriculum are of first importance. All other concerns of the Sunday Church School leader are, in a way, subordinate. Everything he does is directly or indirectly to the end that the program of pupil activities may be as fruitful as possible in Christian growth.

Rightly understood, the word curriculum is a good one. In its derivation it means "race track." Thus the curriculum is a path, prepared and fenced in, along which the pupil is being guided. It will be found later, however, to include not only the track on which the pupil runs, but also the race which he runs and the personality change which takes place in the running.

A curriculum is a series of activities through which a learner is guided by leaders so that desirable sorts of change take place in his living and greater abundance of life results.

THE NEW CURRICULUM

The view of curriculum which has developed within Christian education since 1925 has been shaped most largely by Dr. William C. Bower. From his point of view, the curriculum is that part of the pupil's stream of experience which is brought under consideration in the school for enrichment of meaning and increase of control.[1]

Curriculum in Terms of Experience

A pupil is passing through certain experiences in his various life situations where he has problems with which he needs help. The Sunday Church School is equipped in leaders, materials, and procedures to assist him at given points. So certain experiences are brought under consideration in the school for educational results. The curriculum consists of the learner-and-leader dealings with those experiences.

In that view the curriculum is seen as a series of educational events involving: the material, historical and contemporary, employed—content; the techniques concerned in using it—procedure; and, as a basic ingredient, the pupil's "becoming" in, with, and through the above—experience. In Christian education the events of the curriculum include: (a) the lesson studied, the pupil's work studying and being instructed, and *primarily* the reconstruction taking place in the pupil as he studies; (b) the worship service in which the pupil engages, the communion with God which he enjoys, and *primarily* the change going on in him as he communes; (c) the social affair planned for the pupil's enjoyment, the fellowship he has in it, and *primarily* the social development which he is undergoing as he participates; and (d) the service enterprise which the pupil undertakes, its performance and *primarily* the growing of his personality as he does his good deed.

An important precaution must be observed regarding that analysis. It suggests a fragmentation which falsifies the concept

---

[1] William C. Bower, *The Curriculum of Religious Education* (New York: Charles Scribner's Sons, 1925).

to that extent. Learning takes place in wholes. The curriculum properly is constituted of units of work with interrelated aspects. Study-and-instruction, worship, fellowship, and service should be woven as varied colors into a total pattern which constitutes the design of the experience.

Thus, all in all, Bower considers the curriculum as life—life undergoing reconstruction, life in the process of being enriched and controlled, life being made richer as to meaning, life being socialized, life being brought under control to larger self-realization.[2]

Curriculum in Terms of Activities

Here, curriculum was defined earlier as a series of activities through which a learner is guided by leaders with the result that desirable sorts of change take place in his living and he consequently has greater abundance of life.

That definition is not meant to be different in essence from Bower's. It uses different language because it aims to bring the definition into harmony with the terminology and approach represented throughout this book. The term "activities" is considered preferable to the more vague, subjective, and passive "experience." Also, since we learn to do by doing, the objective and the method

---

[2] "The experience curriculum will, then, consist of a body of carefully selected and organized experiences lifted out of the actual, ongoing life of the person or of the social group; of a critical study of the situations themselves for their essential factors and their possible outcomes; of the ideas, ideals, attitudes, and habits that have emerged from the past experience of the learner and of the vast stores of historical subject-matter that have descended from generation to generation and that contain in organized and available forms the best that the race has thought and felt and purposed. One will miss the time-honored text-books and schedules of things to be learned. Instead one will find a body of experience that is feeling its way from point to point of meaning and control as it moves out into the uncharted areas that skirt its everwidening frontiers, and rich body of source material in which the learner may see his own experience reflected and interpreted, and by the aid of which he may deepen his own insights into reality, widen the range of his own outlook upon life, and bring his own experience under conscious and certain control in the light of the most dependable knowledge, the worthiest ideals, and the highest purposes of the race." (From *The Curriculum of Religious Education*, p. 179.)

of education alike are activities.

Curriculum in terms of activities, too, is concerned with the pupil's stream of experience. The pupil desires, and the Church School leader aims at helping him, to move from his present status to a more desirable one. That is to say that the two have a mutual purpose for the pupil to live his Christian life on a higher level than at present, with the corresponding increase of abundance. It is also to say that the pupil is to change so that he will be performing more desirable and satisfying Christian activities. Since he will learn to do by doing, the means by which he moves toward his higher achievement is the performance of ever-increasingly desirable activities. Certain activities in his total system of current living can be affected by the school. They become his curriculum so that the curriculum is a series of constantly improving activities. In actual fact, some activities are being introduced anew; others are in process of elimination; still others are increasing or diminishing. Yet the word "improving" covers all types.

THE PLACE OF THE BIBLE

Bible lessons have been viewed so long as *the* curriculum that the use of the Bible in the new curriculum needs immediate consideration.

Functional Outlook

When the Bible is used to promote growth in the direction of the objectives of Christian education, it is being used educationally. The particular way of utilization now gaining currency is known as *functional*.   Historical research discloses that this is the way Jesus used the Old Testament and the early church used the then new New Tetament. Also, it is in harmony with the manner by which the Bible arose—life, then oral tradition, then record. It reverses that process—record, oral tradition, life.

In the functional outlook, the Bible is utilized as a resource to show the direction for and give support to the ongoing Christian faith-life of persons and groups. The materials are employed to enrich and control present religious experience. They are used to show Christian people the kind of activities which are appropriate to their abundant living and move the people to perform them.

Perhaps the particular manner of functional use can be expressed best by a contrast. In both the older and newer types of curriculum, the purpose is that pupils shall "live the Bible way." In the older curriculum, the approach is as if to say:

"Here is the Bible.

"Listen to what it says.

"Go, do that."

In the newer curriculum, the approach is:

"Here we are with this problem in living.

"What shall we do?

"Let us see what help the Bible can furnish."

The focus in the former case is the Bible; in the latter, persons within their life situations. Perhaps better, the starting point in the former case is the Word in its written form. In the latter case, it is the persons in whom the Word is to live again. Always, the Bible is being used as a means of grace.

General Possibilities

In general, the Bible is utilized functionally in the new curriculum as a "resource." We go to it as to a storehouse of materials for fostering Christian growth with consequent increase of abundance in living. Figuratively, it is a pool of the water and a granary for the bread of Christian existence; it is also a sun for light; and a "pile" of power for Christian living. As such, it is capable of enlightening the Christian person or group; of directing, nourishing, and empowering them as well.

More exactly, the Bible can aid development in the primarily intellectual area; it provides meaning, deepens insight, furnishes standards of appraisal and shows direction for effort. It can aid development in the primarily emotional area as it subdues or stirs feeling, provides proper outlets for expression, restrains or liberates the spirit. Also, it can aid development in the primarily volitional area by developing purposes, reinforcing motives, lending steadiness, and releasing power. In totality, it integrates personality.

These potentialities of the Bible to effect educational results are called "teaching values." A value in general is a resource, a thing worth while to satisfy a felt need and bring a desired satisfaction. It is a tool for a task; a solution for a problem; a way out for an interest; the answer to a desire; something you can utilize to help you advance your abundance of life. Teaching values are values which produce growth; change in knowledge, attitude, skill; development toward objectives.

Teaching values of the Bible, then, are potentialities resident in a passage of Scripture to effect educational results. The teaching value of a passage is its usefulness to interpret, evaluate, redirect, and empower human experience. A passage has teaching value when it is convincing, conclusive, effective for functioning to enrich and control personal and social life; when it is capable of becoming, indeed, a means of grace toward salvation; when it can be laid parallel with a human aspiration, need, interest, or purpose so as to transfuse Spirit into spirit.

Teaching values of the Bible are like naval craft which come alongside other vessels to render some special service: to put aboard a pilot; to bring a doctor; to supply food, water, or fuel; to put out a fire; to pass a line for a tow; to ease the ship into a berth. In functional use of the Bible, similarly its teaching values are brought to bear upon human activities.

More Specific Uses

The Bible can be utilized in that way for a minor purpose—enrichment, and for a major purpose—control. Those two interact, each being in some degree a by-product of the other. The minor purpose is to *enrich* the Christian life of persons and groups. Biblical materials may serve to help pupils have more abundant life whether or not they control conduct to any considerable degree. It is worth while dealing with the Bible just for the sake of knowing it and being in the company of those who do. It is history; it is literature. There are scholarly, aesthetic, and fellow-ship values which alone (if must be) make its use worth while. In some detail, these values lodge in such categories as: vocabulary, imagery, fund of knowledge, sense of beauty, devotional attitude.

The major purpose in educational use of the Bible is to *control* the Christian life of persons and groups. Objectively, first, biblical materials may serve to help pupils by (1) *guiding* them in the performance of Christian activities. It (a) presents *examples-in-performance* of activities desirable and undesirable. (Examples: Christ's prayers, Peter's denial.) It (b) gives *statements-of-principle* concerning the performance of activities desirable and undesirable. (Examples: the Ten Commandments.) Objectively, second, biblical materials may serve to help pupils by (2) *stimulating* them in the performance of activities. It (a) shows *values* and *penalties* associated with various activities desirable and undesirable. (Examples: the Beatitudes.) It (b) brings *sanctions* and *disapprovals* to bear upon various activities desirable and undesirable. (Examples: "Go and do thou likewise"; "Thou shalt not . . .") The subjective service of Scripture is to energize pupils so that they may accomplish what they have been guided and stimulated to do.

Method

The teacher's principal purpose is not to expound Bible: it is to help people "live the Bible way." One angle, and only one, although its importance is not to be undervalued, is to study the Bible with the pupils. That may require an element of exposition, but exposition should be kept at the minimum necessary to effective biblical utilization.

There are six modes of handling the Bible in teaching:

1. Start and end with facts in and concerning the Bible largely for the sake of the Bible. (Bible study with the idea that "the Bible ought to be known.")
2. Start and end with facts in and concerning the Bible with more or less expectation that there will be (a) enrichment or (b) issue in

faith and practice. (The first step toward functional outlook.)

3. Start with a stated pasage; "apply" it to a related life problem. (The usual Sunday Church School lesson.)

4. Start with a stated life problem; seek and consider passages related to it. (Start with "What is God like?" and refer to biblical passages.)

5. Consider life as it is developing; seek related biblical passages as needed. (Like "Bible study" in a camp situation where immediate needs are met by seeing "what the Bible has to say on that.")

6. Work at Bible study for biblical knowledge at present, but with the long-range purpose of more intelligent utilization of biblical materials for the guidance and stimulation of Christian living. (Example: to study the Old Testament prophets as such with the view that their messages can later be utilized more effectively.)

The first three modes above are typical of traditional Christian education; the last three represent the forms of use in developmental circles. The fourth mode had a considerable vogue in curricular guides published about 1925. The movement is towards the fifth, the thoroughly creative idea. Unfortunately some leaders have not recognized the importance of the sixth in relation to the fifth. Many portions of the Bible are so complex as to require rather exacting study on a content basis before they yield their values for effective utilization. Unconsidered use of such material may result—does often result—in grievous error. There is a place for content study. It should be understood, however, as a secondary and not the primary level of functional utilization of the Bible.

CURRICULAR ACTIVITIES

Curriculum, as defined on page 171, includes the guided Christian educational activities of a pupil not only in the Church School but also outside the Church School. The Christian learning activities which a pupil performs in his home, public school, place of work, and community in so far as they are affected at all by guidance, are a part of his Christian curriculum. Increasingly, Sunday Church School leaders realize that they must do more about those matters which are external. When the pupil is in the formal program of the school only an hour each week on the average, the school must direct to some degree, and foster educational results in, the life of the pupil during the other hours if objectives are to be accomplished.

Out-of-school Activities

The Sunday Church School leader is properly concerned with pupil activities involved in *living the Christian life under guidance in home, school and work, and community.* The following are sample out-of-school activities which the leader may consider including and doing something about in the pupil program:

1. Living the Christian life in the home:
    Example: Engaging in helpful service in the home. (This may be fostered as an aspect of such a unit as "Our Homes.")
2. Living the Christian life at school and work:
    Example: Influencing companions and colleagues for the Christian way of living. (This may grow out of evangelism enterprises conducted by the school.)
3. Living the Christian life in the community:
    Example: Improving recreational facilities and practices in the community life. (A strong fellowship program in the church is indicated.)

In-the-school Activities

The major curricular activity for which the Sunday Church School leader provides is, of course, *living the Christian life under guidance in the Church School.* In practice, it is usually conceived as involving four divisions or "aspects" of curriculum, namely:

1. Studying and receiving instruction about Christian matters
2. Worshiping in Christian modes
3. Enjoying fellowship in Christian groups
4. Serving at Christian enterprises

The meaning and guiding of those four types of pupil activity will receive detailed consideration in Chapters XI, XII, and XIII. Since, however, they should be handled as interrelated phases of curricular units in a total pupil program, "units" and "program" need consideration first.

UNITS OF ACTIVITY

The Christian curriculum is properly a total program of interrelated activities. However, there must be divisions. So, for convenience as well as effectiveness, those divisions are organized and handled by pupils and leaders as "units of activity."

What is a unit of activity? Blair says: "A unit of work is a number of worth-while experiences bound together around some central theme of child interest and need." [3] Hewitt thinks of each group in the Church School as being engaged with a "slice of life." [4] Each such slice of life will deal with some center of interest. That center of interest will be developed through "major activities or experiences, or units of work." Each major experience or unit of work," she writes, "will make use of lesser activities of various types."

We shall define a "unit of activity" as *an educational enterprise which is to develop as a constellation of interrelated religious activities centered around some specific objective of Christian growth.*

In the light of that definition a Church School becomes a group of persons engaged in units of activity moving forward with desirable results in Christian growth. Also, the task of the leaders of the school is to take the steps which insure the initiation and continuance of a series of well-selected and efficiently managed units for everyone. Central in that task is the necessity to plan the curriculum a a whole, building and continuously rebuilding a total curricular program.

BUILDING A TOTAL PROGRAM OF UNITS OF ACTIVITY

In Chapter II Christianity was defined as a system of activities of a certain type. Chapter IV classified the activities of the Christian religion in terms of eight major objectives. The individual activities, it has been recognized, will be legion. Living a Christian life consists in performing all of them on the highest level possible for the person in his present situation. In Chapter II, also, Christian edu-

---

[3] W. Dyer Blair, *The New Vacation Church School* (New York: Harper and Brothers, 1939), p. 23.

[4] Mildred Hewitt, *The Church School Comes to Life* (New York: The Macmillan Company, 1932), p. 50.

cation was said to consist in making such changes in an individual's system of activities as would result in greater abundance in his Christian living. The same chapter showed that the method is performance, learning to do by doing. Thus the activities are at once the objectives and the process of Christian education.

It was inevitable that this chapter should define the curriculum of Christian education as a series of pupil activities. Those, it has appeared, are performed while living the Christian life in the home, at school or work, throughout the community, and in the church. It was found, too, that those performed for educational purposes in the Sunday Church School are largely those which emerge in the processes of studying and receiving instruction, worshiping, fellowshiping, and serving.

Since, in practice, those curricular activities are properly handled in "units" of activity, a Church School is essentially a group of persons engaged in a series of units of activity, all moving forward together with results in desirable Christian growth. Thus, it is the Sunday Church School leader's responsibility to lead in building a program of pupil activity—constructing a curriculum it is usually called—or, better, arranging for the initiation, continuance, and conclusion of a series of units of activity.

The need for program building

That responsibility is met most often by adopting the denominational series of lessons, hymnbooks, and the like. Leaders then direct the publishers to ship a set of supplies at quarterly intervals. Those are distributed to teachers and pupils who use them with little further consideration.

Although those denominational materials have been prepared by expert writers who adjusted them for typical pupils at the various age levels in the average situation, a considerable amount of dissatisfaction will be encountered. Pupils are individuals, not averages; groups differ; and times change. A third of the pupils of the class will find the materials too easy; another third will find them too difficult. Half the class may be deeply interested just now in something else. An up-to-date teacher may find the helps too old-fashioned; the traditional teacher cannot approve "this new-fangled stuff."

Such facts suggest the need for a custom-built program designed to fit the immediate situation. It would be meant to help each pupil meet his immediate needs and fit his personal attitudes and interests, taking account of his full life. It would consider each group's particular outlooks, and problems. It would recognize differences in the ability, interest, education, and outlook of the leader as well as of the pupils. It would fit the school's tradition, equipment, administrative policy, and organizational setup. It would consider new issues constantly appearing in an infinitely complex, varied, and fluid social order.

Continuous program building

Such a pupil program would be always in process of building, constantly under reconstruction. If the developmental approach is really followed and creative use of techniques actually employed building the program would be, to a considerable degree, not only a year-by-year but a week-by-week and Sunday-by-Sunday affair. "To a considerable degree" is used since there is no need, and certainly it is not desirable, to lose foresight and sequence out of the process. The program can have general outlines shaped long in advance while lesser adjustments are made as it proceeds. When a family goes on a vacation tour, it may spend the winter laying out the major lines of its journey although it will be making adjustments day by day and hour by hour en route.

Co-operative program building

When properly done, the building of the program is a co-operative effort by pastor, director, superintendent, teachers, pupils, and parents. The Sunday Church School leader with his colleagues and their helpers in other educational phases, all of whom constitute the Church School Council, would meet from time to time to outline or construct and reconstruct the larger pupil program. Divisional workers, departmental workers, and teachers would confer at other times to develop the various units of work. The teachers and pupils would plan the items of the sessions as they proceed. At appropriate times, too, the parents would be permitted to contribute their judgment and experience. Since, throughout, the major interest is the pupil whose development determines the direction of the effort, his role in the planning should be a major one.

Total program building

In the matter of providing a total program, the word "total" deserves particular attention. Recalling the eight major objectives of Christian education, page 64, the various types of Church School, page 14, and the major types of activity which constitute the pupil program, page 179, imagine the plight of the pupil who participates for many years in all of it, unless there is some unification of aim, and practice! There is stern necessity to unify it all in such a way that the pupil's total experience can be an integrated one.

In contrast with a total program, consider further the typical situation. Most churches have many agencies working at the task— agencies whose programs are largely separate and distinct. There are Weekday and Vacation Church Schools as well as Sunday Church Schools, along with young people's societies, camps, clubs, and others, each having its curriculum. Worse, in most of the agencies, there are really several separate curricula. There is the curriculum of study and instruction, the curriculum of worship, the curriculum of fellowship, and the curriculum of service, and if they happen to gear together it is often by accident.

Thus pupils collect a bit of knowledge here and another unrelated bit there. They begin to develop an attitude in one place and then shift to another place where a little effort is made at the development of another. There is a start of a habit here and a little progress on another there. Out of all these jig-saw puzzle pieces the pupil is expected to develop the complicated design of a Christian life.

Those persons are needed, expert or otherwise, who can sit down with their helpers at appropriate intervals to lay out creatively a *total* program which will tend to unify the experience of the pupils.

Such persons will take into account all the general objectives of Christian education and the present standing of the pupils in relation to them. They will keep in mind all the various schools and sessions in which the pupils are participating; out-of-school matters, too. They will remember all the types of activity which go to make up a total program. Then they will arrange for a progressive series of rounded units of work, which, after engaging the pupils for the requisite period of time, will lead on to the next such units to meet the total need.

Procedure in program building

The factors in the process of building a total program are somewhat as follows:

1. Enlist the entire school in the work, under the most competent pupil and staff leadership possible.

2. Formulate the objectives which become, in due time, the process. These involve general aims, of course. Yet the particular task at this point is the determination of specific aims.

3. Formulate the probable main lines of the various separate units of activity to be worked at.

4. Allot those units to the several groups, providing for variety and balance within the lines of interest and need manifested in pupils' life situations.

5. Examine and evaluate available materials and make tentative selections.

6. Adjust all matters pertaining to organization, equipment, the time element, leadership, method, and the like.

7. Let the units be carried to conclusion.

8. Keep records of the experience.

9. Evaluate the work.

10. Arrange for a sequence to follow.

It will be observed that the conducting of a Church School on such a basis is an expert's job. Yet, is it the right way? If so, more experts are needed. Besides, if there is no one with time and ability to do such a creative piece of curriculum construction, every possible effort can be made in that direction. Once the need is understood and accepted, instances will be found in which some larger or smaller thing can be done. There is no need to wait for the day when it will be possible to go "all out" for a total program. While the full procedure is desirable, one does what one can do now.

As an example, the responsible leader with that ideal before him will not, like a certain pastor, insist that the teacher must always use just the prescribed lesson for the day exactly as provided in the denominational quarterly. Instead when a Junior teacher comes, to say that the boys of his class need different lessons, he will help that teacher find what is needed. Wherever, in his school, a few workers have the capacity for even a limited amount of such constructive work, he will give them scope for their endeavors.

MATERIALS IN THE PROGRAM

In every pupil program, even a specially constructed one, there is need for materials in terms of books and similar supplies. The main items will be pupil and leader resources, guides for completing the units of activity, perhaps what usually are called "lesson books."

The full adoption of the developmental approach in Christian education with creative use of the various techniques would require something in the way of a library for pupils and leaders. It would contain reference books of a general nature as well as books dealing with specific areas of related study: Bible, history, biography, literature, psychology, sociology, missions. There would be, also, journals dealing with current developments and a filing cabinet containing a wide variety of pamphlets and clippings. Films and recordings would be available, too. Further, this would be the place to consult the records of procedure in previous units in the school: analyses and descriptions of life situations; the resources used; the data gathered; the principles arrived at; the experiments undertaken and the results achieved.

Most churches cannot themselves maintain all such resources. The pastor and other leaders in the school will need to co-operate by lending what they have. Homes can share their resources. School and community librarians usually welcome requests from church workers who need materials not otherwise available.

Providing for Particular Needs

To be sure, most schools are not ready for ideal procedures. There are four types. (1) Those which build their programs creatively, perhaps prepare their own guides, and select special materials as they proceed in the various units of activity. They will need the sort of facilities described above. (2) Those which have accepted the ideal but serve it only as far as possible. They may build their programs, then select printed guides from various sources to serve the program they devise or employ creative units where there are workers who can manage them. (3) Those where some standard series of guides, usually a denominational series of lesson materials, has been adopted with the idea of doing some creative unit now and then or substituting some elective guide to meet a special interest or need. (4) Those which adopt and use an established series of materials just as they have been planned by the publishers.

Each of those ways has its advantages and its limitations. Only those schools with personnel having the necessary capabilities should undertake anything more difficult than the third procedure listed. Many, however, could venture that far in the direction of the newer type of program. Particularly for such schools, the following sections are included.

Selecting Printed "Lesson Materials"

Almost every school will be selecting some form of printed pupil and leader guides, usually called "lesson materials." These should be selected democratically. When feasible the pupils as well as their teachers, the administrative staff, and the parents should unite in the task. First, of course, the objectives should be well understood by all, just as the conditions of leadership, equipment, and the like must be kept constantly in view. Then samples can be secured from publishers for examination by everybody concerned. The leader himself will make certain that he is fully informed and that the best educational point of view is understood by all before the final selection is made.

The International Uniform Lesson Series

A majority of the Sunday Church School pupils of the United States and Canada use International Uniform Lessons.

The International Council of Religious Education has The Committee on the Uniform Series which develops outlines for *International Sunday School Lessons: The International Bible Lessons for Christian Teaching, Uniform Series.* That committee represents approximately forty denominations. In its annual meeting it prepares outlines for the lessons of subsequent years including lesson titles, Scripture text, memory selections, and devotional readings. There are "suggestions," also, for the handling of the materials and related home daily Bible readings.

The Committee on the Uniform Series operates on a principle which has modified the uniformity ideal considerably. It seeks to make suitable adaptations of a basic text to the four age groups— Primary, Junior, Intermediate-Senior, and Young People-Adult. The gradation is achieved by planning the outlines on a common core of Scripture for each Sunday with particular blocks chosen out of it for the separate groups. The lessons are based on a six-year cycle (1945-1950) which aims to cover all portions of the Bible which are fruitful for group study. At least one quarter each year is a study of the life and teachings of Jesus.

When the outlines for a given year have been completed, they are printed and furnished to the various co-operating denominations or to independent publishers. Editorial writers then prepare the quarterlies which are the familiar equipment of nearly every school.

Those lessons are furtherest removed from the developmental approach in Christian education. They do have certain advantages. They tend to systematize instruction and integrate it with worship, fellowship, and service. Their popularity makes possible the provision of many definite teacher and pupil helps. They solve many publication problems. They fit certain situations, particularly the smaller school, with a minimum of effort and difficulty. Yet there are many points at which they may be rated as least desirable of all instruments for use in study and instruction. Even as improved in 1945, the lessons continue to be fragmentary, disconnected, material-centered, and less effective because of the transmissive techniques they induce. They tend to foster superficial moralizing about biblical verses instead of penetrating insight into the possibilities of Christian livng.

Graded lessons

There are many types of so-called graded lessons. Their general idea is to provide separate, and supposedly better adapted, lessons for each age group or department of the school. Several of the major denominations, as well as private presses, have prepared their own graded courses. The International Council of Religious Education has provided outlines which may be used in producing such lessons.

The International Council has the Committee on the Graded Series working at two enterprises: *The International Bible Lessons for Christian Teaching, Closely Graded Lessons;* and *The International Bible Lessons for Christian Teaching, Cycle Graded Lessons.* The former aim to parallel the year-by-year development of the pupil from ages 3 to 17 with materials adapted to each year. The Cycle Graded Lessons keep in view a larger span of development, the three-year period covered by each department. The outlines prepared by the committees vary in content but provide somewhat the same features described above under the uniform series. The work of the committee is guided by careful research studies, meant to reveal the range and details of experience in the several areas of relationships met by the pupils for whom the curriculum is being provided.

The writers of graded lessons have approximated developmental Christian education in varying degrees only. Here and there we see gratifying efforts to get away from the typical emphases and procedures and provide life-centered units where the creative use of techniques is largely employed. Too often, though, graded lessons are largely a parceling out of biblical materials which seem to be suited to the capacity of a given age. As a result, many graded lessons show such slight advance over uniform lessons that schools might better accept the advantages of the latter.

On the other hand, the better graded lessons offer decidedly improved materials. They are better adapted to pupil interests and needs. They are not so fragmentary. They introduce materials from many sources, extra-biblical as well as biblical. They are prepared, usually, on a developmental approach or some modifcation of the transmissive. As for group (departmental) graded versus closely (age) graded lessons, the former are advantageous for practical reasons in most situations.

To complete the record, International lesson committees work also with *Society Topics, Weekday Church School Curriculum, Home Curriculum for Adults, Curriculum for Camp and Summer Conference, Vacation Church School Curriculum,* and *Graded Lessons for Older Young People.*

Prepared elective units

Many of the presses now have available for use in Sunday Church Schools, particularly for the Young People's and Adult Divisions, what are usually called "electives." If a group wishes to study, for example, the choosing of a vocation, some work of the Church, or a particular aspect of the Bible, it can secure the leader's guide and pupil's manual for that study. Such materials merit much wider use. They often approximate the best school procedures in learning and teaching. They can be chosen to serve genuine interests. They develop initiative. Wisely used they can help to meet real individual and social needs.

Criteria for Selecting Materials

Many items crowd into the picture when determining the criteria by which materials are to be selected. Elaborate studies and schedules are available but simplicity must be maintained here. Too often price is made the fundamental consideration. Sunday Church Schools exist for educational purposes, always a costly matter. Thrift is commendable, yet a few additional cents spent for better materials may prove to be a worthy investment. Unquestionably,

Sunday Church School pupils should be using books instead of "quarterlies." As for other criteria:

Do the materials represent the best of Christian experience?

Are they in line with the objectives to be served and do they promise to be effective in attaining those objectives?

Are they manageable under the conditions in which they are to be used?

Do they represent the most forward-looking educational methods which can be employed in the situation?

Are they of the highest possible quality in literary form and physical make-up?

Are they rich and ample in content?

Using Materials

However fine the materials selected, the manner of use will determine their efficacy. The more vital things regarding use are discussed in later chapters, particularly the next which deals with teaching. Here, several incidental factors will be considered.

Installing new materials

When new materials have been selected, care must be exercised in their installation. Whether the new materials are a whole new series, a hymnbook for the school, or a course for a class, all parties need to have the whole purpose well in hand so that the initial reaction will be favorable. Should any considerable part of a group make up their minds that they do not like this new thing, they become unteachable and so spoil all possibility of the highest educational results.

One of the most important demands at the present juncture in Christian education is to interpret the underlying philosophy of the materials. Not long ago, a pastor introduced a new series in his Weekday Church School. The leaders had been accustomed to the type of texts which duplicated the Sunday Church School work in content and employed the most pronounced sort of transmissive and memoriter procedures. The new series represented the denomination's most progressive publications. Wisely, the pastor distributed the new leader's guides well in advance of the first session. Within a few days one teacher came exclaiming, "Just look,

I can't do this. We need maps, and blackboards, and tables. Besides, I don't know how." Then and there the pastor undertook to show that leader, and later all the others on the staff, the meaning of the new idea in Christian education. They responded favorably, caught the idea, and did well with their new type of work.

That experience leads to an incidental statement: the frequent complaint that the new approach requires better teachers is not necessarily correct. What is a good teacher? Is it not one who gets results? Very well, is it easier to get results by the new methods? Workers may need to be re-educated, it is true, but given that retraining, the same workers can, as a rule, do better work with the new materials than with the old. Besides, and most important, all have some background of experience. For example, this is the way of education in the home, on the street, in the office or shop—almost everywhere except the school. Further, a growing number have appropriate experiences as pupils and teachers in public school where things are increasingly being done this way.

The practice of instructing workers in the use of new materials could profitably lead to a quarterly meeting for a similar purpose. One denominational children's leader feels that her time with teachers is spent best when she sits down with them and they all go through the guides for the next quarter together. The local Sunday Church School pastor and superintendents would find such a meeting exceedingly helpful when the new "books" for each quarter arrive.

Handling the materials

Once the materials have been selected and installed, how shall they be handled? For example, shall the lesson books be given out to leaders and pupils for permanent possession or shall they be the property of the school to be used over again? The question is often debated pro and con, but the basic principle is easily established: handle the materials so that they will produce the greatest educational results. If they have been prepared for pupil use and possession, then give them to the pupils, but follow through the process to see that they are used in the way intended. If they were prepared so that the disposition is optional, and there is no serious financial stringency, it is well to get religious literature into the home that way. Teacher's materials should always be made the property of the teacher so that passages may be underlined, notes written on the margin, pupil reactions and suggestions for procedure another season noted in blank spaces. In all cases, neat and thrifty care of property should be encouraged.

TIME SCHEDULES

The majority of Sunday Church Schools meet on Sunday morning for one hour. A typical schedule might be:

> Worship, 20 minutes
> Announcements and similar matters, 10 minutes
> Class Session, 25 minutes
> Closing Assembly, 5 minutes

Some schools meet after "church"; a majority meet before. There are, too, various fellowship and business meetings on weekdays.

Such a schedule raises questions about length of session, balance of worship and study, value of closing assembly and the like, even on the traditional level. With the "new curriculum," it is unsatisfactory. There must be work time, if possible, and considerable flexibility so that various aspects of the unit activity may be completed without too much regard for the ringing of bells. Further, there are problems having to do with the proportionate arrangements of subjects, the time which should be spent on a given unit and like questions which need to be worked out in the democratic way by the persons involved.

In relation to the present development in curricular theory and practice, certain general trends are noticeable. Some schools are lengthening the session to an hour and a quarter, an hour and a half, or as much as three hours. More attention is being given to a certain amount of "departmental instruction" such as that discussed in Chapter XIII. The closing assembly is often omitted.

There is a strong tendency also to modify the proportion of

time given to worship and study. As a general observation, teachers have not been getting enough time for class sessions. It would be better in an adult group to have not more than five or seven minutes of hymn-singing and prayer before the study of the lesson would be taken up. The adults are expected to attend a later common service of worship; a miniature "church service" in the Sunday Church School may detract from that. At any rate, adults should have more time for study which is profitable, too, and more appropriate to the school idea.

As for the Young People's Division, there is a tendency to make the same adjustment of schedule with similar purposes in view. It should not be done, however, unless there is opportunity elsewhere for the young people to plan and conduct their own worship; they should not be denied that educational opportunity. In the older children's groups the typical division of time may be about right in general, but there should be flexibility in harmony with the particular plan of each day's session. The younger children should have an entirely different schedule—one which allows for spontaneous worship and informal procedure generally.

How shall these matters be adjusted in the one-room school? Without begging the question, let it be said that some unified total Sunday morning program is essential. That would provide for emphasis on children's worship at a given point in the schedule while the major worship is for the elder member of the church. If the Sunday Church School service and the common service must be two separate units, then something like the typical schedule above will apply. The children should, however, have recognition during a few minutes of the major service, at least, and the young people should have regular opportunity to plan and conduct the Church School services.

Everywhere time should be economized. An efficiency expert might well pale at the manner of using session time in the typical Sunday Church School. Whether there be one hour or three hours, there is not a minute to be wasted by insufficient planning and ineffective procedure.

Chapter XI

GUIDING PUPIL ACTIVITIES (I)

(Especially Study and Instruction)

Three additional chapters are required to consider fully a Sunday Church School leader's dealings with the curriculum.

The program of pupil activities described in the preceding chapter, although built and going, must be guided. In that task the leader has many and varied duties to perform. Some may be quite immediate ones in which he deals with the pupils themselves. Most of his duties, though, are more remote ones in which he works through other staff members, particularly teachers. All his organizational and administrative activities have an important bearing on this work and the supervisory task described in Chapter VIII is most intimately related to it.

TEACHING

Essentially, the topic here is teaching although more than usual is meant by that term. It is usually taken to mean only a teacher meeting a class in session. Here, though, teaching includes all formal and informal guidance of the pupil in study and instruction, worship, fellowship, and service activities within the school or out of it.

Description of Teaching

Earlier chapters have described the nature of the teaching function in a general way. *To teach is to help folks learn.* Learn means change. That includes initiating new activities, eliminating old ones, increasing or reducing the functioning of an old one. Help means guide—guide in a creative experience of living. Experience of living means doing real things. Creative means putting the emphasis on dynamic motivation, self-chosen goals, self-directed procedure, and original results. This does not, however, require the exclusion of such things as a proper proportion of transmission, an element of teacher direction, even compulsion where necessary; such techniques as lecture and memorization; materials by way of content; the forward look.

Teaching in terms of objectives

It is possible to describe teaching largely in terms of objectives. One of the teacher's first tasks is to help the pupil locate and define the highest objectives. While the pupil's own objective is to have first consideration, it is to be chosen always in the light of the best social checks, including the teacher's views. The teacher needs to know and take account of the pupil's present interests, likely needs, and the fields of human relationships involved; then he helps the pupil interpret the situation and choose his goal. After that choice of a proper objective, the teacher's task is to help the pupil win through to it. Also, since learning by doing is the procedure, the doing wholly or part by part, of the activity represented in the objective, is the process of learning. The teacher makes available the circumstances for that activity and guides the pupil in the effective practice of it.

Teaching in terms of guidance

Guidance is, more or less, a synonym for teaching. Hence teaching is described when the task of guidance is pictured. The following are important items from a long list of the innumerable activities of guidance which a teacher may be called upon to perform:

Being one of the group in the highest sense—the more mature member of a fellowship of learning
Getting each pupil to do what he needs to do most
Knowing each pupil's experience, interest, and capacity
Imbuing pupils with spirit
Giving special help to those with special problems
Securing voluntary acceptance of rules and responsibilities essential to individual and group success

Arranging time schedules
Calling forth ideas from the group
Providing a "looking ahead" element
Helping keep the focus on real goals and seeing that there is step-by-
    step progress toward the objective
Showing results of good and of bad activity
Setting an example
Explaining rules or principle involved
Seeing that equipment and materials are provided and cared for
Sharing personal experience with pupils
Opening up new activities

Teaching in terms of principles

Finally, teaching may be described in accord with its principles. Each type of education has its own outlook. In the view of Christian education described here, teaching proceeds from such a basic platform as that outlined in the short paragraphs below.

The basic purpose of a teacher is to help pupils learn by whatever technique is most efficient.

The basic procedure in teaching is not teacher-telling-pupil but leader-guiding-pupil-in-performance.

The basic unit of a teaching experience is not a "lesson presented" but a pupil activity guided.

The basic organization of a teaching task is not a textbook to be followed but a unit of work to be completed—an objective and all that is done for its attainment.

The basic control the teacher uses is not dictation and compulsion, but counsel and eliciting of inner discipline.

The basic pupil function on which the teacher depends is initiative, not imitation.

The basic stuff of the teacher's craft is not some social inheritance such as a book or an institution but the growing life of a pupil.

LEARNING AND TEACHING

Since to teach is to help folks learn, it is essential in teaching to recognize how pupils do learn. Another way of putting it is: to consider the procedures pupils employ in completing their units of learning activity. In this whole area we must keep in mind the learning cycle as well as the teaching cycle yet carefully distinguish them. The former is the sequence of pupil activities which results in educational growth. The latter is the sequence of teacher activities by means of which the pupil activities are directed.

Meaning of learning activity

A "learning activity" is an activity which is to become the object of a pupil's learning process. The activity is to be (a) introduced into or eliminated from the learner's system of activities or (b) increased or decreased as to the frequency or facility of performance in the learner's system of activities.

From one point of view, the major learning activities in Christian education are identical with the four aspects of curriculum treated in the four chapters of this section. Better, though, they are identical with the objectives on page 64 or, in general, the types mentioned on page 179. In more detail here are samples from a long list of activities of pupils in Church Schools:

Appreciating (music, poetry, Scripture, and the like)
Attitudes, developing and maintaining (to school, its people, and in general)
Discussing (includes conversation, conferences, debating, and others)
Evaluating (ideas, plans, activities of self and others)
Giving (includes sacrificing)
Handling materials, tools, objects, equipment (includes operating)
Leading and following (as officer, committee member, or member of school)
Music, making (includes study, practice, composition)
School management, fitting into and helping with
Worshiping and conducting worship services (includes praying)

Elements of a learning activity

The basic pupil procedure in learning is performance. In the simplest activity performed—and more complex activities are largely combinations of smaller ones—there are three types of elements when considered as to time relations. They are *preparatory, consummatory,* and *anticipatory.* Preparatory elements grow out of native readiness, past experience, and current insight. They carry the learner up to the performance of the act. He performs it, in the consummatory element. Then there are left in his physical and

mental structure the anticipatory elements which become preparatory to the same activity or a related one on a later occasion. When
it is said that we learn to do by doing, it is meant that we make
use of preparatory elements of an activity to carry it to performance and by the performance store up anticipatory elements which
will function in a later enterprise.

These elements may be primarily mental as well as primarily
physical. In schools, the pupils do a great deal of learning to think
in a given way about a situation by anticipatory thinking in that
way about it, teachers directing their thinking into those channels.
Later, in more direct encounters, they bring the sediment of that
anticipatory thinking to the actual enterprise as preparatory elements for performing the total consummation. They have learned
to do the thinking about the thing by thinking about it, and that
has helped them toward the consummation of the total activity.

A six-year-old girl composed a hymn—words and music. Back
of it was a long line of enterprises in which she learned to do the
various preparatory elements of the consummation by doing them.
It would be impossible to mention everything, but the more direct
route of her learning may be described.

At an early age she had sat with her father on the piano stool
enjoying the Christmas carols. One day she started singing them
with him. Later he guided her fingers as she played a few measures
of "Silent Night." In due time she decided to learn to play "Come
Hither Ye Faithful" and worked at it long and hard until she was
able to pick out the tune.

During the same period she was being introduced to poems
which she learned to love. Soon she decided to do a poem herself.
Her father encouraged that impulse by writing down her production. Frequently thereafter she had poetic moods in which she
would place pencil and paper in her father's hands and ask him
to take her dictation.

Composing poems doubtless suggested the composition of piano
tunes. They were occasional and brief at first. Later, though, she
invented her own form of musical notation so that her tunes could

be preserved. Then she wrote several longer ones.

In each of the separate steps described above, preparatory elements growing out of a previous activity led to consummatory ones and they to further anticipatory ones. Then, in due time the various streams of anticipatory elements merged and a poem became a hymn with a tune composed to fit it.

That is the way a pupil learns. And, incidentally, that is the way a teacher teaches ideally—being at hand to provide help when the creative spirit is stirring the learner.

Steps in a learning activity

At several points in the example of learning described above, one might have observed the young composer working through some or all of the following steps in a complete learning activity:

1. Being aware of the situation
2. Discovering the possible activities to perform
3. Evaluating those possible activities
4. Choosing an activity for performance
5. Desiring to perform the activity
6. Resolving to perform the activity
7. Outlining the procedure
8. Providing the conditions
9. Executing the activity
10. Experiencing satisfaction or dissatisfaction with results
11. Evaluating the activity in retrospect
12. Planning to repeat, alter, or discontinue the activity

The order of those steps may not be always the same. They may overlap in a given case or some may be omitted in certain activities. Nevertheless, the list is representative and complete for a typical learning activity. A good way to think it through is to apply it to an imagined service enterprise in a Sunday Church School. (It is probably helpful to observe that the past experience of self and others will be used at many points.)

The laws of learning

As defined above, to learn is to change in one's system of activities: (a) to initiate a new activity; (b) to eliminate an old activity; (c) to accelerate or decelerate an old activity. In all education, it is recognized that the effectiveness of a learning experience (a, b, or c) is in proportion to the three factors listed below with a statement of the laws of their working.

Readiness, the learner's state of preparedness or unpreparedness for the change. If the learner is "ready," the change will take place with relative quickness and permanence. If the learner is "unready," the change will take place not at all or slowly and impermanently.

Effect, the amount of satisfaction or annoyance which the learner experiences in making the change. If there is much satisfaction, the change is more quickly and permanently established. If there is much annoyance, the change is more slowly and impermanently established, if at all.

Exercise, the frequency or infrequency with which the learner practices the change. The more frequent the practice (positive or negative), the more quickly and permanently the change takes place. The more infrequent the practice, the less quickly and permanently the change takes place.

It is to be understood, however, that the operation of those laws is subject to their interdependence. As examples, there are important relationships between effect and readiness, and readiness and exercise. For teaching purposes, though not as a statement of the laws in sequence, a rule can be stated as follows:

Strike while the iron is hot.

Foster practice with satisfaction.

Let annoyance attend the wrong.

Helping pupils learn

The nature of the teaching task should now be still more clear. It is to help pupils learn—help them do and *by doing,* change— ideally represented in coaching the direct performance of a real task. It is to assist pupils while they complete a unit of work, providing the necessary guidance and stimulation for seeing it through. It is to make available an effective setting of time, space, material, and social relations for an educational experience. It is to help revive anticipatory elements which become preparatory for the consummation of a learning activity; help provide conditions for the consummation; help husband the anticipatory elements for later preparatory use. It is to lend the helping hand at each of the various steps of a complete learning activity. It is to help the pupil observe the laws of learning.

Principal Ways of Teaching

Many terms have been used to describe the procedures which a teacher employs; "methods" is perhaps the favorite, "techniques" is another. A competent teacher at work in the classroom is an exceedingly versatile person doing many different things always adapted to the ever-changing situation and personnel. His task, really, is living with the pupils in such a way that they learn more rapidly and effectively. We can scarcely talk of "techniques" or even "methods" of living. Those terms are too precise and inflexible. Similarly, they do not describe the complex and shifting practice of the teacher. So "ways of teaching" is about the best we can do for a general descriptive term. Each "way" involves its detailed techniques which vary from situation to situation and sometimes comprise a rather precise group which may deserve to be called a method.

There are many "ways of teaching" and no two lists will be the same. The list below aims to be rather complete. It is arranged alphabetically as to the chief words.

Cultivating *appreciation*

Making *assignments*

Counseling

Providing *demonstrations* and *displays*

Leading *discussion* (includes conference, conversation, debate, forum, panel, round table, symposium, and others)

Coaching *dramatizations* (formal and informal)

Conducting *experiments* (social and other—the laboratory idea)

Directing *games* (play in general)

Guiding *handwork* (includes crafts and hobbies)

Arranging *interviews*

Lecturing (includes commenting, also use of resource leaders)

Conducting the reading or reciting of *literary gems* (biblical or other)

Securing *memorization*

Leading *music*

Guiding *participation* in administrative affairs

Using *phonograph* records

Holding *planning* sessions (and evaluation sessions)

Guiding *prayer* experience

Employing *projectors*

Doing *questions* and *answers*

Using the *radio*

Fostering *reading*

Conducting *"reading around"*
Using wire (or tape) *recorder*
Directing *research* and *report* (includes seminar and other forms of group inquiry such as committee work)
Conducting *reviews*
Coaching *speaking* (choral or other)
Telling *stories*
Directing *supervised study*
Directing *surveys* (includes opinion polls)

Testing
Conducting *textbook-study-and-recitation* (includes socialized recitation)
Taking field and museum *trips*
Employing *visual aids* (not otherwise mentioned, including picture study)
Conducting *workshops*
Guiding completion of *workbooks, notebooks, and creative writing.*

More formally, of course, teaching in Sunday Church School means dealing with the four classic aspects of "curriculum": (a) study and instruction; (b) worship; (c) fellowship; and (d) service. These will now be treated one by one in the remainder of this chapter and the next, in each case with an emphasis on the leader's tasks in relation to them.

DIRECTING STUDY AND INSTRUCTION

Study-and-instruction is a twofold way of dealing with the more intellectual factors in curricular units of activity. In study, the pupil takes the spotlight; in instruction, the teacher. Always, though, the pupil's learning process is the central fact. There can be no true instruction by a teacher unless the study attitude is present in the pupil. Study, therefore, is the more significant of the two components while instruction takes the lesser role as being meant simply to render the pupil's study more effective.

In actual practice, study and instruction are centered usually around "lesson materials" so that the leader's task in directing this aspect of the curriculum will usually be shaped by the type of materials used. The various possibilities by way of materials were discussed in the preceding chapter. Here a general point of view must be taken with the understanding that the leader will adapt his activity to the problems and possibilities which arise under the conditions in his school. Always it is expected that the leader will be working toward the point where he will no longer limit his school to any particular set of lesson guides when the larger advantage might be served by another type or by constructive work in program building.

In the discussion which follows, there will be some limitation to an older and more narrow concept of study. That is but an accommodation to the existing situation. Study is properly the pupil's whole fact-finding, data-gathering, deliberating, and problem-solving process with respect to that creative experience of living with which he is dealing in his unit of activity. That is much more than the usual home study and ordinary supervised study practice which Sunday Church Schools have in view. That typical sort of study is too largely concerned with mastery of materials only. Nevertheless, it must be taken as it is so that the leader may direct it into the better usage which is to make it truly the intellectualizing phase of a unit which is based upon the principle of performance—living and learning in the Church School.

Study

Among the activities through which pupils achieve Christian growth, the study of Christian topics has always been viewed as an important one. It is important from two angles: (a) people learn to study by studying, which is a significant Christian activity; and (b) there are necessary knowledge elements involved in other Christian activities. Yet there is grave reason to question whether the Church has been very successful at fostering study. Sunday Church School pupils do not, according to their teachers' reports, give themselves to study with any great diligence. Also, the results of tests, of biblical knowledge, for example, are woefully discouraging.

How shall Sunday Church School workers get their pupils to study the Bible and subjects like the history, organization, work and worship of the church, as well as the special problems of morals and theology? That has been and continues to be a problem even in the newer approach.

Study outside of the school

Study usually refers to the activity of Sunday Church School pupils at home before they come to the sessions of the school. Under typical conditions, the problem is how to get them to study their lesson quarterlies at home.

On this matter a personal testimony may be suggestive. I used to study my Sunday School lessons with my father. We had a place to keep our books and when he would get out his materials from their place, I would get mine. We had, among other things, a Bible Cyclopedia in three brown volumes. I still can see some of the pictures on those pages as vividly as if I had consulted them yesterday for tomorrow's lesson. If we wish to get home study of Sunday Church School matters, we must inevitably enlist such parental co-operation in providing time, place, materials, equipment and, above all, example.

But many persons now question the desirability as well as the possibility of fostering home study on any such basis. Almost inevitably on Sunday morning, only a few members of the class have done their home work. Those prepared pupils answer or ask questions while the unprepared sit as more or less disinterested onlookers. Worse, if the teacher works with the unprepared, the others start some activity of their own. Under the circumstances, we probably cannot expect much else. Where in all their educational experience, save in Sunday Church School, are pupils expected at intervals of seven days to get out a paper-covered manual, read a few pages on a subject, and memorize the answers to some factual questions or think superficially about some problems? They are accustomed to dealing with real books, often a considerable number of them, and proceeding generally in a quite different way.

Nevertheless, there can never be a religiously literate people and spiritually regenerate race without a great program of study among Christian people. It is the business of the Sunday Church School to initiate and foster such study. How shall that be done? Perhaps the result can be attained by supervised study described below, by such methods as research and report, and by direct effort at the promotion of reading. A certain percentage of qualified pupils will "look up things" and make a report to the class when proper plans have been made. Others, properly guided, will do post-session study of things in which they have become interested and about which they want to know more. Not a few will read a good book highly recommended by a leader whom they like and respect.

Supervised study in the school

Excepting those rare classes where the teacher can depend upon the majority of the members to prepare at home, and laying aside all reference to other techniques, general study of the lesson could be done better at a period of supervised study in the Sunday Church School schedule. In many cases, the whole class session could be profitably conducted somewhat as a supervised study experience. On a minimum schedule the teacher might guide the pupils for ten or fifteen minutes of reading the helps, referring to maps or other materials and getting themselves ready for the subsequent discussion.

This procedure does not apply to all age groups and cannot be adopted easily in the one-room school. It will fit best into those schools which are extending the length of the class session perhaps by encouraging the pupils to attend the chief service for their worship activity. Many schools, however, use it with success. More than one denomination has revised its lesson materials in this direction.

Whatever the particular means, it is important to initiate and guide programs of study so that the typical Christian learns how to continue some personal self-education throughout his life, making use of the vast range of available publications in the field of religion and related subjects. That is in addition to the necessity for study in the school because of its relation to all other school activities. Supervised study is the best means now in sight for such results.

Instruction

Being instructed about Christian matters is the type of pupil activity for which the most ample provision is made in typical Sunday Church Schools. Thus the directing of this item of pupil program is one of the leader's major responsibilities as things now are.

Instruction has a tendency to crowd out all other considerations in the process of education. When people think of education, they seem to think first of a teacher instructing a group. That view is trebly shortsighted. In the first place, teaching and instruction are not co-extensive; second, education is not primarily teaching, but learning. (As stated earlier, study is the more significant item here and instruction is but helping the pupil arrive at better results in his study.) Finally, study is but part of the learning process just as instruction is only a part of the teaching process. There are four aspects to the curriculum of Christian education and the basic procedure in all units of learning is *learning by doing.*

The pupil undergoing instruction

Instruction has been considered usually in terms of "presenting a lesson," viewing it solely from the teacher's standpoint. The newer approach is from the pupil's angle. He is being instructed, engaging in instructional activity. The teacher, as instructor, is only helping him with his learning process. He hears stories, listens to lectures, does handwork, views pictures, and participates in discussions. By those means he is gathering data, developing attitudes, coming to conclusions, and seeing solutions about the problems of his unit of activity. As an important by-product, too, he is developing his capacity to profit educationally from further such experience.

Roughly, the instructional techniques by which pupils proceed in their units of activity parallel the ways of teaching listed on page 201. Most of them are of ancient origin. Many are old in Sunday Church School work, but several are relatively new. In the former class are listening to lectures, memorizing, answering and asking questions, listening to stories and studying textbooks to be recited later. While those continue to have a place still in Sunday

Church School practice, recent Christian education tends to reduce their frequency while it emphasizes dramatizing, discussing, doing handwork, reading, doing research and reporting findings, and the like.

One of the most amazing developments in the history of Christian education is the present "boom" in the use of audile and visual materials and equipment. Even an outline, and there is space for no more, will suggest the rich possibilities in that way of teaching.

Audile and Visual Aids (including audio-visual)
I. Visual
    A. Non-projected
    B. Projected
        1. Opaque
        2. Transparent
            a. Still
            b. Silent Motion

II. Audile
    A. Phonograph
    B. Public address or sound system
    C. Radio
    D. Recorder (wire or tape)

III. Audio-visual
    A. Sound filmstrip
    B. Sound Motion
    C. Television

The teacher instructing

The instructional techniques used by teachers to assist their pupils in effective study, broadly conceived, are included among the ways of teaching, page 201. Again it should be said that "ways of teaching" is a broader term for the procedures of a teacher while "techniques of teaching" or, perhaps, even "methods of teaching" designates more precise and detailed ones. Further, instruction is only one aspect of teaching. Yet the examination of that list will enable the reader to select some way of teaching and think of the instructional techniques which are included within the general procedure related to it.

"Lecturing" is a good example. The pupil is working on a unit of activity meant to answer his question, "What shall I do on Sunday?" and get him started on better and more satisfying use of the day. That unit will have as its central feature the doing of the right things on Sunday. Nevertheless, thinking the right thoughts about the matter is a part of the doing. Consequently, some preliminary exploration of principles is in order and that may involve study and instruction. The pupil wants to know, for example, what light can be shed on the matter from the Bible. Using a concordance, he finds such a passage as "The sabbath was made for man, not man for the sabbath" (Mark 2:27).

"But what does it means?" he asks the teacher. The teacher replies that you cannot answer a question like that on the spur of the moment. He'll prepare to speak on it next Sunday. (This assumes that there is not time or material for the student to look up the matter himself.) The pupil comes next Sunday with a questioning and ready mind. He'll ponder as he listens. That is the pupil's technique under lecturing. The teacher will have prepared himself by study, planning, outlining, and making notes for an informal lecture which he will deliver according to the techniques of lecturing in so far as he understands and accepts them as good procedure. That is his body of instructional techniques.

The example illustrates another important feature about present tendencies in the use of techniques, namely their creative use. The larger meaning of creative use of techniques has been discussed, particularly in Chapter II. It is made effective in the teaching which results when pupils ask for guidance to do something they want to do as they move toward their objectives. They may ask, "I'd like to know more about that, please tell us," and an informal lecture follows. "I want to look that up," and a plan of study is arranged. "Let's have a play about that," and a dramatization results. "Please tell us a story about that," and there is a storytelling. "I love that verse, please help me memorize it," and the teacher conducts a drill. "This is what I want to make," and a handwork enterprise follows. "I feel like writing a poem," and the way is cleared for a poem to be produced.

To repeat, when thinking of this aspect of learning and teaching it should be recognized that schools using developmental approach will have the pupils working at a unit of activity in which the major procedure is in the direct performance of activities although as many kinds of instructional techniques as may be necessary will be employed. Instruction is but a part of a unit of activity, and an indirect one at that. Pupils still learn to do by doing. Instruction is meant to be employed only as an aid to doing and, while pupils are guided in doing by instruction, schools which stop with the teacher's performance of instructional techniques may not have completed their educational task at all. The pupil's part in the process is the vital thing.

International Uniform Lessons

Something like half of all Sunday Church School classes are using International uniform lessons. If teaching is to be improved, that is the point at which the leader can well take hold first. What shall he do? The general answer is to start where the classes are now and move step by step to the kind of procedures in which he and his constituency, after careful study, believe.

The experiences of a certain leadership education class may be helpful with suggestions. The theme of the course was "Teaching International Uniform Lessons." The group included seventy-five teachers of Young People's and Adult Division classes in a city of 50,000 population.

Plans for the course were discussed and outlined at the first session. Each student received pencil and paper to write several questions about his work which he wanted to have answered. Later fifty representative questions were mimeographed as the objectives of the course. The following are interesting and significant items from that list:

Some leaders say questions and answers are better for adults than lecturing; how put this program in effect among older people who prefer the lecture method and will not answer questions or discuss things?
What is a desirable general lesson plan?
How can we get them to discuss their ideas on the lesson?

How can the superintendent be limited in his use of total time?
emphasis be attained by the teacher, avoiding mistake of making lesson
period a kind of "home-made sermon" by an amateur with the result that
the majority of Sunday School goers know very little of actual Bible content and use?

Is Bible message, or message applied to modern life, more important?
Should Sunday School pupils be given homework?
How can proper combination of content emphasis and application
What is your advice, to a lay teacher, on controversial questions?

A second thing each student did in the planning session was
to write a brief description of his way of teaching a typical lesson.
Representative replies are reproduced below to exemplify the sort
of thing which is taking place in most young people's and adult
classes using uniform lessons.

"The class of men I teach consists of farmers and industrial workers
who read the Bible very little. I strive to supply them Bible information—
the doctrines of God and the gospel message—so they can think upon and
ponder these facts. As I ask questions to stimulate discussion, they do not
indicate they have studied the lesson."

"I teach young people sixteen to nineteen years of age. I usually outline my lesson before anything else. When I begin to teach, I review the
previous lesson and then lead into the present one. I get information from
several books including my teachers' journal; I try to compare certain
things in each lesson to our own present age. I use examples to illustrate
my point. I try to bring the pupils into the discussion by asking them
questions or by having them ask me questions. At the conclusion, I summarize my lesson."

"With my adult class I use primarily lecture and discussion methods.
Occasionally there are assignments. Sometimes these are not in connection
with a lesson. They may refer to something in the church—the significance
of symbols, for instance. We use the question-and-answer outline in the
adult quarterly. Main difficulty—perhaps teacher talks too much."

"I first decide on a purpose or aim in the lesson, and after necessary
introductions as to background, I apply the thought to practical Christian
living with biblical references which I try to have members make, find,
and read. This often produces discussion. I am never able to complete
this lesson using all I have prepared, due to lack of time. I find real Bible
study requires more time than we are granted."

Later sessions of the leadership course included such procedures
as informal lectures, presentations by the denominational writers
of the lesson books, demonstration of the use of audile and visual

aids, and creative discussions in which several major questions from the list of fifty were considered.

A principal feature of the course was demonstration lessons in which someone would teach the group on the basis of a forthcoming lesson. The best work was done by a young seminary student who used the first lesson in a short unit on the church.

This young man, with his class of seventy-five teachers who themselves would teach the same lessons he was considering, began with a pre-test a week in advance. It was a series of thirty-five true-false questions covering the area of the prospective unit of study. The following is a section:

Instructions: Encircle T for true; F for false:

T F 1. I read the denominational journal.

T F 2. My congregation should take more active part in interdenominational community Christian enterprises.

T F 3. I believe women should be given larger place in the work of the church and should be paid salaries as ministers receive salaries.

T F 4. I think the American church should not give so much money to European churches.

T F 5. The purpose of worship is to glorify God.

T F 6. The pastor should not express in his preaching any attitudes on matters of labor and capital.

T F 7. If one's belief is right, one's actions do not matter.

T F 8. There is a World Council of Churches.

T F 9. I believe there should be more variety in the worship services of the church and Church School.

The demonstration session itself began with a report on the pre-test results. The teacher told his students about the things they had done well and their more grievous errors. This was to arouse their sense of need and challenge their interest in the work to follow. After the results of the pre-test had been discussed, he explained the divisions of the unit and showed how a proper consideration of the designated lessons would enable the students to increase their knowledge and understanding of the church and its work.

Then the teacher started the first study, a somewhat inspirational treatment of the nature of the church. He began by reviewing, with his students, the history of the church. Their next task was to consider basic data on the denomination at the present time. Then they thought for a moment about their own local congregations and the work done or not done in their communities. Throughout, the findings of the pre-test were guiding the discussion and stimulating the sense of need and interest for the information which was being made available. The blackboard was used at many points in the development.

The study just described was itself sufficient material for a unit. This, of course, is one of the fallacies of the uniform lesson plan. It sweeps over the territory too swiftly. Consequently, classes should be more ready to drop certain lessons in order to finish others, even to drop a whole quarter and study some elective unit which meets the class interest and need. The principle of stress and neglect in accord with the group situation alone makes the use of International uniform lessons tolerable.

As the second and last major division of the session which the young man taught, he dealt directly with the nature of the church. It was an effort to arrive (the history had helped as a background) at a definition. The usual descriptions of the church were reviewed; then the group worked co-operatively to write its own statement.

A striking feature of this session was the fact that no mention of the biblical text was made until the end. In the last few moments it was brought forward in a manner almost thrilling. That quietness which indicates emotional stress swept over the group as the teacher concluded by reading the most fitting parts of the lesson text. The students had been well prepared for them and they served as the climax of "the lesson."

As the students left the room, the teacher distributed printed materials pertaining to the church. If he had finished his unit, he could have continued that practice. For example, he could have secured material from denominational mission boards when the group studied the outreach of the church. These would have been an invitation for home reading and study.

Also, if the teacher had been able to go on with his unit, he could have planned to continue the informal lectures and creative discussions using audile and visual aids when desirable. He could have planned, most of all, to have direct learning by doing: for the lesson on worship, student participation in the worship services of the school; in connection with fellowship study, fellowship meeting of the class planned in part by the entire group; concerning the outreach of the church, some work done by the class to extend the community relations of the school.

Always, of course, it is to be remembered that thinking is part of doing and when people even think about these topics treated in the lessons, they have done something. Also, it is never to be forgotten, as stated in Chapter X on the use of the Bible, that there is a time for the study of Bible content as content. However, practice should get beyond merely intellectual considerations to something which is more completely a creative experience of actual living and learning by doing in real life. This is the point at which the users of uniform lessons are most likely to fall short. It is likewise the point at which the leader who wishes to improve the work done by his group will need to endeavor most vigorously to help.

Summary

The leader's task in directing study and instruction is clearly a large one. He will foster in his school the creative use of the modern techniques in so far as he can believe in them. He will provide the conditions under which they can be employed, and encourage and develop his teachers to do effective work with them. Undergirding that effort, he will help his teachers to see that teaching is really something bigger than what they have typically understood by instruction. From the teacher's point of view, the major effort is to coach and direct the performance of Christian activity using instruction as a significant partial method to be employed only as necessary.

Executing a unit of activity, including the planning and evaluating stages should, also, involve the other three aspects of curriculum — worship, fellowship and service — in an interrelated experience of great variety. The next chapter will consider these other three aspects of the activities within the curricular program. The following one will deal with unit management.

Chapter XII

GUIDING PUPIL ACTIVITIES (II)

(Especially Worship, Fellowship, and Service)

Formerly the words "school" and "teaching" meant study and instruction and not much more, but recent decades have been working a vast change. Now public schools recognize many features beyond those typical classroom experiences as regular parts of proper school content. Similarly, Church Schools recognize the proper place of the three additional aspects of curriculum which comprise the topic of this chapter.

We are concerned about worship, fellowship, and service in terms of Christian growth through, in, and for them. Christian growth takes place *through* each—pupils grow as they have experiences of these types. In addition, pupils expand their capacity to find increasing abundance *in* these activities and they develop the abilities which prepare them *for* the promotion of finer enterprising of these types in the church.

DIRECTING WORSHIP

In many schools the pupil activities in these areas will be guided by the administrative leaders of the school themselves. In other schools the pastor, director, or superintendent will direct the program through other staff members. Whatever the situation, the activities deserve fullest attention. Always, however, they are to be properly related to one another and to study and instruction so as to provide a unified program which, further, is integrated with the total work of the church. In this way worship will hold its fundamental place in the pupil's participation in Christian education.

Definition of Worship

Worship services are to be planned and purposeful experiences in which human concerns are brought into God's presence, and commitments are made in the light of his revealed nature and will. Worship is a pupil activity that involves several components: an outreach of the self toward God; a felt inreach of God toward the self; resultant communion; some thought about things of God and godliness; an emotional reaction to the same; and some response in peace, purpose, or action.

That is a paramount instrumentality for fostering the central elements of growth. It is an important area for development in the ability to have increasingly higher experiences of it. Also, the cultivation of skill at planning, conducting, and fostering increasingly effective services of worship is properly an outstanding objective of a school. Yet the typical Church School has "opening exercises" which are dull, monotonous, unprepared, and conducted without much thought of their educational value or even their religious significance.

Planning a Program

The directing of Sunday Church School worship should begin with the planning of a program of worship for the entire congregation. The pastor and all other persons in authority where worship is involved will need to consider the whole congregational situation, purpose, and practice. In this planning, the Church School people should represent the educational ideal of growth through, in, and for worship. Out of the planning should come a clear-cut understanding of the mutual relationships and special emphases of the common congregational services and all other services of worship, especially those in the educational agencies.

A total program would provide for a variety of satisfying worship experiences to meet the needs of every member and result in the three types of growth mentioned above. The Church School leaders, doubtless, would be made responsible for a stress on variety of worship, worship of the more informal type, worship adapted to the immediate circumstances of the pupils, worship graded to the various ages, and worship planned and conducted by the pupils themselves.

Planning Services of Worship

Worship in the Church School can be rich. Whether it is rich depends, first of all, upon the leader. The materials to help him are available, for example, an abundance of books; the people are waiting for somebody to do something; only rarely will his hands be tied in any way. Perhaps the leader will need to start the improvement of worship in his school by introducing some new features in his own conducting of the services. Instead, he may work with a committee or individual members of his staff and membership. In either case he will remember that the final goal is a situation in which the pupils themselves, with proper material helps and adult coaching, are planning and conducting the services.

In planning single services, there are three considerations—*the elements, their selection,* and *their arrangement.* To be sure, there should be planning not only for a single service but also for series of services. This is in contrast with the typical lack of any preparation beyond random selection of hymns, reading of the next responsive selection in the hymnal, and calling upon the pastor for prayer. There can be some general planning for the year, more detailed planning for the quarter and meticulous planning for the single service unless the conditions are favorable for spontaneous worship.

Elements of Services

Setting

The setting of the service has much to do with its effectiveness. "Atmosphere" is an indescribable but very real part of it. There is a quality in the leader's manner, the pupils' demeanor, and the very physical effect of the room which can inspire or frustrate worship. Good architecture, decorations, equipment, furniture, heating, lighting, pictures, and symbols are the more tangible parts of the effective setting. Careful study for skillful approach is neceessary to promote favorable psychological conditions.

Music

This element always has held a prominent place in worship and offers perhaps the highest value of all as a means of creating and expressing religious sentiments. The low quality of much Church School music is correspondingly distressing. The best musical, literary, educational, and religious standards should prevail in its selection and rendition. Hymnals deserve careful selection and wise handling in use. Hymns deserve similar attention in study, selection, playing, and singing.

There could be a much wider variety of music both instrumental and vocal. There is room for more instrumental music of a high type by way of prelude and interlude, as background for meditation and as continuity for the program. Solos, quartettes, chants, and responses make for variety in vocal music. Development of choirs deserves earnest support. Excellent results are being achieved by the varied use of choice recordings. Throughout, the ideal of growth in ability to have lofty religious sentiments through music should prevail.

Orchestras are of uncertain value in Sunday Church School work. The idea behind many of them is expressed in an observation report: "If it does no other good, at least it brings to Sunday School some of the young people who play in the orchestra." That is not sufficient reason for maintaining orchestras; they should contribute to worship. But they are managed only rarely in such a way as to serve that purpose. Nine out of ten of them drown out all possibility of hymn singing. That fault is recognized in such reports as the following: "As I arrived, the orchestra was blaring away at a hymn." "One of the first things I would do in that school is to get mutes for the orchestra." "In the men's department, a hymn was announced. Unsuspecting visitor that I was, I opened my hymnal to sing. No one else did, and soon I knew why. A cornetist turned his trumpet to the rafters and made them ring. He had a good time; others chatted; I fumed. Nobody worshiped."

Fortunately, it is possible to describe the work of one good orchestra. It plays in an assembly room with a well-fitted stage.

The members assemble behind the curtain and must be in position with their instruments tuned ten minutes before opening time. On the stroke of the hour the curtains are drawn and the orchestra plays a selection chosen for its religious quality. Then the hymn leader takes his position. He is accompanied by a smaller group of instruments properly muted, different ones each Sunday. The people sing and the total effect is worshipful. Then, when the orchestra has finished its work, the curtains close and no bustle, noise, or confusion is seen or heard.

Scripture

Bible readings, if they be devotional in character, are legitimately a part of any service of worship. The typical procedure where International uniform lessons are used, is to read the lesson for the day. That has its value, yet tends to introduce instructional material into the devotional period.

The Bible is too sacred to be read poorly. Its reading needs preparation in advance, including the study of all difficult words or ideas, and the practice of effective expression. Variety in the use of Scripture may be had by the introduction of free telling, memory recitation, musical settings, and unison reading along with reading by superintendent or pupil or responsive reading. A few words of introduction, explanation, or interpretation are not out of place in the use of devotional Scripture.

Prayer

The heart of the worship experience, it would be expected, is prayer. It should be the most carefully guarded feature of the service. Casual calling upon the pastor, careless reading of some formal prayer, constant repetition of the Lord's Prayer exclusively—all should be avoided. Let the leader set the prayer as a jewel in the midst of the service and let it be in itself a gem.

Young persons can take the part of the leader and do it beautifully if prepared and carefully trained. Prayers should be brief, with sincerity as the keynote. Variety of form and procedure is desirable although there should be no straining after novelty. Collects, litanies, sentence prayers, and silent prayer will provide dignified variety where prayers by leaders only have been the practice.

Devotional arts

The term refers to a variety of things "seen and heard" such as pageants, stories, sermonettes, objects, pictures, and the reading of extrabiblical literature. Special attention should be given to the projected picture as a focus for worship. There are further possibilities in projection as well as recordings. All of these may be employed to provide variety in worship. They should have the devotional tone, leaving that which is largely instructional for the class session or special period of departmental consideration.

Offering

There is nothing either educational or devotional in passing an envelope around the class just as the teacher is starting the lesson. There is, however, high educational value in making the offering in a religious manner and with a worshipful setting. Offerings are received properly within the service of worship.

Liturgy

Most services are conducted according to the liturgy of a hymnal or some modifications of the same. Liturgical services have both their values and limitations. They are orderly and uniform. They train for similar usage in common congregational services. On the other hand, they may engender monotony, perfunctoriness, and disinterestedness. They tend to make leaders careless in preparation. When they are used, it is most important to recognize the seasonal variations and give attention to the leader's expressiveness. Thorough education and re-education in the meaning of the forms is essential, too.

Selecting Materials

Out of the wealth of such materials it is necessary to select for each service of worship that which is best suited to the hour. Six principles will be listed and defined below in alphabetical order.

Adaptation. The materials must be adapted to the pupils as to age, interests, and experience in worship. *Completeness.* There should be relatively complete development of the thought or theme for the day and inclusion of a variety of materials to make a rather completely finished product. It is a bit difficult, for example, to think of a service either without prayer or only of prayer. *Familiarity plus variety.* The service should be neither so familiar as to foster perfunctoriness nor so novel as to invite attention to the technique. We cannot worship well on a hymn which we have sung for the third consecutive Sunday or on one which we have never seen.

Fitness. This principle requires that the materials used be the best in every way to foster the highest possible experience of worship in that hour. It involves full consideration of the objectives, the needs of the worshipers, the quality of the materials, the circumstances in equipment and leadership. *Participation.* Each worshiper should have full opportunity to take part in the service. It is to be, as far as possible, not something done for him, but by him. He will sing, not be sung to; pray, not be prayed for. *Unity.* Every service should have a theme, usually one which expresses the objective. Around it are gathered the hymns and other features. Themes may follow the lesson for the day, the great holy days of the church year and holidays of the national year, also such vital pupil experiences as the beginning of school. Throughout, it is aimed that "outward expression shall parallel inward experience."

Arranging the Order

When the materials have been selected as wisely as possible for effective results, they must be put into the most fitting sequence. There are four principles, here listed alphabetically. *Alternation.* Music and reading, standing and sitting, and the like are mixed so that variety of expression is achieved. *Climax.* The opening event is chosen with special care. Then the service proceeds to a height where it closes. *Familiarity plus variety.* There is need for some variation in the weekly fare. Yet it is impossible as well as undesirable to have a different order every Sunday. Perhaps one order, with slight variation from Sunday to Sunday, will serve for a month.

It may be even one service for a quarter so far as general outline is concerned if there be some change each month and a bit of variety each Sunday. *Practicality.* Awkward and embarrasing effects will be produced if the order of service does not take into consideration such practical elements as the necessity for rising and sitting, the movement of leaders, ability to read, skill in singing, and the like. Let only those materials be used, and used in only such order, as will "work" under the conditions. Special attention will need to be given this item by the adults who are coaching younger people.

Conducting Services of Worship

When the program and the service have been planned, artistic conducting remains as an essential if the objective is to be attained. There are many important considerations at this point.

Proper rooms and equipment

In many, perhaps a majority of schools, pupils of widely varied ages are crowded into unattractive rooms having poor light and ventilation, and filled with more or less distraction. On the other hand, a few buildings, recently built or remodeled, provide children's chapels as carefully appointed as the places of worship for adults in their chief services. Every school needs to take its facilities in hand and strive to achieve the best possible physical setting for its services of worship.

The ideal room would be well lighted, with sunshine if possible, although seating should be arranged so that the worshipers do not look directly into the light. Heating and ventilation should have requisite attention. The room should be decorated in a dignified way with plainly tinted walls and a bit of colored border. The windows should be neatly curtained or draped, pictures carefully chosen. A few flowers, real ones, tastefully arranged, are desirable when possible. The movement for what is called a "worship center" has made a fine beginning toward creating the consciousness of worship. A type which is adapted to the character of worship experience in the age group and can be varied in its appointments with seasons and themes is better than mere duplication of the chancel furnishings. Creative designing and pupil participation in providing and caring for it are important.

There should be chairs of suitable height, rubber-tipped if there is no carpet; a plentiful supply of hymnals and Bibles; and, very important, a cabinet for putting things away. A prime requisite is a good musical instrument, kept in tune. The tasteful and correct arrangement of the furnishings dare not be neglected.

It is written that Paul and Silas were able to worship quite heartily in a dungeon, but they had attained a degree of spiritual maturity scarcely to be expected of typical Sunday Church School pupils. Hence, if any group must use basement facilities for worship, let it be an older one that will find the situation less distracting. Besides, the room may then be changed. There was one basement room which had long been used by children. It was unventilated, undecorated, dim, and unlighted. Dampness, even, showed on the walls. Then certain circumstances made necessary its conversion into an adult classroom. Before long that room had water-proofed walls, softly tinted decoration, indirect lighting, a rug on the floor, and curtains at the windows!

For many schools, the most suitable space for worship is the main place of assembly for adult common worship. The use of that equipment for worship by children is too often overlooked, in the larger churches particularly. Inspiring surroundings, great organs, lovely windows, are unfortunately denied the children. Why do we not use the best for those of whom the Master said that the kingdom is constituted?

Freedom from distraction

Services of worship should be conducted under conditions in which attention is upon worship alone. This will require co-operation by everybody concerned. The program must be carefully and appropriately planned to hold the attention of the pupils so that they will not create disturbance by their lack of interest. The leader must be prepared so that there are no delays after the service has started. The pianist must have a copy of the day's program so that she can proceed without hesitation. The pastor, superintendents, secretaries, treasurers, librarians, and sexton must all understand that their proper responsibility is to worship, keeping silent and not moving about until the worship has been concluded. For this portion of the schedule the leader of worship is the sole commanding figure upon whom attention is fixed as he guides pupils in communion with God.

When worship is conducted at the opening of the morning session, a most important factor is restraining late pupils from disturbing those who have come on time. Simple justice demands it. Also right procedure would do at least three things: raise the tone of worship; train the pupils in punctuality; train the future members of the church for proper reverence and deportment with regard to adult common worship. There must be careful study of etiquette in this matter as well as proper arrangements. One practical help is to admit late pupils to the back of the room, if the building is suitably constructed, letting them provide themselves with hymnals there and enter the worship from that point.

In order to provide for concentration upon worship alone, announcements will be excluded from the service. Even a minimum of directions will be given. Hymn numbers will be posted on a board, written on the blackboard, or mimeographed along with the complete service if it is different, as in many cases it should be, from that suggested in hymnal or quarterly.

The passing of papers or other supplies during worship is a gross misdemeanor. So, also, is noisy counting of money. Talks by the superintendent or any visitor should be eliminated if they are not specifically worshipful in character. Stopping the pupils in the midst of a hymn to correct their singing is undesirable. So is that type of song-leading which introduces contests between boys and girls to see which can sing more loudly, frequent exhortations to sing out, and similar pyrotechnics.

When, then, shall making announcements and other such things be done? At the special period in the time schedule called "departmental instruction" described in the next chapter.

Providing the proper approach

As the time for the service draws near, it is necessary to get the pupils into a frame of mind appropriate for worship. This requires that the leader arrive early. Other workers, too, can do their part by being in their appropriate places, greeting the pupils, helping them get to their seats in a quiet manner, and providing them with the necessary hymnals or other helps.

Workers should remove their hats and coats and be at home. Pupils, too, should have a place to hang up their things and have them out of the way. The earliest arrivals may be put to work helping with arrangements. Some profitable pre-session activity is possible for all, even if it is but quiet conversation. Listening to music is another possibility—soft music on the piano or with records. Then, when the moment for beginning has arrived, a hand signal to arise, the chords of a hymn, or the superintendent's standing in his place should be sufficient.

Right techniques

There are ten general suggestions for proper technique. Know the purpose of worship in general and have definite and specific aims for each service. Know the worshipers and be sensitive to their needs. Know materials available for use and the principles of combining them. Enlist the co-operation of all persons involved. Provide the most favorable setting possible. Have preparations made long in advance in the interests of poise, ease, and a finished service; then arrive early and be able to proceed with freedom of spirit. Start promptly; keep moving quietly and reverently; lead the service to its conclusion; and close it there. Eliminate every possible source of distraction. Expect order, and in all kindliness, tolerate nothing less. Worship.

Spontaneous worship

Much of the above has had in view a typical school with a more or less formal service of worship, likely at the beginning of the hour. Current trends favor, especially for the younger children, spontaneous and informal moments of worship at any appropriate point in the progress of a unit of activity, quite regardless of time schedule. Somewhat similarly, certain schools have worship at the end of the session. This allows for preparation in advance. It provides an opportunity to use worship as an integrating activity in concluding the work of the morning, and to send pupils home under its inspiration.

Leadership

There are many personal characteristics which an ideal leader of worship possesses. Some of them are: reverence, dignity, self-command, sincerity, good voice, pleasing appearance, friendly disposition, quietness, religious enthusiasm, positiveness. Most of all, however, the ideal leader of worship is one who can be, while leading others, the chief worshiper himself. Dinner or business forgotten, with thoughts fixed upon God, he worships and the pupils follow.

The planning and conducting of worship should pass to the pupils as rapidly as they can be rendered capable of handling the responsibility. Here, for example, is a Young People's Department in its Sunday session on the day before Christmas. Plans have been made by the appropriate members well in advance. As the visitor enters, he is greeted by a young man who ushers him to a seat. Looking about, he observes a profound orderliness enforced by the young people who know what they are about. In fact, throughout the session there are very few adults in the room, only a superintendent sitting near the back of the room and a few teachers in appropriate places.

Preceding the worship, the president of the department requests a meeting of his group on a certain weekday night. Then the young people worship. One young woman takes her place as leader; another is pianist. The order of worship has been written on the blackboard so that there are no announcements of any kind. The only spoken words are words of worship. They sing. A young man leads in prayer. Others assist their fellow students in making the offering. Finally the young people go to their class sessions, spiritually uplifted by communion with God.

DIRECTING FELLOWSHIP

From its beginning with Jesus and his disciples, the Christian Church has been recognized as a particularly intimate social group. Within its membership men, women, young people, and children can experience a warmth of human interrelationship which is akin to the divine relationship in which they have their highest realization. We all sing heartily when the hymn is "Blest be the tie that binds our hearts in Christian love."

The Place of Fellowship

The spirit, sense, and practice of fellowship is worthy of cultivation. Christian persons should grow through their experience of it, appreciation for it, and skill in promoting it. They should be educated from fellowship to constantly higher fellowship for themselves and others, even others the world round. That is not an insignificant factor in the abundant life at which Christian education aims; it is even, in a sense, the only hope for peace within or without.

We have many ways of promoting Christian fellowship experience. Some of it will be a by-product of study, worship, and service. Consider the greeting and visiting enjoyed by many congregations after the benediction, or the "fun" people have while working upon a pageant. There is also planned fellowship. It may follow a worker's conference meeting when refreshments are enjoyed after the more formal program is finished. Planned fellowship takes the form also of a day's picnic or an evening's game or party. (While this usually is called recreational activity, fellowship is the more inclusive and desirable term.)

Although fellowshiping is closely associated with play and the play spirit, it should not be despised or considered of little importance for that reason. Martin Luther wrote favorably about education through play, although as late as the 1850's Sunday School leaders in a convention were debating whether it could be right for a Sunday School to have a picnic. It is a far cry from that debate to the present situation as seen in the use of church gymnasiums and social rooms. Playing in the Christian group as a legitimate area of Christian activity has been growing in favor in recent decades. Its fruitfulness for wholesome religious outlook is being increasingly appreciated and the trend will scarcely be reversed, particularly in view of present social conditions.

Educational Aim in Fellowship

The fellowship program of the Sunday Church School, needless to say, should have the educational aim. It is not to be merely "bait" for attracting and holding the young people of the church. Too often it has been said that "if we don't let these young people have parties, we'll lose them." Rather, if you don't cultivate the Christian fellowship experience of all the people, you will lose an opportunity to help them develop fully into wholesome Christian personalities.

The program should do more, also, than conserve the leisure time of people so that they will not spend it to their moral, physical, and spiritual detriment. There can be the positive value of helping them turn leisure time into pursuits which are physically, morally, and spiritually profitable. The fellowship program of the church should help people find life more abundant through happiness in associating with the Christian group so that they will grow through, in, and for it.

A Program for Fellowship

The congregation which takes seriously the fellowship aspect of its life will want the Sunday Church School to give attention to this element in all units of activity and arrange for special units in which it is a central interest. The leader will likely have to guide the pupils in some of the events himself and direct his co-workers for effective practice in their share of the task. In addition, most leaders will need to develop the whole program within their churches. Several steps to be taken in that direction will be discussed.

The first step is to *accept the task*. Many churches have not yet done much thinking about the promotion of fellowship. Others are reluctant to launch out into a program. A majority need to give attention to its desirability, convince themselves of its worth, and determine to do whatever may be possible. And, let it be understood, this means more than having a "social" now and then, particularly the type designed to raise money.

The next step is to *discover the facts.* This refers to a study of the congregation itself and its fellowship value for the various age groups on the one hand and of the community recreational situation on the other. In both areas, the average church is due for some awakening facts! It will be found that, while the church has its doors closed six days a week, young people in particular are being seduced by commercial interests for useless if not dangerous forms of fellowship. Meanwhile, the thing many young people want the church most to do for them is to care for their fellowship interests.

To *organize for fellowship* is a third step. This will mean a determination of the functions which the pastor will serve, also the places of other leaders and committees who will see to it that fellowship interests are given full place in all program building. There must be those who will care for interchurch co-operation and community relationships, too.

At this point another important step is to *adopt standards.* Here, as in some other instances of church activity, standards have been relatively low. Some of our "drama," parties, athletics! The fellowship activities should be of the finest types and on the highest level of which the group is capable. They must be practical, of course, the kind which the group can manage. They should stress true sociability. They should be compatible with and conducive to spiritual development. And they should be educational, which is to say that they should lead on to finer things in the realm of fellowship and otherwise. Among other proper tests of a program are these: Have the young people learned to know one another at their best? Do they more fully appreciate the fellowship which they have in the Christian Church? Are they learning wholesome methods of play? Have they been introduced to right social techniques? Are they more loyal to the Master?

These things having been done, the church is ready to *provide a program, leadership, equipment and finance.* The program will include a wide variety of activities. Some will be primarily physical—athletic games, sports, hikes, and the like. Others will be primarily mental or cultural like reading, dramatization, lectures, and study groups for pleasure as well as profit. Social activities, including parties, socials, and picnics will round out the program. There is a wealth of literature to assist the leaders who wish to plan a program of this type for the classes, departments, Church School, or entire church. The program should be graded to the interests of participants, should be planned for all year round, and should be balanced as to the types of things included. While much of it may appear in other units of activity, some may well be the center of concern in a particular unit. Great care must be taken so that it does not become a detached organization, program, and objective on its own as are, for example, many church athletic teams.

Nothing is more important than leadership. That fact will be attested by congregations who built a gymnasium without providing leadership and found it desirable to close the gymnasium. A leadership education program is essential, too. It is possible to do fine things with little money and little equipment if the leader is wise. At the same time many churches can well begin to plan for more equipment—homemade, if possible, on a service enterprise basis. Financing of fellowship is best done by a budget allotment, although there are affairs where pay-as-you-enter may be desirable.

The final step is to *educate.* We need to educate for fellowship through fellowship experiences. The whole constituency is the first concern. Yet, out of that constituency should come the trained leadership which understands, has the right personality, and can be further equipped in leadership courses to carry on the program.

Here is a procedure which is full of weal and may be full of woe. Half-hearted, careless, and unsupervised efforts will always be worse than none. Earnestness and intelligence about it will result in the cultivation of helpful leisure-time interests and the learning of techniques for wholesome leisure-time pursuits. By-products will be found in increased church loyalty and church service. Altogether it is a vital means for the fuller attainment of the Christian educational objectives.

Guiding Fellowship Events

It would be perhaps a rare person who could be highly effective as a leader of worship and at the same time an expert at recreational leadership. Possibly an administrator's major effort in this area should be directed toward making sure there is an adequate program, supervising teachers for the recreational aspects of their units, and seeing that recreational leaders are trained. Nevertheless, many a leader will be required himself to preside at a banquet or handle a picnic or see that a party comes off with the right sort of good time for all.

There is a science of recreational leadership. As with worship, good books are available and should be placed in a library where they can be consulted frequently. Out of the great wealth of material, several important items which stand out for primary consideration are listed below. They will apply, some of them, to any type of fellowship activity; in other cases, to certain ones only—physical, mental, cultural, or social.

1. Keep this aim in view: wholesome, joyous, healthy leisure-time activity, building well-rounded Christian character.
2. Understand principles; seek experience; know sources of games, stories, and other materials.
3. Use fellowship qualities like these: tact, wit, honesty, alertness, cheerfulness, friendliness, good judgment, spirit of fun, sportsmanship; bring to bear such skills as athletics, teaching, singing, storytelling, leadership.
4. Know the group.
5. Be prepared, in general, for the event, and for each item in the event. Have some extra ideas. Don't have to go hunting for ideas, rules, or any equipment while the participants wait.
6. In planning the event: have a theme and keep to it; have variety in the program; put games in psychological sequence, mixing active and quiet items; be familiar with novel ideas; recognize importance of first item in event; visualize things beforehand, work them through, try them out; arrange to have sense of fellowship from the time invitation is received; remember decorations and refreshments are as significant for fellow-

ship as anything else; be sure to include plans to "clean up."

7. In leading the event: use helpers, well-prepared, too; get attention quickly and as quietly as possible; get it before speaking and hold it; keep control, don't let the group get away from you, securing discipline through group action when possible; explain things clearly; keep expectancy alive, making use of the surprise element; keep things moving, with only necessary relaxation and rest; get everyone into the fun.

DIRECTING SERVICE

"Service" is that element of the program in which pupils learn to contribute more fully to the welfare of others by performing acts of helpfulness. Since sharing is undoubtedly a better word than service, this is the area where pupils learn to share by sharing. Learning to be good stewards of money, energy, time, and talent by being such stewards is still another way of describing it.

The life of Jesus is often epitomized in terms of his service and the importance of his teaching on service by word as well as example is universally recognized. Thus it is proper to single out this activity for special attention in Christian education. Regrettably, though, service has been largely subordinated to the least of all places in the amount of time and attention given to it in the typical school. As McKibben has said "Church School workers in general are perhaps more lacking in appreciation of the general nature and significance of service training and expression than of any other element in the total program . . . Practically all that some of the leaders know of the service program is represented in the most traditional conception of missionary education."[1]

No one can measure the harm that has been done by two classes of people. One is the group who rightly may be called "social gospellers." They have overstressed "service" to the extent of undercutting it by the neglect of other matters which are represented, for example, in worship. The other group is made up by those who have glibly labelled all efforts at social action as "social gospel." Christianity can no more ignore social implications than individual expressions.

---

[1] Frank M. McKibben, *Improving Religious Education through Supervision* (New York: The Methodist Book Concern, 1931), p. 140.

To be sure, when persons or groups get one-sided in their emphasis, correction is needed. Too often, though, the correction overdoes itself. So, just now, there are trends away from the social emphasis toward the ecclesiastical—worship, organization, theology —which may, in turn, get out of hand. The sanctuary must not become a retreat from life instead of a center where life's burning issues are appraised in the light of the Word, determination is born to meet them in the Christian way, and the enterprise of reconstruction is planned and begun.

Educational Aim in Service

There are two principal areas in which education for service takes place: participating in church and Church School life; engaging in "social service."

Serving in the church and Church School

We have always considered it desirable to give our pupils tasks to perform for the school. We have made them secretaries, treasurers, librarians, and ushers. Now and then we have allowed them to do substitute teaching or assist in departments with younger children. We have encouraged them to earn money for the church or school by various, if not sometimes doubtful, devices. We have even allowed them to usher or sing in the choir for the chief services of the church.

Often, though, there was some doubt about the procedure if it meant taking them out of classes. We viewed it as stopping their education. Actually, we were by such means coming closest to educational truth. All of those activities represent the valid employment of learning by doing. In this way pupils have learned many of the things they really know about the church and have gained most of the wholesome attitudes and useful skills they possess in regard to church affairs. They do need "Bible" and "history" and "doctrine," but also this. Our problem is to get the right balance and timing.

There are still unrealized possibilities. For example, young people may well have much more to do in their churches and

Church Schools. As a goal, the young Christian completing his work in the Young People's Division should have had some experience in each type of church work. He will have done all he can in and for his class, department, and school by way of holding office, serving on committees, planning and conducting sessions, participating in the directing of units of activity. He will have engaged in congregational evangelism. He will have had experience in carrying mercy to the needy. He will have helped to promote Christian fellowship through assisting in recreational programs, club work, class, departmental, school, or church socials. He will have become familiar with the stewardship work of the church by his own intelligent contribution to its enterprises and by participating in its program of support and benevolence. He will have had some part in the conducting of services of worship.

Engaging in "social service"

Education in service which would not look beyond the local congregation or even the whole church would not be worthy of the name. In each pupil's program there should be units or parts of units of activity which provide opportunity to participate in the work of established community agencies of social service and church institutions of mercy. It is still better, of course, to have direct contact with individuals with whom he may share.

The giving of Christmas baskets is perhaps the favorite practice in this area. It has its real educational value, particularly for those who make the direct contact with their beneficiaries. One small group of young people, for example, will never forget their touching experience of presenting a Christmas basket to a barefoot, twelve-year-old girl who was bravely trying to take the place of mother in a one-room slum home. That was an experience in sharing; she shared her spirit, the young people shared their food. Social workers have good reasons for discouraging this personal delivery of Christmas baskets. Perhaps it does embarrass the recipients, and the young people may remain untouched. But always necessarily? At any rate, where does the educational value lie for recipient as well as donor? Some of us think that selected young people can be prepared to do, personally, their deeds of Christian helpfulness.

Yet, service should go far beyond Christmas baskets only, into lively study of the community near and far and constant work to uplift conditions wherever one's slightest influence can reach. Even when using only the typical Sunday Church School lessons, this is an element not to be neglected. When choosing elective units, some of them should be in this area and no pains spared to carry out their suggestions of things to do. When building a program of units of activity, this element is to have a large place.

Program of Service

The Church needs a constituency that is intelligent about service—its meaning as the sharing of welfare with all, its place in the Christian program, the need and the opportunity for reciprocal relations. Proper attitudes are just as important—strong and abiding motives of good will, dependability, and devotion that lead to unfailing action. The ultimate purpose is skill—ability to carry forward, perhaps even in full-time service in the area.

If all the constituency is to be educated in service to that end, a leadership must be prepared. In the whole leadership program of the Church there is need for the introduction of opportunity and materials which will lead to understanding, attitudes, and skill for education in service.

The major element in a program of service is the providing of opportunities for service. This should get beyond the raising of money to dealing with actualities. Giving is highly important and there are many things which no one can do except by gifts. However, the whole financial program of a congregation can be wisely studied at this point and adjustments made to render the giving more fully a form of service. Beyond that, the leader will concentrate on providing service enterprises so that this aspect of the pupil program is truly a creative experience.

With that background, the leader can well co-operate with his workers to develop a comprehensive program of service for the school which will integrate with that of the congregation, denomination, and world-wide church. It should be comprehensive for all age groups and adapted to them. It should be flexible enough to include all reasonable interests and furnish the special purposes of various units within it. It should represent balance among the competing demands for service enterprises to be undertaken in the home, church, community, and world. It should not neglect the possibilities of vocational choice in this field.

Standards and Principles for Service Enterprises

In full accord with the importance of education in service is the seriousness of proper precaution in handling individual enterprises. The leader will need to check upon such standards of selection as those which follow. Is the enterprise:

Acceptable, heartily approved by the group?
Actual, not just something to do—genuine?
Adapted to the group, attainable by them?
Balanced, a part of a program that will include various types and outlooks, needs, and peoples?
Correlated with other aspects of curriculum, part of a unit?
Educational, fertile of understanding, attitude, and skill?
Helpful, really not pauperizing recipient or givers?
Important, dealing with urgent need, necessary enough to be challenging?
Manageable, practical?
Planned by group?
Progressive, part of step-by-step experience?
Studied, preceded by careful study, even a survey?
Valuable in genuine sharing?

There are established principles to be employed in carrying out service enterprises. Among the most important ones are these:

1. Appeal to spiritual motives.
2. Use direct procedure; connect giver and recipient personally wherever other principles will not be violated.
3. Follow through; don't start and then give up.
4. Guard the best interests of both giver and recipient.
   a. Avoid as giver: formal, perfunctory giving; imitation, motives of social approval only; blame; patronizing; professional attitudes; sense of superiority; and sentimentality.

b. Avoid for recipient: defense and escape; dependence or parasitism; laziness; loss of proper pride; panhandling; simulation of need or illness; and whining.
5. Go in the spirit of real comradeship.
6. Make it a creative experience.
7. Remember that the best service is preventive service.
8. Recognize that in many instances it is best to work with the regular social agencies.
9. Provide for full participation of the school group.
10. Be assured of competent guidance.

Chapter XIII

CONDUCTING OTHER GROUP SESSIONS AND DIRECTING UNITS

In the three preceding chapters on the leader and the curriculum, his duties with regard to the pupil program as a whole and each of its four major aspects have been treated. Yet the subject cannot be concluded there. For one thing, there are several types of group session common in Sunday Church School practice which yet lie somewhat on the periphery of the main stream of curricular endeavor. They are here called "other group sessions" although it is desirable that their "otherness" be eliminated and they become as fully integrated into the curriculum as possible. These are to be considered in the first half of this chapter. As a second subject for the chapter and a final consideration under curriculum, unit management requires attention.

OTHER GROUP SESSIONS

A basic activity of every Sunday Church School leader is to conduct the meetings of various groups. It is an activity in which his ability or the lack of it shows most prominently as well as one in which major steps toward fruitful service are taken. The leader's manner of handling business meetings, leading departmental sessions, and even announcing the numbers of special day services will determine largely the attitude which pupils, parents, and church members will take toward him and the school. More important, the leader himself will be in charge of these items so that they are his own chief teaching opportunities. Departmental instruction, special day services, incidental teaching, and business meetings are all to advance the objectives of Christian education.

General Principles

There are certain "practical" principles which a leader must observe to make the most of his opportunity in any meeting. Ten of them follow:

Be prepared with a program worked out and thought through.
Arrive early and start the meeting on time.
Provide for something worth while to happen.
Achieve the chosen purpose if possible.
Win the members to the program; don't try to drive them.
Suit the occasion with appropriate dignity, reverence, or good humor.
Keep the program moving.
Don't talk unduly; listen also.
Be tactful in handling difficult problems and persons.
Observe the special principles of the particular type of meeting.

Departmental Instruction

The term "departmental instruction" refers to a portion of the time schedule of the Sunday Church School hour in which the entire department, division, or school, in an assembly, participates in some activity of study and instruction. It can be a vital part of the whole pupil program if proper ideals and procedures are observed, and many schools could use the idea advantageously. In alphabetical order below, several older practices and newer ideas are examined. Let it be said that these are in addition to the idea of using departmental time, when appropriate, for the initiation and completion of various items in the continuing units of activity which constitute the major program. Indeed, all these departmental activities should be as far as possible a part of a total unified and integrated pupil program. As elsewhere, too, the pupils ought to have the fullest possible participation.

Catechism

In many schools, the pupils recite portions of the catechism, usually as a part of the "opening exercises." The superintendent will ask, "What is the fourth commandment?" and the pupils will read the answer. Then he will inquire, "What does this mean?" and again they will read the answer.

This is not worship. It is an effort at instruction in the sense of refreshing the memory of the pupils. Its efficacy may be questioned. Yet, the underlying purpose is commendable. Some effort at real departmental instruction in the catechism is to be approved in the "catechetical church." When a problem has arisen upon which the catechism can furnish light and inspiration, departmental time can be given to its study, not merely its recitation. Certain lessons in the typical series also suggest using time in this way. Further, there might well be certain units of activitiy involving the catechism in which the departmental program could be used to expedite its progress. Visual aids in "teaching" of catechism might be employed and the pastor or other resource leader used.

Films and recordings

A major problem just now is the difficulty of getting teachers to use the new audile and visual aids. Actually, too, there are almost insurmountable obstacles to be overcome by those who would use them gladly if the conditions were more favorable. Departmental instruction time is the way out of some of these difficulties. A film can be viewed or a recording can be heard and followed by departmental or classroom discussion.

"The lesson"

In many schools, the superintendent introduces the lesson in the departmental assembly before the class session, or reviews it afterward. Teachers do not like the practice and can scarcely be blamed. They wish to prepare their own introductions to the lessons and they expect to handle them in their own way. Likewise, they do not like to have the lessons worked over again after they have finished with their own conclusions.

It may be desirable now and then to have a resource leader make a presentation which will bear upon the later work of each class. Perhaps, too, the superintendent can sometimes agree with his teachers that he will present a particular aspect of a lesson. There are possibilities also in having a teacher who has traveled to the scene of some biblical event tell the whole group about it. Other life experiences of the various teachers may be handled similarly. A still more legitimate employment of departmental time in this respect is having the whole group work upon some activity which is related to the class session but not in any way a duplication of it.

Memorizing

When Sunday Church Schools have memory "requirements" for promotion from each department, the pupils often "learn" them in a departmental period. Having such requirements is questionable; handling them in a mixed group of varied background and ability is still more so. On the other hand, there are legitimate occasions for using departmental time for memorization. Future services of worship may be prepared in part by departmental memorizing of hymns or Scripture. Special programs to be given for other departments or guests at the special seasons suggest further needs for memory drills. As far as possible, of course, memorization should grow out of an appreciation so deep and a sense of need so finely met that it is largely a by-product which requires only a bit of drilling to make it permanent.

Missions

In an earlier day, Sunday Church Schools would have "Mission Sunday" perhaps once a month, with a missionary offering and a missionary story told in the various departments or the entire school. A different point of view has now been achieved. It is well put by Harner and Baker:

"1. We will have special missionary courses, but all our teaching should be permeated with missions.

"2. We will have special periods of missionary emphasis, but all the year should be permeated with missions.

"3. We will have special missionary auxiliaries in some cases, but all auxiliaries should be permeated with missions.

"4. We will have special misionary sermons, but many a sermon should have the missionary spirit.

"5. We may have summer missionary conferences, but all our camps and schools should embody the missionary emphasis.

"6. We may have a few individuals who are missionary enthusiasts or specialists, but all Christians alike are entitled to the responsibility and the joy of sharing in the missionary enterprise." [1]

In the light of those things and the chapter by the same authors entitled, "The Sunday Church School is Basic," it becomes apparent that the Sunday Church School leader is properly the chief missionary educator in the church. Clearly, too, his work is to be carried out in more ways than having a special Sunday once a month. Study and instruction, worship, fellowship, and service elements in all units of activity will have the missionary flavor and many of the units of activity will center on missionary objectives. Yet this does not set aside the possibility of good to be accomplished by departmental instruction in missions—the mission story, the mission exhibit, a film presentation, some work for mission enterprises, a visit by a missionary. Special attention, too, can be directed to missionary giving. Needless to say, all types of missions should have their fair place.

Temperance and peace

For a long time, temperance "talks" or "demonstrations" have been given and more recently world peace has received similar treatment. As with all proper Sunday Church School objectives, it is now realized that these matters should be fitted into the total program as integral parts and not as added externals. There can be special units of activity. Putting it in terms of typical schools, these features can be emphasized best in appropriate lessons. Nevertheless, speakers and programs under appropriate circumstances and on given occasions can be used advantageously in departmental time.

Stewardship

Stewardship, like missions, should permeate the entire program of the church and Church School. The time comes, however, for special consideration of the giving of time, energy, money, and talent. There must be calls for personal service and contributions

---

[1] Nevin G. Harner and David D. Baker, *Missionary Education in Your Church* (New York: Missionary Education Movement, 1942), p. 29.

to social enterprises. In connection with the giving of money, there should be abundant opportunity for all members of the school to participate in budgeting and hear reports of expenditure. All this can be a part of the departmental instruction program.

Preparation for worship

At more than one point, this book has reported the growing appreciation of worship as a religious activity of major importance for which Sunday Church School leaders are to provide educational opportunity. While, like all other things under discussion in this section, worship is handled properly as a part of total units of activity, outstanding contributions to worship experience can be rendered in the time of departmental instruction. Worship services themselves should not be interrupted for guidance in the meaning of worship, the significance of hymns, and the proper rendition of musical numbers. Frequent sessions of at least ten or fifteen minutes in the departmental program should be held for such purposes. Pupils can be reminded of the meaning and significance of worship. They can memorize portions of future services. They can study the words and music of hymns. They can learn new hymns for subsequent services.

Special Day Services

It would be interesting to know when Sunday Church Schools began having Christmas and Easter services and still more interesting to see some of those early programs. Most of us remember the earlier ones in our own Sunday School days. We may picture, for example, a tall cedar in the chancel of a country church, a tree with popcorn strings and tinsel decorations set with real candles that twinkled like the stars outside. Near the tree was the shepherd scene placed on green paper grass, with toy sheep and miniature shepherds and a sister's doll bedecked in angel's wings poised in song above it all. The church was packed to the doors while everyone sang, heard the children speak their pieces and do their exercises, and listened to the preacher and choir outdoing themselves in speech and music.

Values

Such fond remembrances suggest the fine educational possibilities in these programs. They deserve the careful attention of all leaders, especially superintendents. They bring the whole church fellowship together, often by families, in a common experience. They put the children in the midst. They give the members of the school things to do co-operatively and for others. It is an outgoing religious experience as well as an intaking one. The church becomes important for the time. The content of the program is vivid and the memory remains.

Purposes

If there is any one supremely important suggestion to be made in this matter it is this: that leaders and pupils consider the proper aims or objectives of these programs. When a group of some fifty workers were asked, "What is the aim of special day services?" the first answer was, "To show off the children." Others followed: "To make some money"; "To draw the parents who never come otherwise"; "The children like them." Christmas, Easter, Children's Day, and similar programs have no real excuse for being used unless they serve the purposes of Christian education. They should be planned and conducted so that each participant's growth in grace will be furthered and each hearer, whether he be pupil, parent, friend, church member, or worker, will be informed, inspired, and cultivated.

General procedures

The objectives will need to be recognized first in the choice of songs, "pieces," exercises, pageants, or plays which are to constitute the program. They must be chosen not because they are "cute" or merely attractive in any other way; rather, because they allow the participant to express his religious feelings in a way which will share his experience with others.

The objectives must be kept in mind when the parts are assigned and rehearsed, too. There are ways of asking people to take part, rather of offering them parts, which suggest the spirit in which you would like them to perform. The spirit so inculcated can easily be lost, however, in rehearsals which are conducted in the typical bedlam of such occasions. A worker who told how the pageants she conducts are rehearsed in quiet and order, indeed, with the reverence of a full performance, presented the proper ideal.

The attainment of the objectives must be aided and abetted by the superintendent's attitude and manner as well as the words of his announcements and explanations during the rendition of the program. More than once a superintendent has told how hard the children and teachers have worked preparing to entertain their hearers. Instead, let him announce that they have wanted to share the stories they have heard and the songs they have learned to sing so that others, too, will be helped as they have been.

Rally day

Properly viewed and dealt with, this day can be one of the most significant for the Sunday Church School. The key to the matter is in the area of purpose: this should be Christian Education Day in the congregation. It can well climax the Christian Education Week or Month in which the meaning and program of the educational work of the congregation becomes better understood and more richly appreciated. The use of a speaker from the outside, usual *piece de resistance,* is questionable. Too often he is not acquainted with the school and does not represent the real purpose of Rally Day. Rally Day is a time for welcoming back those who have newly "rallied" to the winter's work in the school. It is a time of dedication by all, including the whole congregation, to this work. It is a time to rejoice in the school. Nothing could be better than a day of doing just those things in the midst of a program that is typical, yet special in the sense that everyone tries to outdo himself at making it the best day of the school year as a beginning of better days to come.

Trends

Recent years have seen different types of programs developed. The play or pageant tends to displace the agglomeration of "pieces" and exercises. If the latter are used they are chosen and arranged in a structure that has some unified impact under a theme or progression. The "White Gift Service" at Christmas suggests the use of such services for a purpose. Most recently the use of projected picture programs at Easter and Christmas has been effectively employed. Yet there is danger that a "spectacle" take the place of pupil participation in the presentation of a program.

As a special objective, the superintendent on all these occasions has an unusual opportunity to interpret the school to parents and outsiders. They do come to these programs, many of them to these programs only. The superintendent will never scold them; he can suggest further items of co-operation which will help in the school's work. Mainly, however, he will commend them for the part they have had and the interest they have shown, and he will seek each time to leave them with one definite new item of information about the school.

"Incidental Teaching"

There are times when the leader is engaged in matters that are highly important although they do not seem to be directly related to the learning-teaching process as usually conceived. We call them, therefore, incidental teaching, the other side of incidental learning.

Transitions

In typical Sunday Church School sessions there is occasion for groups to pass from one form of activity, aspect of the session, or part of the building to another. Smooth handling of these transitions will contribute to the saving of time and otherwise work toward the general efficiency of the school.

Bells or buzzers are sometimes needed to co-ordinate the various groups or signify the beginning or close of an activity. Their use should be reduced to a minimum; in the case of loud gongs, eliminated entirely. Lights are better. Calls to order in any conspicuous way are unnecessary if adequate handling of better devices is employed. The passing of classes, so often a moment of bedlam, can be done quietly and in perfect order. The use of music will solve nearly every problem in this area. The prelude and interlude, soft music or marching music, will indicate the transitions, serve as a background for tying together the whole program, and give an atmosphere that is conducive to the proper purposes of the school.

Before and after sessions

All pupils should arrive early; some will come unduly early. This is an opportunity to lengthen the hour. To be sure, leaders must arrive still earlier and be ready. Then they can put some pupils to work—very valuable work educationally—helping to make ready for the session. Others can read from a browsing table, look at pictures, start completing some enterprise, consult an atlas or encyclopedia, present a question that has risen during the week, perhaps go to a music corner.

There is, also, post-session work to be done. Pupils here, too, should be guided to do as much as possible, although it is largely in the nature of housekeeping. They can put away all items of equipment which are stored in cupboards or cabinets. They can clean up any scrap paper or the like and in every way put things in order so as to leave the room "shipshape."

Before and after session is an excellent time for the incidental cultivation of the Christian grace of fellowship. Every pupil deserves a quiet but hearty greeting from as many leaders and other pupils as possible. Nothing will do more to make one want to come again and again although that is not the chief value in fellowship. Further opportunities for fellowship appear when a new pupil or visitors attend. Throughout there is opportunity for attaining good Christian etiquette. Pupils should be sent home with the gracious good-by which is but an informal benediction.

Business Meetings

Sunday Church School leadership includes an element of business management so that Chapter XV is devoted to it. Here, too, there must be mention of the business meetings for which the leader is responsible as well as other incidental business meetings of pupil and worker groups. The leader's principal concern will be the monthly staff meeting.

"How can we get our workers out for the regular teachers' and officers' meetings?" That question is raised in almost every Sunday Church School conference on administrative matters. Usually the inquirer expects some panacea to be proposed. Suppose, however, the solution were approached from the viewpoint of providing better meetings? That objective is not easily attained. The ten principles listed above are difficult to practice. The leader is unable to get the people to attend regularly for the regular Sunday sessions, much less for business meetings. The business may be relatively unimportant, anyhow. The meetings tend to degenerate into a pronounced informality which drags them out interminably. Unless the superintendent talks, most of it will be done by one or two others and there is often a hobby-rider who is difficult to handle. What to do?

Several answers can be proposed. First, do not have a meeting unless there is worth-while business to transact. Most people have too many meetings to attend. Besides, the routine matters can be handled better by an executive committee so that general meetings deal only with policies of larger interest. Second, see that an order of business is prescribed in the constitution of the school; in following it carefully a spirit of some dignity and precision will be cultivated. Third, make it a matter of pride to study and follow parliamentary practice, using Robert's Rules of Order; it is good education to do so. Fourth, open and close even an informal meeting with prayer and continue throughout in the attitude appropriate to the Master's business. Fifth, view every formal monthly or quarterly meeting of teachers and officers as an educational opportunity. In fact, every monthly workers' meeting should have a fourfold program including, besides business, worship, education, and fellowship.

UNITS IN THE PROGRAM

It has been emphasized and reiterated that the pupil's proper task in the educational work of the church is the completion of

successive units of activity in which he learns to perform Christian
activities by performing them. Studying and being instructed about
Christian matters, worshiping in Christan modes, fellowshiping
with Christian groups, serving at Christian enterprises are the major
interrelated factors, with the activities mentioned above as fully
integrated as possible to make a total program.

Thus it is essential for the leader to understand unit procedure.
If it is not now being used in his school, he may wish to introduce
it. If his departmental superintendents and teachers are using it,
many adjustments of his plans and schedules to provide for pupils
to work in this way may be needed. His workers as well as his
pupils will want him to be familiar with the type of work they are
doing so that he can understand, encourage and appreciate it. He
will himself want to be informed about unit procedure so that he
can help to make it more effective.

Meaning of Units

As defined on page 180, a unit is an educational enterprise
which is to develop as a constellation of interrelated religious activities centered about some objective pertinent to Christian growth.
That general way of organizing the learning-and-teaching procedure has been in the vanguard of educational thought in various
forms for more than a generation and its validity for directing learning effectively is widely recognized. The essential point of the
concept is the handling of the pupil's work in meaningful wholes
of complete and real experience.

The manner of unit procedure is meant to be the lifelike way
of learning. The steps in a learning activity listed on page 199
describe it in detail. More simply, the pupil is challenged by something he must do to satisfy some aspect of his personality and meet
the social demands upon it. He analyzes the situation; he gathers
data and deliberates upon them; then he decides how he will act.
He carries his strategy to its conclusion and gets his result. In
retrospect, he evaluates his achievement (and perhaps his process)
and links it all with his future.

The completion of a unit will be seen to involve much that does not appear on the surface in thinking about a pupil's "going to Sunday School." This is not just presenting himself, singing a few songs, keeping quiet while someone prays, listening respectfully while someone reads Scripture, hearing the lesson story, perhaps answering a few questions about it, putting an offering in the envelope, tarrying a moment for another hymn, and then leaving.

It is having a sense of need, a problem, an interest about which he feels keenly and wants to do something. It is sharing that center of concern with a group of pupils and with leaders. It is planning to see it to a conclusion. It is studying about it, worshiping about it, fellowshiping in the process, serving in relation to it. It is doing things, fitting into situations, getting somewhere. It is learning to perform in many areas and one in particular. Then it is getting ready to do the next thing, something about which a new concern has developed, likely in the process of dealing with the former one.

Properly, the leader of a Sunday Church School is fundamentally a person who directs a program of such units of activity while they are being completed by the various groups in his school. He does it largely by providing the conditions of staff, material, equipment, time, and organization in which they can be completed. Through those conditions he aims to make available the most effective study and instruction, worship, fellowship, and service experiences possible as teachers guide learners in the performance of their wide variety of self-chosen and self-motivated tasks.

While that is the proper situation, the leaders directing the program of units in a typical Sunday Church School most often will be following the denominational schedules and the groups will be following printed guides for pupil and leader. Sometimes those guides do scarcely more than use the word "unit"; sometimes, also, "unit" is used for a subject-matter division. Too often, too, teachers have no understanding of the meaning of a unit or experience in unit procedure; consequently they follow the book slavishly and do not accomplish the full purpose. As a result, one of the leader's tasks will be to help his teachers study the underlying philosophy of unit procedure and the details of unit management. It is described below in the form which is followed when groups are doing creative work but the same general procedure is represented in the better printed guides.

Unit Management

There are four stages in the management of a unit. However, the group does not necessarily finish one stage and then move on to the next; the four may overlap. It will be understood, too, that no two units will develop in exactly the same way. Only a general picture can be painted.

First stage: preparing and beginning

In a well-planned pupil program, one unit of activity follows another in a related and cumulative manner. As the pupils and teacher work with one unit, they discover the next problem they wish to attack. Consequently, preparation for a subsequent unit will be taking place while the present one is being completed. "Let's do this next," one pupil may say and the entire group accepts the idea. Then the group starts using some of its time to clarify its new purpose, make its plans, assemble its materials, and otherwise get ready for the unit to come.

Beginning refers, of course, to the opening sessions in which the new unit is being initiated. In preparing, and particularly in beginning, certain purposes belong uppermost. The pupils should get a clear understanding of the learning situation and their objectives regarding it. The teacher should ascertain the pupils' abilities, needs, interests, knowledge, and experience. Each pupil should discover his special needs with reference to the unit. Likewise, those past experiences which can contribute to the enterprise should be raised into mind and associated with the new unit. Out of all this, the pupils and the teacher alike will arrive at their mutual purposes and special objectives.

By the time those things have been done, teachers and pupils have a good overview of the work they are undertaking. This may be developed further by discussion, reading, viewing a film, hearing a recording or having an informal talk by the teacher or a resource leader. Then more definite plans, including the detailed work to be done and methods to be employed by the entire group, its committees, and its individual pupils, should be outlined. That may result in a written or mimeographed statement of problems, objectives, and assignments. Always, of course, there should be an element of flexibility.

After the general plan has been laid out, the real work of the unit is about to begin. In the process up to this point, however, the teacher may have discovered certain pupils who are going to need special help. Likewise the general nature of the help needed by the entire group will have appeared. All can work together to assemble the materials or to make other special arrangements for the various experiences which are likely to be needed. This working together, the close correlation of all individual or small group enterprises, is important in all stages but particuluarly in this stage of getting the unit going.

Second stage: working

Although this is the major undertaking, many of the processes described above will have to be continued or repeated at intervals. Further planning, reclarifying the problem, re-examining objectives, arranging for additional experiences, finding more materials—all those things will have to go on continuously.

The purpose of this working stage is to see that the group and individual interests and needs are met as completely as possible. Meanwhile, too, initiative should develop and self-direction should grow through abundant opportunity for creative achievement. General habits of good work and proficiency in the use of techniques and materials are important by-products.

In this stage the teacher will prove his real ability to guide and help pupils. Any of the "principal ways of teaching" on page 201, or other forms of guidance, may be used. These will be selected and employed always to help the individuals and the group make the most effective attacks upon the various angles of the problem. The pupils will be handled so that they will ask for suggestions with regard to content or method. They will attend carefully to all the experiences which the teacher helps them arrange and submit their results for correction of error or for approval.

Throughout the typical unit there should be abundant opportunity for socially contributing and receiving. The members should share their findings and otherwise help one another mutually toward the best possible results. Each should feel his obligation to contribute something real to the periods of discussion. Any one should be ready to give a demonstration, make a report, or share his personal experience. Those same goals pertain to committees, too.

One responsibility of the teacher, as difficult as it is important, is the control of time. Time presses forward rapidly. The pupils may become interested in following some tempting bypath. It is possible to fritter away a session doing practically nothing. There is danger of overexpanding the unit. The teacher will need to help the pupils determine the proper time in which to complete things and help them to keep on the main track so that they meet the schedule. If some highly important new subject develops, it can be the center of the next unit. Thoroughness must be emphasized.

Third stage: concluding

"Concluding" means more than just ending the unit. It means integrating the various aspects which have been considered from time to time in the group and committees, or by individual pupils. It means bringing things together to a vivid focus and working them into the permanent structure of the personalities involved.

There should be opportunities for final re-orientation of the individual pupils and the entire group. In some units there will have to be special effort at final mastery of some knowledge or other form of activity. Things may need to be summarized and reviewed. Wrong notions must be discovered and corrected, bad habits eliminated if possible. The notebooks, workbooks, and portfolios used in some units have value here. Discussion is an important means. Tests and measures are an obvious technique. Records of procedure are valuable, as are reports of conclusions.

Above all, the results of the unit in relation to future situations ought to be provided for. In many cases an opportunity to do something for an audience or other group will serve this purpose well. Demonstrations of the processes mastered, exhibitions of products made, talks, oral or written reports, dramatizations—all those are good. The basic idea is doing something of the nature which the unit was meant to help the pupils learn to do. Has the activity been really learned? That is the question and it is answered in the affirmative when pupils do things that promise further action in the future.

Fourth stage: evaluating and planning

Concluding leads naturally to evaluating and both to planning the next unit. The final check for errors and omissions, the review, and the final summary will lead a group to survey its achievement and evaluate the character of work done. Testing the pupils on their achievement may have the same result.

Something more direct, however, can properly be done. It is to list the results of a unit particularly in terms of habits, attitudes, and appreciations as well as knowledge gained. For Christian education, of course, all these must be in terms of Christian growth and must certainly go beyond matters of attendance.

At least an informal conference at the end of every unit is suggested. A pupil who participates in an evaluation session often discovers that he accomplished more than he had realized. This develops personal encouragement, enthusiasm for the school, stimulation toward more effective work in the oncoming unit. It is profitable for older groups to consider, also, the techniques employed in the process of completing their unit. That will guide more effective work in the forthcoming unit and should be an important step toward the final product of the school, namely, an individual qualified to profit educationally from everyday experiences and to undertake some effort at Christian growth outside the school.

The stage of planning merges into the stage of preparing. At this point in the progress of a unit, the teacher leads the pupils to summarize their new interests and decide upon something to do next. If, of course, the pupil program is determined by the denomi-national outlines, and published materials, this step will be less important. It has its place, though, for introducing the prescribed unit, seeing its value, relating it to past experience and getting ready for its effective use.

Repeating, this description of stages in unit management deals with the creative construction and management of a unit. A typical school will have its printed pupil and leader guides. However, they have been constructed according to the outline above. This treat-ment should clarify the idea back of those guides and enable the leader to see what his pupils and teachers are being guided to do with results in helping them do their work more effectively. In more advanced schools, the leader can encourage his workers to proceed with units on this creative basis.

Summary

Sunday Church School pupils learn in a curriculum—a series of activities organized into units. In those units the major activities will be gaining possession of significant religious facts; participat-ing in inspiring services of Christian worship; having enjoyable fellowship on a Christian level; dealing with enterprises of Christian service. Throughout, all should be interrelated so as to provide a unified pupil program thoroughly integrated with the whole church program.

Leading a Sunday Church School means guiding pupils as they move on in that curriculum. More specifically, it deals in the man-agement of the individual units and the use of certain special tech-niques of leadership in each of the four major aspects of curricu-lar activity. More broadly conceived, it includes the organizational, administrative, and supervisory tasks of the leader, especially the management of the whole curriculum. Thus the Christian educa-tional leadership task is guiding a group of pupils engaged in a creative experience of living the Christian life on the highest level possible for them week by week, making every necessary provision for them to live and learn effectively in the church as a school.

Chapter XIV

MANAGING PHYSICAL EQUIPMENT

Each Sunday morning nearly twenty million American Sunday Church School pupils assemble in several hundreds of thousands of buildings with an average of perhaps three times as many rooms. The pupils sit in millions of seats and use half a hundred million hymnals, lesson books, and Bibles.

There is but one purpose for all that equipment: to provide the conditions within which Christian growth can take place most rapidly and effectively. The buildings and all they contain are to be silent teachers themselves and tools of the learners and leaders who comprise the schools. It ought not need to be said as one pastor wrote: "I think we have wasted money from time to time in some types of buildings because we forgot their purpose." Do we forget that this equipment is an instrument which the congregation is to use in educating itself?

The forms of equipment are widely varied in nature and quality. A few schools have facilities superior to the best in public schools while, in most cases, the equipment is exceedingly meager. Yet conditions can be improved in almost every school by cultivated vision and earnest effort. That is a happy fact. It is not impossible for skilful workers to have good results with relatively poor facilities; Jesus could convert the most commonplace locality into a thrilling classroom. Yet the Master's followers need the best of physical aids to do his educational work at its best.

BASIC NEEDS

The basic demands on Church School buildings are provisions for management, for comfort and convenience and, fundamentally,

255

for the curriculum. Offices and committee or conference rooms are needed for the management of the school—at least an office for the superintendent, secretaries, and treasurers. Comfort and convenience require cloakrooms, lavatories, and an abundance of cabinets and other storage space.

The curriculum demands space for instruction in groups of varying size and shifting constituencies—an assembly place for the entire school, well-equipped separate classrooms, corners where an individual can carry on some enterprise of reading, writing, or construction. Closely associated is a library. There is, similarly, need of space for worship, formal and informal, in large and small groups, broadly or closely graded. This may include a chapel. The fellowship aspect of the curriculum calls for such things as parlors, a fellowship hall with stage and kitchen, play and scout rooms, and possibly a playground. The service enterprises require work and storage space.

Only an unusual congregation can provide all those things, of course. Yet the total picture can be kept in mind by those who provide and manage the equipment, even in a small church. What the congregation has or can have will depend in considerable measure upon the leader's vision.

DEMANDS OF CURRENT TRENDS

The need to reconsider physical equipment is becoming increasingly urgent as the Sunday Church School equipment becomes the educational setting for the entire congregation. As such it may be a beehive of constant activity, not merely a place where "opening exercises" and classes are held one hour each week. It is for weekday and vacation schools and other groups as well as the Sunday Church School. It must provide for various types of Sunday sessions and a great variety of weekday activities. It is used not only for worship and instructional activity but also for fellowship and service enterprises.

The integration of the Church School with the whole church organization and the unification of the total enterprise have bearing upon equipment, too. For example, the adoption of a unified Sunday morning program might modify building plans in a marked way. In particular, some "conference room" with a table about which leaders and pupils representing many phases of the school and total congregational work could gather for mutual planning might be a central feature both as a symbol and a fact.

The chief factor affecting physical equipment is the progressive adoption of developmental approach and creative use of techniques. These require more space, to be used more informally, in various types of activity. A large number of rooms of different sizes and furnishings will be needed—rooms for committee meetings, counseling interviews, and conferences; work space for construction and storage rooms for tools, supplies, and unfinished work; a library of resources for pupils and leaders; all those and the usual space for play, study, and worship.

An important development whose history can almost be measured in months is the demand for provisions to use audile and visual materials and equipment effectively. All our present arrangements are makeshift. The entire educational plant should be considered in terms of wiring, screening, darkening, projection, amplification, and storage.

There are still other demands upon equipment arising out of previously mentioned factors in current Christian education. They include facilities for writing, supervised study, dramatics, more emphasis on art and music, the larger use of discussion procedures. There must be special consideration for larger nursery departments and the revival of adult religious education. Leader and pupil cooperation in management, along with the organizational work of the various classes and departments, has meaning for equipment, too. Children's chapels, worship centers, music centers, and reading centers should be developed further. The recognition of individual differences suggests provision for elective courses and interest groups which demand frequent changes in groupings. The trend toward larger co-educational classes is significant.

In general, the physical equipment must be designed to reflect the emphases on pupil instead of leader activity, more informality, and larger freedom. The Church School is to be a place where pupils live and, by living there under guidance, learn to live the Christian life on increasingly higher levels.

TYPES OF BUILDINGS

Sunday Church School buildings are of three general types: the Akron; the "large-small"; and the "haphazard." The better ones of the older types were erected on the Akron plan. That plan was originated, it is said, by Mr. Louis Miller, superintendent of the First Methodist Episcopal Sunday School in Akron, Ohio. While seated in a natural amphitheater viewing his Sunday School pupils at a picnic, he conceived the idea that such an arrangement would be desirable for the school at work. An Akron-type building is much like a theater. There is a superintendent's platform or stage on the first floor with assembly space in front of it and classrooms around the sides. The second floor is a gallery with classrooms built on a slope and open at least in front. All classrooms look toward the superintendent's platform, radiating from it like the spokes of a wheel.

As its chief advantages, the Akron building was meant to provide for "togetherness" and "separateness." In practice it provides too much of the former and not enough of the latter. The mass meeting which results may engender enthusiastic spirit but it is more conducive to noise and confusion than reverence and learning. It is utterly unsuited to current trends.

The better buildings of the newer type, here called "large-small" for want of a better name, are characterized by large spaces for worship and departmental instruction, smaller spaces for class sessions. Most of these spaces are separated by permanent walls although there may be exceptions for the younger pupils. They often occupy rooms having a central space for worship or other large group activities and screens or semi-permanent partitions around the sides and one end of the room to provide small group meeting places.

The majority of buildings may be called haphazard or improvised. They have been built more or less as afterthoughts or, perhaps, rebuilt as necessity dictated without a plan from the beginning. They reflect quite accurately the Sunday Church School's adoption into the church after arising and developing as a philanthropic lay movement.

The present trend in the erection of new buildings and remodeling of old ones is toward the large-small type mentioned above, with more flexibility about them now than twenty years ago. Some churches are rebuilding their Akron type structures along those lines; also, in cases where the building facilities have been more or less haphazard, those who aim to improve them are trying to achieve some approximation of that type.

The situation really awaits creative genius applied to some functional development, the sort of thing we are providing for better homes, offices, and factories. It would take the view that there is a task to be done and ask what kind of equipment could serve the purpose most economically and effectively. A real vision of the task would eliminate anything bizarre in character and maintain continuity with the historic past. Yet there would be any change that would expedite the program toward its objectives through more serviceable means.

STANDARDS FOR BUILDINGS

For creating a new building, for remodeling an old one, complete schedules of standards have been set up. They can be found in several available books and pamphlets on church and Church School building. Those who are undertaking an extensive building program should also consult denominational and interdenominational committees as well as reliable and well-informed architects and Christian educational consultants. In all cases it is to be remembered that Christian education is on the march so that much earlier thinking and writing on the subject is obsolete at least in the sense of being incomplete.

Five important standards will be given as general principles only. The details for a building as a whole and for its separate departments must be sought in fuller treatments of the subject and always in the light of the immediate situation. It is necessary first to ask, What is or ought to be the educational program of this congregation? Then plans can be made with abundant attention to flexibility for the present and adaptability for future developments.

Beauty

Since there is a close kinship between beauty and religion, the note of artistry must enter into the planning and construction of a building. Order, symmetry, strength, grace, and color should impart their ministry to each pupil's religious growth. It was realized by a five-year-old boy who, finding himself in a rarely beautiful church auditorium, said, "Mother, let us stay here where it is so soft and quiet." Cleanliness, orderliness, and good repair, it should be needless to say, are essential to beauty, and provision should be made for service, in easy cleaning for example. The exterior with grounds and lawn, so often neglected, is almost as important a consideration as the interior. The whole ensemble should equal or surpass to some degree the average home of the community.

Utility

While the artistic should modify the merely practical, it should not overpower it. There should be something of the monumental in each building, yet it should be more than a monument. Floors, ceilings, windows, and walls ought to be not only a symphony of beauty but also an instrument of educational achievement. The artistic builder should not be blinded to his real purpose—the creation of an effective setting for the growth of persons in the Christian graces. Utility as a first consideration, with beauty as its handmaiden, is the ideal. Let objectives determine means.

Comfort

Austerity held a large place in religion during the Middle Ages. Perhaps there is not enough of it now. Nevertheless, people expect to be comfortable in church, and pupils find a hindrance to their educational growth in the distraction produced by discomfort.

Among the most important factors in comfort is temperature. The heating system must be adequate for severest winter with provisions for proper control at all times. In summer the building should be capable of management to keep it cool. Proper lighting is another major requirement. There should be abundant light of pleasing softness, not shining into the eyes of the pupils. Adequate ventilating facilities should make it possible to keep the air fresh at all times. An item so often neglected is the acoustical factor and, closely related, sound proofing. Safety is requisite, too. No oversight should cause the pupils in a building to be insecure because of fire or other hazards. As to size, there should be neither sense of overcrowding nor of seclusion. Assembly rooms for large groups and individual rooms for classes should be ample but not spacious. Many of those ideals might be summarized by saying that a Church School building should be at once a temple, a schoolroom, and a comfortable home.

Economy

Buildings are good not merely because they are big and costly. Indeed, they begin to lose their value as they draw too far away from the daily living conditions of the pupils, or place too great a strain upon the financial resources of the constituents. There is point, too, in the query whether the church is not socially blameworthy for the undue expansion of equipment used with relative infrequency. On the other hand, the false economy of cheapness and artificiality should be carefully avoided.

True economy comes from careful planning to accomplish the maximum service with a minimum of space, to make every dollar buy the most in permanent values, to exalt simplicity and avoid elaborateness. A particular point of economy is the multiple use of equipment. A room may serve one function on weekdays, another on Sunday; one on Sunday morning, another in the evening. A platoon schedule may be arranged to use a children's chapel or the church auditorium for at least two departmental services of worship each Sunday morning.

Adaptability

It is but a step to the ideas of flexibility and expansion. The seven-day program of religious education is a reality in some churches, and will become more prevalent. New forms of Christian education arrive with each new decade. Populations shift so that a Church School building large enough today may be too small tomorrow. The growth of a church itself and the expansion or change of its program, are to be kept in mind. To create a building which can be enlarged or modified, which can take in a weekday or vacation school, an expanded young people's or adult program, a community service program, should be the ideal.

USE OF BUILDINGS

Some years ago there was an era of erecting new educational buildings. Many of them met a considerable number of the standards mentioned above. We might have looked forward to a great era of effective Sunday Church School work. Yet one thing was omitted from the calculations of some who built. They forgot that, after all, Christian education is a matter of personalities meeting personalities, while physical equipment, although important, is secondary. Thus, numerous congregations erected their structures at a cost which exhausted their financial resources so that it was impossible to provide adequate leadership in the program for which the building had been provided.

There is danger of making the same mistake again. An era of postwar building is in progress. One billion dollars is one estimate of the amount to be expended. A man who knows nation-wide church conditions says that he knows scarcely a congregation which does not plan some form of building activity. When asked, however, whether he knew any congregations which plan to add an educational worker to their staffs, he said, "No, not one." Yet a pastor writes: "As I see it, the greater problem is not the need of equipment but of a trained and consecrated personnel."

Perhaps the practice of a small Pennsylvania town will high-light this issue. The town is in serious need of recreational facilities but it cannot afford an expensive building; besides, a building would be of doubtful value without competent leadership. So it has employed a full-time community director of recreation who will organize and direct the use of available physical and other facilities to fuller results. Similarly, church leaders who envision a more adequate equipment for their educational work may best proceed according to the following schedule: (a) provide for future leadership; (b) plan slowly, wisely, and broadly; (c) provide for financing without undue strain; (d) build; (e) use the building under capable leadership.

More generally, those concerned in the use of the building will be the sexton who must be fully responsible for its cleanliness, good repair, heat, and ventilation. Next, the superintendent and his helpers must have eyes to see that these matters are not neglected and minds to plan for effective employment of the various rooms. Finally, pupils should be led to revere, preserve, and strive to beautify the building and its grounds while using it to their fullest educational advantage.

FURNISHINGS

Types

When the floors, ceilings, walls, doors, and windows of a building have been provided, the Sunday Church School leader has yet to discharge no small amount of his responsibility for effective equipment. There remains the provision of proper furnishings and supplies. When the outstanding items of this nature have been listed, one is astonished at the large array of them, many being more or less essential. Here are a few, listed with the understanding that, of course, no church likely will ever need or have all.

Blackboards: either permanent or movable types make available certain forms of teaching not otherwise possible.

Bulletin and service boards: necessary for displaying notices, pictures, poems, and similar materials.

Chairs: not folding ones that clatter, creak, and collapse, but substantial ones. There are definite standards of height, form, and type. Some with tablet arms are needed.

Chapel furnishings: the pews and chancel furnishings of a real children's chapel or the homemade, simple provisions for a worship center.

Coat racks: without these, pupils create disturbances with hats and coats. Teachers should use them, too, removing their wraps and being at home while they worship.

Curtains, shades, and drapes: these to contribute the homelike atmosphere.

Dramatic equipment: depending upon the situation, there may be a fully equipped stage with costume and property lockers or simply the sheerest requisites for informal dramatizations.

Fellowship furnishings: these may be easy chairs, lamps, and the like for a parlor; kitchen and pantry facilities for serving; games and related equipment; craft tools and supplies.

Floor coverings: linoleum or asphalt tile is best in general unless there are hardwood floors, then a few rubber runners are desirable. Rugs are preferable in social and children's rooms.

Maps and charts: these make concrete and real the biblical and missionary facts and scenes. How can one teach about Paul without a map?

Musical instruments: good pianos, in tune! And why not use organs for the children, too? Recorders and record players are now being used. There may be orchestral equipment.

Offering plates: to receive the offering in a worshipful manner.

Office equipment: it is difficult, indeed, to imagine a present-day educational program without typewriter and duplicating machine available for frequent and ready use.

Outdoor equipment: some churches have playgrounds and others have scouting and camping programs which require appropriate equipment. The bulletin board, properly, should be used educationally. A garden or landscaping area with the necessary tools can be an adjunct of the Church School.

Phonographs and recorders: already there are records of Bible and missionary stories in considerable numbers, and it is difficult to think of studying church music without this type of equipment.

Pictures: one superintendent recently visited seventeen young people's rooms and saw not one picture on the walls. Pictures should be well-chosen, good reproductions, placed at the proper height and location. Another related need is a file of mounted pictures for class uses.

Projection devices: visual and audile aids are rapidly assuming outstanding importance. Along with the machines there is need for a library of filmslides and filmstrips.

Public address system: in the larger schools this equipment is now recognized as almost essential. Now educational uses for it are multiplying.

Radios: this is another audile aid which can be useful, particularly for weekday sessions. No doubt television sets will be in use soon for Church School purposes.

Screens: these or other forms of partitions for classes are an insistent demand.

Servitors: may be built into the walls so that materials can be passed into and out of the classrooms without creating a disturbance.

Signal system: only if needed as, for example, in a large school.

Tables and desks: the leader's needs must not be forgotten. Tables for the pupils have been popular but they are passing in favor of chairs with tablet arms. Display cases and tables are needed, too.

Standards

For all these items there are certain standards. The first, naturally, is utility. The leader will seek to provide for his school all those furnishings which will serve toward the highest attainment of its objectives. The furniture should be comfortable, durable, attractive, of a kind that fosters orderliness and quiet. It seems necessary to add, not castoff. While the financial stringency under which certain schools operate is to be respected, many are needlessly furnished with a conglomeration of second-hand pianos, desks, chairs, cabinets, and pictures. There is, for example, a leading church in a large city where one recalls bookcases with missing shelves, chairs with broken rockers, portraits of somebody's grandfather, and a sofa with springs protruding. If possible, let people send the second-hand furniture to the proper place while the school buys that which will dignify the cause.

Use

Leaders will need to give careful attention to the use of their available equipment. A first consideration will be its effective and artistic arrangement in the various rooms, a combined educational and housekeeping problem. The items of cleaning, repairing, keeping in good order, and conserving are further responsibilities.

In a well-regulated school, pupils will be as careful of the furnishings as in a home. There is scarcely any excuse for the carelessness which prevails in some schools. It is but another evidence that somebody has not given thought to the bad educational results of a program carried on under those conditions. Reverent regard for the Church's property is a proper objective.

SUPPLIES

After the building has been erected and furnished, the next step is the provision of all the necessary supplies.

The leader will first consider Bibles, hymnals, and lesson quarterlies or textbooks. Bibles should not be neglected. There was one school which insisted on the name "Bible School," yet a supply teacher one Sunday could not find one except on the pulpit. A plentiful supply of hymnals of high musical and religious quality, kept in excellent repair, should be conveniently at hand. Lesson materials for teachers as well as pupils, of the best available types, should be supplied in sufficient abundance to warrant full use on the part of all. Additional supplies worth mentioning are record-books, paper, scissors, paste, pictures and the miscellaneous items needed for handwork, dramatics, and recreational activities. Now, too, we must think of films and records.

Five standards for measuring the adequacy of supplies may be listed: *condition, fitness, quality, quantity,* and *thrift.*

No ragged, torn, and worn Bibles, hymnals, or lesson books should be tolerated if they can be replaced. At least, they should be kept clean and fully mended. The same standard should apply to all other items.

The supplies should be as closely adapted to the school's purposes as possible. Only the finest treatment of Christian topics should be studied; only the choicest hymns should be sung. All should be graded to fit the ages and interests of the pupils using them.

It is regrettable that we do not use beautifully bound and printed textbooks with the best of religious pictures. At least we can insist upon these qualities in our hymnals and Bibles. Let them be well-printed, well-bound, beautiful accessories to worship and study.

One visits school after school where supplies are so limited that halfway through the quarter there are not enough quarterlies for effective lesson study. "They take them home and leave them," someone laments. "What if they do?" one may reply. "At least one piece of religious literature got into the home." Besides, it is not impossible for teachers to work with parents to help pupils remember.

To be sure the church should and must be economical in its use of supplies, but the virtue can be overdone. Expenses are very moderate at most. It seems foolish to do everything else, then fail at this one vital point of providing materials that are fine, fit, and sufficient. Could Jesus have meant this when he said: "Ye cannot serve God and mammon"?

MAKING PRESENT RESOURCES MORE EFFECTIVE

Vision is of vast importance in the use of the physical resources available to the majority of schools. A man who visits many of them said he had never stepped inside a single one without seeing certain conditions which could be improved if taken in hand by a leader with vision.

The typical leader is prone to let the real or assumed limitations of the present building restrict the program. Some daydreaming about the things which would be done if the school had the physical resources might be wholesome. Then the main outlines of an ideal program ought to be worked out. Next, the school might make an inventory of its present resources and determine what steps can be taken with things as they are. Very often some slight adjustment is possible as a first step toward the ideal program. Then other steps can be taken one by one until the maximum possibility is exhausted. By that time new equipment may be possible.

So often a way can be found to do what had seemed impossible. A nook for Boy Scouts, a place for a stage, room for the nursery department, provision for a parlor—often these have been arranged in relatively meager surroundings by somebody who had in mind a full picture of the needs of a complete Church School plant. Since it is not necessary to carry on the whole educational program under one roof, neighboring buildings can be used. Another important way out is to use the main place of assembly for worship as educational equipment. Small churches use this space regularly for school purposes and many larger churches might use it profitably. Multiplied use of other rooms will help, too.

There was a certain primary room. The possibilities of the

room itself were good. But two discarded sand tables stood at one side. There were at least a half-dozen different types of chairs, many needing paint and repairs. When the children worshiped, they sat facing the light from a half-dozen unadorned windows. There was not a single attractive thing about the room unless it was the collection of pictures cut from old charts and hung on the panels of the doors dividing that room from another.

Someone caught a vision. Then the women of the department painted the chairs green with black stripes. They put curtains at the windows. They brought plants to provide a bit of green on the window sills. They tore down the charts from the walls and put a few attractive pictures there, planning to change them with the different seasons of the year. They faced the pupils away from the light, and re-organized the seating and the other furnishings to give the room a homelike appearance.

In another church an additional room was needed. There had been a basement where the rats scampered about among a few of the pastor's extra crates of potatoes and carrots. The men's brotherhood got a vision. They cleaned out the basement. They provided proper heating. They painted the walls a light color. They put curtains on the windows with the aid of the Ladies' Aid Society, which also put rugs on the floors and installed comfortable chairs.

In a third church the Junior Department used a rectangular room with an alcove in which the ladies had stored their sewing machines, quilting frames, and tables for serving. All the walls were the dirtiest of grey, with the woodwork and floors painted in the same color. The windows had neither been curtained nor washed. Then somebody saw the possibility of making a children's chapel. An altar and lectern were installed in the alcove, and the piano was placed just below. Seats for a junior choir were installed. The walls were painted a light color; the chairs were painted in tones which matched. The windows were curtained and the floor was covered with linoleum. The result was a children's chapel which, with movable screens, made also a choice room for the instruction of the departmental classes.

SECURING NEW EQUIPMENT

Many Sunday Church School leaders have long been thinking of a new or remodeled building and others need one almost without daring to hope for it. There are few schools, indeed, which do not need some new items of lesser equipment. How shall they proceed?

To start is the important thing. Perhaps the leader's first work is to sell the school to its constituency, that is, to develop a deep loyalty and contagious enthusiasm about the school among pupils and friends. The next step is to make the group conscious of the school's need. If it is a new building, he will be particularly zealous to work with the pastor, committees, church council, and influential members of the congregation. If it is a smaller item, he will likely work more directly with his helpers and pupils.

After creating sentiment and securing a realization of the need, representative leadership may be required. If a large building project is in view, there will be a building committee. This committee, appointed by the congregation, should include the best possible talent with liberal consideration of the educational point of view. In smaller projects other workers, and pupils, too, may be given leadership.

Planning will follow. As many members of the constituency as possible should have an opportunity to share. In the case of a building program, an architect will be chosen. Great care is necessary in that matter. The typical architect has no experience in educational building and no knowledge of current Christian educational theory and practice. Too often he is guided by his boyhood experience in Sunday School or the numerous Akron-type buildings he has seen. Insistence upon the use of skilled advisory assistance of Christian educational specialists is vital. From the beginning it should be understood by all that the building is to provide for a total educational program and some adaptation of the large-small plan is to be followed.

Throughout, attention must be given to financing the new equipment. The important thing is to start. A fund for such purposes will always win support. It can start accumulating by free-will offerings in general or at stated times or seasons, although the ideal way from the financial standpoint is to place the item in the church or Church School budget.

The smallness of the amount of money spent upon Christian education in general and upon equipment in particular is pitiful. More money should and could be spent. It would be a capital investment with immeasurable returns for the church. Yet, money is not as important as faith and imagination. So often one hears, "But we can't do that," followed by some explanation, such as, "We're just a one-room church." But, are you sure you cannot do it? Have you tried? And do you need to remain a one-room church? Isn't there some way to carve out or add an educational room or two? Many leaders have found it possible.

A schedule of activities for those who are conducting a more elaborate building program follows:

1. Foster congregational realization of the importance of educational work and conviction about the present need. This is the sound foundation for the entire enterprise.

2. Assemble a proposed organizational setup and outline of activities to be housed. What is to be done with this instrument? Give much thought to the ideal program of Christian education for the congregation. Confer with recognized educational authorities. Have conferences and study groups on the proposed program. Take full account of current trends. They must be faced since a building is erected for future leaders as well as present ones and failure to consider their interests is inexcusable.

3. Survey the needs of the congregation in relation to the community.

4. Do not fail to consider leadership needs in connection with this advance in physical equipment.

5. Complete the organizational requirements of committees for the project.

6. Select and confer with consultants in church building such as denominational and interdenominational bureaus of church architecture.

7. Select architectural service for planning and executing the structure. Make sure about competence in the field of education. Beware of bargains.

8. Study, revise, and approve tentative plans. Do not let the lion's share go to the elaborate and monumental items. Do not copy other churches; plan for this particular group's needs now and in the foreseeable future. Provide for expansion. Keep the building flexible for use. If housing and equipment cannot be provided for all needs at present, decide on the most important first units.

9. Plan and conduct promotion and publicity, in an educational manner.

10. Study financial methods and adopt a financial program. Prepare a complete budget for all the different items, and plan and conduct any necessary financial campaign. Let the original budget provide for appropriate and adequate furnishings. Do not use discarded items from old buildings, such as the pews from the old church.

11. Arrange for the selection of contractors, probably by bid. Check on all legal phases, including legal title to property. Have carefully prepared contracts.

12. Arrange for selection and purchase of equipment and furnishings.

13. Keep careful check lists of requirements throughout the period of building.

14. Conduct leadership education classes to carry out the enlarged and improved program made possible by the new plant.

WHAT LEADERS WANT

Twelve pastors replied to a letter asking them: "What do you and your workers want most if and when you get a new educational building and other physical equipment?" A symposium follows. The paragraphs are listed in the order of frequency of mention. Figures in parentheses after a few significant items indicate the number of times they were mentioned.

Separate classrooms. These would be bright, light, airy. They would be equipped with blackboards (4); maps (2); pictures (2); cork panels (1). They would have chairs and tables for certain age groups, for others, chairs with arms for writing (2).

Departmental rooms. The purpose is assembly space for worship and work. The children's departments were in view particularly. The rooms would be bright, light, and airy and not in damp basements. There would be appropriate chairs and tables. Bright (not gaudy) paint would make them attractive. There was one mention of space for activity and project work. There was also one mention of a nursery room for children to be kept during the adult service of worship.

Provisions for worship. This might be a chapel (4) or a large assembly room, likely to be used on a platoon schedule (4). Otherwise it would be in the departmental room with a worship center. One pastor commented, however, that the families should worship together.

Auditorium. This would be used in one case for an assembly of the entire school once a month or more frequently for special features. In most cases it would be a fellowship hall with stage (3); kitchen facilities (2); and other recreational equipment (4).

Projection equipment. This was mentioned five times.

Miscellaneous. The following items were mentioned once each: public address system; space also for Scouts and Weekday and Vacation Church Schools; provisions to avoid distraction; safety from fire; library for workers; library for the congregation; facilities for hanging up coats and hats; plans to receive offerings as an act of worship; display and browsing table; provision for secretaries and treasurers to work inconspicuously.

Unquestionably those visions are in the right direction. Doubtless, too, they represent stern realism with respect to possibilities. Yet, are they possibly too modest? One can wish that the horizons were broader and the sights lifted higher. "Operation Christian Education" cannot succeed brilliantly unless it is equipped generously.

A world of weary adults may rightly wish to rest its soul before a monumental altar, elaborately adorned. Yet the overindulgence of that tendency may be a major ecclesiastical peril of the next few decades. One cannot forget the Ladies' Aid Society that purchased an eighteen hundred dollar carpet for "the church" while the Sunday Church School grievously needed new hymnals and there was "no money" for them.

Chapter XV

FINANCING THE SCHOOL

This subject ordinarily receives little attention beyond the passing of envelopes in classes and the expending of funds received in that manner. When, however, a conference of some fifty workers began to consider it, they found it bristling with such problems as these:

What system of gathering funds is best?

How can a school increase its offerings?

Should the congregation use the Sunday Church School as a source of revenue?

How shall the money be cared for?

Who rightly controls the use of the funds?

PURPOSES

Most of those problems begin to solve themselves, as do so many others, when the matter of objectives is studied. To recognize that the financial program of the Sunday Church School has both educational and religious purposes beyond the monetary one is a great gain.

The financial aim

Obviously, the school needs money for its operating expenses and its beneficent work and the adequate provision of such funds is an important charge against the leader. A mistake is made, however, when the financial aim is put foremost. In all religious and educational work a too direct emphasis on this angle defeats its purpose. On the other hand, when a Christian educational service is emphasized, finances tend to care for themselves.

The educational aim

It is better to recognize that the financial matters of the school are an educational opportunity fully as important as any other in the whole round of endeavor. Christianity is a religion of giving in every way, including the financial. So, giving should be viewed as an aspect of the curriculum. More exactly, the handling of Sunday Church School funds should educate youth to *give* for *certain enterprises* in *certain ways*. To give—regularly, freely and cheerfully, even sacrificially. For certain causes—the regular and benevolent enterprises of the Church and other worthy objects. In certain ways—to make a pledge in the every-member solicitation and use duplex envelopes weekly. There is a definite relationship between church financing and Christian growth—pupils are to grow through, in, and for it.

The religious aim

This purpose of the financial program is the most often neglected. The giving of the Sunday Church School offering is seldom done as a religious exercise. It should be done in the form and spirit of worship, to the accompaniment of music, and with a proper consecration of the gifts. Every pupil should be led to view his offering as a return of the Father's own to the Father for his special causes among his children who are needy in body and spirit—the stewardship emphasis of viewing oneself as the manager of a portion of God's resources.

On this point it is a privilege to quote a student from India. "I like the way we do there in India. We have one Sunday a month set apart for offering. The children and parents are told previously. In fact, on Sunday before the offering, announcement is made in the church during the morning service so that pupils can come prepared. The members of the staff and the pupils follow the superintendent in systematic order making a procession around the altar with singing praises to God from the church hymnal. Then, when all have gone back to their respective seats, a passage is read from the Scriptures followed by prayer. After this we have the class as usual."

PROVIDING FUNDS

With those goals in mind, what methods can be used to provide the school with an adequate and stable supply of funds?

Systems

The usual system is a special Sunday Church School treasury to which the pupils contribute every Sunday morning, usually by dropping their money into an envelope passed around the class. In addition, there may be special school or class funds perhaps provided by such semi-commercial enterprises as dinners, lawn fetes, socials, candy sales, or bazaars. Special day offerings on Children's Day, Rally Day, Christmas, or Easter, and offerings for special causes like missions in general or a particular missionary objective are common. The birthday offering is another popular device.

Needless to say, such methods do not fully meet the educational and religious standards set forth above; not even the financial aim in many cases. There are better ways.

Unitary congregational treasury

As a long-range ideal, the unitary treasury for the entire congregation is probably the best system for desirable church financing. By this means the Sunday Church School expenses are paid out of the single church treasury to which each person in the congregation contributes. Every member of every agency makes a pledge and contributes in his weekly duplex envelope at any session of the church program he chooses.

This presupposes a careful consideration of a well-planned budget for the whole congregation. The following actual budget suggests the type of thing in view:

I.	The Program of Sunday Services	$12,650.00
II.	The Program of Religious Education	8,700.00
III.	The Program of Benevolences	4,000.00
IV.	The Expense of Administration	4,630.00
V.	The Maintenance of the Plant	4,343.00
VI.	The Interest on the Mortgage	4,750.00
VII.	Miscellaneous Expense	1,000.00
		$40,073.00

The advantages of the unitary system are manifold. First, it is the only method by which a broad-gauge educational program can be financed. Already some churches are recognizing that the educational activities are not to be a source of revenue, nor should they even be dependent upon self-support. Rather, they are to be viewed as the major investment opportunity of the congregation. One pastor has said: "Many congregations raid the Sunday school treasury. We use all money received in educational agencies for educational purposes. We regard our educational program as our best congregational investment." No schools except Sunday Church Schools are expected to be money-makers, or even to support themselves!

Secondly, the unitary treasury is the only sound plan educationally. Under it, a pupil learns to give from the beginning as he always will give, not to *our class, our department,* or *our Sunday Church School,* but to *our church.* No financial loyalty is developed but the permanent one— to the church which provides for all. Again, the pupil gives not for one but for all purposes of the church. Thus the youngest child, from the beginning, participates in the total life of the church. Having a part in the missionary and benevolent work and the expenses for the ministry and physical upkeep, as well as the educational program, the pupil will begin early to take an active interest in all those activities. At one and the same time, a Sunday-Church-School-centered program is avoided and an expansive educational opportunity is made available. It is a way of recognizing that the Church School is the congregation educating itself.

A diagram which shows the operation of a unitary treasury follows on page 277. It is modeled after an actual design in a Texas church.

Some churches have used a modification of the unitary budget idea in which the church budget carries the Sunday Church School and the school does what it pleases with its money. This is not recommended because it educates for giving away from the church instead of giving to the church.

DIAGRAM VII

OPERATION OF A UNITARY FINANCIAL SYSTEM

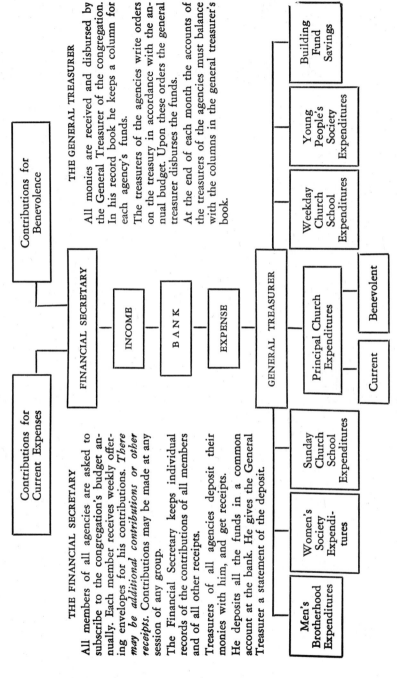

Contributions for Current Expenses

Contributions for Benevolence

THE FINANCIAL SECRETARY

All members of all agencies are asked to subscribe to the congregation's budget annually. Each member receives weekly offering envelopes for his contributions. *There may be additional contributions or other receipts.* Contributions may be made at any session of any group.

The Financial Secretary keeps individual records of the contributions of all members and of all other receipts.

Treasurers of all agencies deposit their monies with him, and get receipts.

He deposits all the funds in a common account at the bank. He gives the General Treasurer a statement of the deposit.

THE GENERAL TREASURER

All monies are received and disbursed by the General Treasurer of the congregation. In his record book he keeps a column for each agency's funds.

The treasurers of the agencies write orders on the treasury in accordance with the annual budget. Upon these orders the general treasurer disburses the funds.

At the end of each month the accounts of the treasurers of the agencies must balance with the columns in the general treasurer's book.

FINANCIAL SECRETARY

INCOME

BANK

EXPENSE

GENERAL TREASURER

Men's Brotherhood Expenditures

Women's Society Expenditures

Sunday Church School Expenditures

Principal Church Expenditures

Current

Benevolent

Weekday Church School Expenditures

Young People's Society Expenditures

Building Fund Savings

Sunday Church School treasury

The unitary treasury ideal, unfortunately, is viewed in many quarters as too visionary and impractical. It is necessary, therefore, to consider the most desirable ways of filling a separate Sunday Church School treasury.

Consideration of the three goals, financial, educational, and religious, gives a ready suggestion—make the methods as much like the regular church method as may fit the purpose. Many schools are meeting the issue by the use of weekly envelopes, preferably duplex. Sometimes the Sunday Church School envelopes are used only by those not yet confirmed or otherwise received into complete membership. Elsewhere the older pupils have two sets of envelopes, one for the school, the other for the church (probably not a good thing).

Those who use such methods have no hesitancy about recommending them. Usually they have given up all other sources of finance save the special day offerings or perhaps some other extraordinary special gifts.

Program

If there is to be an adequate and stable supply of finances for a Sunday Church School, it must have a program as well as a system. This suggests that the leader carry out certain definite policies for developing the giving in the school. He will first disseminate information since no one should (or will long) give money to enterprises of which he knows nothing. Stewardship lessons and literature should find their way into the school and practical discussions of immediate situations are proper in class, department, and school. The unitary treasury plan provides that a statement of needs will be published. If the school is proceeding on an independent treasury it can likewise publish periodically a statement of its needs with a view to educating the people about its requirements.

Closely related is the policy of letting everybody know where the money goes. There was a beginners' department where a superintendent went from pupil to pupil with her hand in position to receive the offering, saying, "Now, give me your money this morning." That is how not to do it! Frequent reports and explanations on expenditures are the proper alternative.

A further suggestion is to make the most direct contact possible between giver and receiver. It was done by a superintendent whose pupils sent their gift to India and received letters from children who were helped by it. One requisite of a financial program is to put the objects of giving within the comprehension of the givers.

If such educational procedures are followed, an eagerness to give is natural. That attitude is the ideal one. There can be no harm in going beyond it to the development of a sense of responsibility to do one's share. Departments and classes can be led to measure up to reasonable expectations so long as the spontaneity of true Christian giving is not lost. The real purpose of the program is the development of a "cheerful giver."

A denominational stewardship committee has done exceedingly interesting work along these lines. Its chairman writes, "I feel we must do a lot more work upstream—among the children—if the church folk of the future are to be better stewards." Accordingly, he and his committee have developed original and effective means for use by local congregations.

They promote an annual every-member visitation among the Sunday Church School pupils in all the congregations of their synod. "Callers" are to go to every home on a designated day. They secure pledges of weekly contributions through duplex envelopes for both current expenses and benevolent causes.

The callers have been preceded, however, by an educational program. It includes general study and special publicity in school sessions. There have been letters to the pupils, too, to explain the plan and tell about the needs of the school. As an especially valuable feature, the letters include attractive leaflets which explain the benevolent enterprises of the church to which the pupils may contribute.

EXPENDING FUNDS

While the securing of adequate funds may be a principal endeavor of the leader, the educational purpose demands careful attention, also, to their wise expenditure. The well-administered school will operate on a budget which provides for its annual receipts to be expended systematically and in accordance with advance consideration. All divisions of the school pool their needs and their resources. Each receives and deposits in the general treasury. Each in turn will disburse the funds allotted to it according to its individual budget.

Budgeting

The designated persons will get together before the school year begins and plan the financial transactions in a general way. They will know by experience and through reports the probable receipts and usual expenditures. The various superintendents or teachers will submit estimates and requests for the forthcoming year. The committee will then make an equitable distribution related to contributions and needs down through all the departments, classes, and other groups of the school. The budget work may be done by a special committee, though preferably by the regular Church School Committee of the congregation. The goal is to make the best possible educational use of the available means. Every effort should be made to employ fully democratic procedures in developing the budget.

The following are typical budget items for which provision is to be made:

Literature: Bibles, lesson books, and library resources for the entire school and for each of the departments.

Leadership Improvement: books and periodicals, fees for attendance at leadership schools and camps, funds for leadership education, program for workers' conference.

Promotion of the School: expenses of the membership committee, publicity.

Fellowship Activity: parties, banquets, hikes, picnics, recreational affairs.

Special Occasions: Christmas, Easter, Children's Day, Rally Day, Promotion Day.

Equipment and Supplies: furniture, decorations, pictures, maps, films, paper and pencils, recordings.

Music: hymnals and other music books; paid leadership, if any; tuning of pianos; orchestral instruments.

Christian Education: contributions to Vacation or Weekday Schools of the church or community; fees for membership in community councils, state, or national agencies.

Service Enterprises: a contribution to the local church for expenses such as heat, light, and pastoral leadership if there is not a unitary treasury; special causes of the whole school such as the support of a missionary; funds to be used for beneficent work by various classes and departments.

Miscellaneous: general expenses of operation and emergeny items.

The cost of paid leadership for the school is not included in the above schedule. It is assumed that an item for paid teachers of classes, supervisors, or a director of Christian education would go into the total church budget if such provision is possible. The expenses of a paid teacher for leadership education classes might be included under leadership improvement.

Control

Who should control Sunday Church School funds? Justice would answer immediately—those who give. It is rarely so in practice. Very often the controlling officers are the church council. These officials usually wish to determine what special offerings are to be asked and how all monies are to be expended. One can understand their desire to raise and use the funds of the church expediently. Yet these men often are not education-minded. As an example, there were those who refused to allow a weekly allotment of twenty-five cents, out of a weekly offering of eight dollars, to be set aside for the expenses of a Vacation Church School. The whole religious educational purpose of the financial program is frustrated when spontaneous giving for chosen causes is thus nullified.

Under the budget method all the contributors, as far as possible, should have a voice in determining the personnel of the Budget Committee, in sending their recommendations to that committee, or in adopting the budget of the school. Classes and departments, too, should have the maximum freedom they have proved their ability to use in handling the items designated for them in the budget. The effort will be to realize the democratic ideal and accomplish in the fullest way the educational objective.

Allocations

There are widely varied practices concerning the purposes to which funds are allocated. Most schools support themselves, con tribute to special causes and, in addition, help to support the general church treasury. All this may be proper but, in general, Sunday Church Schools might well expand their horizons especially in educational matters. They are schools and, as such, should be more conscious of their own needs for effective work and of further educational enterprises they might foster in the congregation and outside of it.

A wholesome change has been developing with regard to the practice at Christmas time. Formerly churches used the funds given by the pupils for religious purposes to buy a "treat" of candy, nuts, or fruit for each of them. Now, in a worth-while Christmas cere mony, the pupils often present gifts for the needy. The appropri ateness of the change is evident. If it is too drastic in some quarters, a transition to a treat of books which have Christian educational value might be effected.

ACCOUNTING FOR FUNDS

Only the finest business procedures should be employed in the handling of Sunday Church School funds. That will win respect for the school and make it a real training ground for future church workers who are to proceed in the same manner when advanced to positions of larger responsibility.

All receipts and all expenditures should be handled by at least two people, keeping two separate records. If the teacher, secretary, or superintendent counts the money he will make one record. When it is turned over to the treasurer, he should count the money again and give a receipt as a second record to the one from whom he re ceived it. He should also make proper reports to the superintendent of the school and the Church School Committee of the church council at designated times. Under typical circumstances, the money should be deposited in the bank each Monday morning.

Expenditures should be made by the treasurer only upon order by the superintendent or other designated officers. Particular care should be exercised to channel all funds to the cause for which they were given unless those who gave have opportunity to consider the change.

Proper books for all transactions should be provided, kept, and regularly audited. Publishing houses offer many types of books and forms although it is often difficult to adapt them to the particular needs of given schools. The best method is to let the most competent person select what fits the need most fully, and then supervise its use.

Let us follow the movements of a dollar given by a member of the school in the offering plate of the adult division. It was duly received by the treasurer of that division. He counted it along with the other gifts of the day and made report of the total offering to the superintendent of that division. Then he passed it on to the general treasurer of the school, who gave him a receipt for the total amount. The money was deposited in the bank. Later the superintendent of the adult division issued an order upon the treasurer for a check to cover some new hymnals for that division. The amount had been determined when the division considered its financial needs for the year and sent an estimate to the budget-making committee. That committee placed the amount in the budget. Now the purchase has been made, and the dollar has been expended according to the recognized procedure.

THE TREASURER

The duties of a Sunday Church School treasurer have become clear although they may be modified to some degree for divisional, departmental and class treasurers, and special conditions may arise in accordance with local conditions.

He will understand the educational and religious aims as well as the financial aims of the school.

He will be the chief official with the superintendent in securing funds for the school.

He will help to devise a financial system and see that it operates.

He will co-operate in fostering the financial program of stewardship education in general and of disseminating information concerning the local church school's place in giving.

In expending the funds, he will furnish the records necessary to the committee which builds the budget and be a chief adviser of that committee. Later, as the year proceeds, he will keep check on the manner in which the budget funds are being received and used.

He will scrupulously count all monies, deposit them, and account for them upon the records provided by the school.

He will pay all bills promptly.

He will issue checks upon proper orders only and exercise care that the budget is being followed at all times.

He will make weekly and other reports to all workers who have use for the same. Statistics on trends of giving in the school are particularly important.

EDUCATION IN GIVING

One factor which remains constant in all situations is the fact that the treasurer's efficiency is not measured alone by the accuracy of his bookkeeping. It is measured even more fundamentally by his outlook and practice as an educator. That does not require that he give frequent speeches on the subject of finances. It means that he shall understand and help others to understand that the Sunday Church School is a place where people are to learn to give by giving. Furthermore, they will give and thus learn to give in proportion as they increasingly apprehend the Christian Gospel and understand the service which the church is rendering.

Stewardship education, it will be seen, is not something to be tacked on as another fragment of the time schedule of the school. It is inherent in the whole program of the school—its organization and administration as well as its more formal curriculum. It should be tied in with instruction, worship, service, and fellowship. It is properly a part of the various units of activity which represent the entire work of the school.

Such an approach is essential to the adequate financing of Christian education. Besides, a Christian economic order will scarcely be achieved elsewhere unless there are experiences of its operations in the church, including the Sunday Church School.

Chapter XVI

SECURING, REPORTING, AND USING DATA

One of the Sunday Church School leader's more unobtrusive but highly important duties, usually carried out with the aid of secretaries, is the securing and reporting of data on significant matters. It includes activities which may range from the simple taking of minutes to participation in an elaborate survey or extended piece of research.

RESEARCH

The current reconstruction of Christian educational theory and practice has resulted in some degree from the application of scientific fact-finding. Some of the spirit and technique which have gone into medical and other research have been employed in Christian education and its related fields of psychology, sociology and general education.

Research starts with a problem. Then it defines the problem clearly. If it is complex, the separate parts of the problem are listed. Sometimes a hypothesis or possible answer is established. Then the data concerning the problem or its various parts are sought. That may involve experimentation, trying things out one way and then another until the most satisfactory way is found. Out of the data a solution to the problem emerges. After it is verified, it takes its place in the body of theory or among the established methods of procedure.

Great industrial plants could not think of neglecting research. They maintain laboratories for discovering new and better procedures. Christian education can do something similar. For example, the International Council of Religious Education has a Department of Research and the various universities foster researches. Even the local Sunday Church School leader may undertake certain elementary enterprises in research to solve the problems and advance the work of his school.

SURVEYS

A survey is, in many respects, a project in research. The typical form in which many Sunday Church School leaders engage is a census of the community to discover new prospects for membership. Other surveys may be undertaken to locate prospective workers for the school, discover the preferred site for a new building, get the facts on population trends, show new needs in equipment and program.

There are certain well-defined steps in the method of a survey. They may be outlined as follows: (1) determining the purpose; (2) outlining the procedure; (3) organizing the workers; (4) training the workers; (5) building up sentiment for proper responses; (6) carrying out the project; (7) tabulating the results; (8) interpreting the data; (9) acting on the results.

It is by the last two steps, namely, the interpretation and use of data, that the value of a survey will be determined. Interpretation is of necessity a somewhat scientific, statistical matter in the more careful surveys. Attention should be given to central tendencies, trends, comparisons, and contrasts. In other types of survey the discovery of strengths and weaknesses is of primary importance. In the case of a census, of course, the major purpose is the securing of names and addresses.

What is done when the data are all in and interpreted is the ultimate issue. Too often reports are made and filed, then lost and forgotten. This does not, however, invalidate the procedure since much good may be accomplished by carefully conducted surveys wisely interpreted and aggressively acted upon.

One of the most interesting and useful forms is the congregational self-survey. An excellent example was one conducted by a congregation in a large eastern city.

Mimeographed announcements included this definition: "The congregational self-survey is the means of taking inventory of the congregation's resources, studying its current program, discovering its strong and weak points, and laying a factual basis for a long-term comprehensive program of improvement. The survey work is planned and carried out by the leaders of the congregation itself without the help of professional outside direction."

The main goals were announced as follows:

1. To get an objective picture of the current program and life of the congregation in all phases of its work.

2. To get a factual summary of the total resources of the congregation.

3. To set the present situation into a historical framework to note the trends and developments.

4. To rethink the stated aims and the present program of the congregation (and all its organized groups) in the light of the original mission of the church and the needs of the present constituency. This is with a view to (a) discovering needed improvements and (b) preparing a comprehensive long-term program of advance for the congregation and its agencies.

These steps of procedure are listed:

1. Advance planning by the pastor with a summary to be placed before a few key officials.

2. Presentation of proposals to the Church Council with a recommendation for approval of all the ideas with the plans for making them effective.

3. Appointment of a "steering committee."

4. Determining main phases of the survey, appointing a chairman for each phase and preparing plans and instruments for conducting each phase.

5. Preparation of a "Discussion Guide for a Self-survey" with questions covering all phases to be used in a series of "survey meetings" for all workers and interested members.

6. Completion of main phases of the survey and report of summaries and resultant proposals at survey meetings.

7. Review of all findings by the steering committee, considering constructive proposals and preparing a comprehensive long-term plan for making an improved program effective.

8. Action on the proposed improvements.

9. Completing the improvements.

Since the building of a comprehensive long-term program was in view, the survey was shaped toward the following specific results:

1. Statement of general aims for the total program, and specific aims for each organization and activity.

2. List of types or kinds of persons for whom the congregation provides a regular or specialized ministry and an outline of the main features involved in such ministry.

3. A challenging standard of membership and a definite policy and plan for maintaining it.

4. A program of evangelism.

5. A comprehensive program for children.

6. A comprehensive program for youth.

7. A comprehensive program for adults with special features for men and for women indicated.

8. A plan for the unified and effective administration of the total program.

9. A program of leadership education to undergird the total operation.

10. A plan and policy defining all community and extra-parish relations of the congregation and its agencies.

11. A plan and policy for maintaining and enlarging the church plant and its equipment.

12. A plan and policy for adequate financial operation.

A final report with the committee's recommendations includes headings which correspond with these items and concludes with "How Each Member Can Help."

Two years later the pastor writes: "I would summarize the tangible results of the survey as follows: (1) adoption of a long-range comprehensive program for the congregation; (2) unification of objectives and activities of various age groups; and (3) practical education of current group of workers on the church and its present-day program."

RECORDS

A carefully devised record system kept in good form can serve more purposes than commonly supposed. One pastor recognized this when he wrote this recommendation for an improved school: "Install throughout the whole school the finest and most thorough record system you can find." In the hands of intelligent users records are more than dead data. Their general purpose is to preserve and render usable certain types of information about the pupils and the school. More specifically, they provide measures of the school's success or failure. They disclose certain faults or values of the school. They can be used to stimulate giving or attendance. They can guide in planning the curriculum and organizing the staff. They can furnish the key to budgetary matters. They can show how to order supplies. They are essential in planning the promotion of pupils.

The types of record kept will depend, in part, upon the size of the school and its means in money and available staff. More practically still, they will be determined by the proposed use to be made of them. Needless to say, it is futile to keep any records which will not be used.

Possible records from which choice can be made on the basis of the factors just mentioned are listed below. No school will use them all. Several can be combined on one card or in one book.

Absentee records which may be kept for each pupil, to show his absences and the type of follow-up used. They may include a follow-up blank for report. It should be remembered that reasons for absence are more important than the fact.

Attendance records which will measure the success of the school in this matter and guide the absentee workers. They often include data on punctuality, offering, and church attendance.

Achievement records indicating the progress of the pupils in relation to Christian growth, and furnishing information for promotion. They may mention participation in class activities, attitudes, special responses, enterprises completed, service training, conduct, grades.

Business records which keep data on transactions of the organization in usable form. On these matters there will also be the minute books and the files of correspondence.

Class records, a small book being the most familiar type. They include names, addresses, birthdays, and similar data on the pupil and show his attendance Sunday by Sunday. There is a summary for the class each Sunday and often each quarter.

Curriculum records preserving the story of the program. They may list the units undertaken with copies of procedures and evaluations. Special care will be taken in any experimental work.

Enrollment records which guide in the placement of pupils and furnish lists of family prospects. They usually indicate name, address and telephone number, birthday, parents' names and church affiliations, church relations, school grade or occupation, other Sunday Schools attended, service interests, and experience.

Financial records which indicate the financial achievements, status, needs, and limitations of the school. The record and report books, bound or loose-leaf, of various treasurers, the check books and order books, the files of canceled checks, cash and budget account blanks are included.

Leaders' records which preserve personal data and show general education, religious education, and leadership experience.

Permanent records which are begun when the pupil has established his membership and follow him through the school with significant data such as his promotion from department to department, his services rendered to the school, and his confirmation. They may be included with his enrollment records.

Personality records which will guide in the planning of a program. They may result from applying personality tests or rating charts. They may show experiences of vocational and recreational interests. They are sometimes in the form of case histories.

Prospect records for the expansion of the school. They may be secured from a community census, by the pastor or other workers, or by reports from pupils themselves.

Registration blanks which gather information upon the entrance of the pupil and assign him temporarily until a class record is made.

Reports to parents summarizing the data kept on record forms of other types. They may mention attendance, attitude, achievement, and punctuality. This type has been the subject of research by the International Council of Religious Education. The evidence shows that such cards, intelligently and carefully used, arouse keen enthusiasm, especially in Primary, Junior and Intermediate departments. They affect attendance, study, conduct, church attendance, and parental interests very favorably in the opinion of those who use them. They were almost unanimously declared to be effective in raising the standards in the schools involved.

Withdrawal and removal records which disclose some of the more obvious remediable failures of the school. In many cases the enrollment cards of lapsed pupils are transferred to this file with a notation of reasons.

Summary records on departments or the entire school tabulating and comparing the data of individual records. They may show enrollment, attendance, or offering fluctuations by days, months, or years. They may record school activities, enterprises, and programs. They may summarize worker statistics.

Whatever the records kept, they should be in a form that makes them easily intelligible, economical in cost and time, and permanent. They should be accurately and neatly kept, always up-to-date. They should be placed where the information will be readily accessible to those who will use it most frequently. Any records made while the school is in session should be gathered quietly and with a maximum economy of effort.

There is no little debate over the merits of card files versus loose-leaf or permanently bound books. While there are many advantages in the former types, permanently bound minute books have desirable features over any other form. Most other records are best kept on cards or in loose-leaf books. Several good record systems are on the market. Advertisements in denominational and general religious journals describe them briefly and provide the names of the publishers.

Whether one record system is better than another must be measured solely by results. Records are means to ends, not ends in themselves. The standard of evaluation is results gained by use. That system is best which makes the largest religious educational results possible in a given school.

REPORTS

The final value of records is determined by the nature of the reports based on them. Reports are of many types—class, departmental, divisional and school, weekly, monthly, quarterly, and annual; reports to superintendent, school, committees, council, congregation, denominational and interdenominational agencies. The purpose is to disseminate useful information for guidance and for inspirational purposes. They mean to call attention to important facts in order to secure effective action on matters which demand attention.

The simplest report, the reading of the minutes of the previous meeting, refreshes the minds of the group concerning their work at that time and starts them in their new work. The usual Sunday Church School secretary's weekly report is meant or should be meant, beyond satisfying the curiosity of the school concerning its record for the day, to encourage the members to larger efforts in membership and finances.

Unquestionably, the function of reports could profitably be studied more widely. It does seem that many would be put in different form if the educational and inspirational purpose were clearly in view. For example, the typical Sunday Church School report of attendance and offerings is a dreary recital of numbers. Actually, however, these figures disclose such vital things as the school's retention or loss of pupils; the abilities of teachers to teach, win, and hold pupils; the effects of rooms and equipment; departmental efficiency; curriculum adaptation; character development and religious growth. A proper report will tell what the figures reveal. Its precise content will be determined by the purpose in terms of response desired and by the persons to whom it is addressed.

The story of the data on the Sunday Church School should be told in more ways than one—by printed as well as oral announcement, on bulletin board or poster, in graph or chart, by letter or bulletin. Always it should be intelligible, brief, clear and concise, and it should include enough description to suggest the response desired.

As a final suggestion, reports should get beyond the school itself to community, congregation, and particularly to parents. Reports should get into the papers, the church bulletins, the church council and congregational meetings. More progressive schools not only send the quarterly report cards to parents but aim to keep parents informed also concerning the nature of work being done in the school so that they can co-operate in emphasizing the same facts and principles of training in the home. This is another way to introduce good educational practice into Sunday Church School leadership.

THE SECRETARY

The average school will have but one secretary with limited responsibilities. A large school may have several in addition to the general secretary. These may be divisional, departmental, and class officers or they may have such special responsibilities as those of membership secretary, absentee secretary, recording secretary, supplies secretary, statistical secretary, and others.

The duties of a secretary of whatever type of school or title will include some combination of items from the following list:

> Handling correspondence
> Conducting or helping with some form of research
> Participating in a survey
> Keeping records of one or more types
> Caring for record systems
> Ordering supplies, storing and distributing them
> Following up absentees
> Handling enrollments or withdrawals
> Interpreting data
> Preparing and making reports of many sorts
> Gathering and preserving historical data
> Taking minutes
> Keeping lists of projects

In carrying out their duties, secretaries meet certain typical problems concerning membership, attendance, and punctuality. Recognized practice would say that a member is a member when he signifies his intention of becoming a member, and he retains that status until he indicates that he has withdrawn or it is otherwise known that his membership has ceased.

Under such a definition, the full enrollment of the school can never be expected to attend since there will be *always* some members who actually cannot be present. The statistics of "average attendance" will, therefore, give an unnecessarily gloomy picture of the situation unless some adjustment is made. The usual plan is to have a distinction between "attending membership" or "active membership" and "non-attending membership" or "associate membership." Often persons who have not attended for three Sundays are included in the latter category and the "average attendance" is computed on the basis of the "attending membership."

In the matter of punctuality, no leeway can be allowed properly. Unless the leader is present ten minutes before the time announced for the session, he is not fulfilling his obligation. If the pupil is not present for the first minutes of the session, he is late, no matter what his excuse may be.

In the interpretation of data on attendance and punctuality, standards are needed to determine the actual condition of a school. While there is no universal agreement, there is reason to say that the minimum for satisfactory average attendance of the "attending membership" is 70 per cent and for satisfactory punctuality 85 per cent of the attendance present on time.

In order to do satisfactorily the sort of work described, a secretary should have the best equipment the church can provide. He should have a room, if possible; if not, an inconspicuous corner. He should have a desk, preferably under lock and key, where he can keep papers without fear of their being disturbed. Cabinets for supplies and records should be supplied.

It will be seen that secretaries, like all other officers of the school, are educators. It is their function to inform, guide, and move the leaders, pupils, and entire constituency into better practices in Christian education. In such a matter as attendance they assemble the facts and then report them to all the persons involved so that attendance will improve. They may show the pupils and parents how lax they have been; they may show the leaders that their program needs to be improved; they may show the congregation that new equipment is needed. The secretary's work is not completed until he has made similar use of all the data with which he deals. His purpose is to advance Christian growth through the use of data secured, preserved, and made available.

Chapter XVII

PROMOTING THE SCHOOL

Every Sunday Church School leader wishes to see his school thriving. That involves more than the enrollment of new pupils. To be sure, the leader does want his school to be increasing constantly in numbers. Yet, he wants it also to be doing its entire work with increasing effectiveness while winning a place of enlarging esteem within the church and the community.

CULTIVATING SPIRIT

A first item in promoting the school in this general way is the development of finer morale. There are vast differences among schools in this respect. Some of them have a pathetic lack of spirit. For example, a worker in a recent conference declared with heartfelt conviction, "Our Sunday School is dead." Other schools have a spirit like yeast working within the loaf to make it light and tasty. It is indeed desirable to accomplish what one pastor expresses as "Enthusiasm! Enthusiasm on the part of all!" What can be done to make the Sunday Church School such an inspirited and inspiring place?

In general, good morale is the by-product of good other things. To have clear-cut educational and practical *objectives* is a first suggestion. If church members have only vague conceptions of the school's reason for being, how can they be expected to consider it important? If parents have only the general idea that it may be a good thing, why should they be careful about sending their children? If the children do not know why they are sent, how can they be expected to go freely? If leaders are not conscious of their goals, what hope is there for a vital program?

Actually the purpose of the Sunday Church School is such a lofty one that the whole constituency might well be radiant about it. To help others live more abundantly in the Christian way—who can quench an enthusiasm to contribute in some way to that cause? The leader who helps everybody become conscious of that goal in the worship, study and instruction, fellowship, and service—every activity—may expect them to enter the school's activities with high spirits.

Having a valuable, challenging *program* is of fundamental importance in cultivating spirit. Suppose the worship period is a haphazard, half-hearted time of hymn-singing, lesson reading, and announcements in an uncongenial setting. Suppose the instructional half hour is a boresome period of droning over a tawdry lesson book with an unprepared teacher. Suppose there is no fellowship program beyond the casual contacts before and after the school session. Suppose the school has no service enterprises beyond the dropping of coins in envelopes.

Our appreciations of values received by ourselves or others are the seeds of our enthusiasms. We become enthusiastic over worship which brings pupils into communion with God, instruction which answers their problems, fellowship which satisfies their finest strivings. The leader of a program like that may expect his school to have not only a fervent spirit but also a lasting one because it is built on a solid foundation.

An inspiring *leadership* is another requisite for a spirited school. "Our school is dead" was not said of a school whose workers were keenly alive and enthusiastic about their work. What the teacher says and does is not the only factor observed by pupils. There is also the manner he employs. Pupils admire the worker who radiates joy in the religion he professes and the task which engages him. They will give their loyalty to a school whose workers thank God that he has called them to a Sunday Church School staff.

Schools which have spirit go out of their way to cultivate human *fellowship*. A man spoke recently of the barrenness of life he would suffer if he should need to withdraw from the church with all the friends and acquaintances he has made by church contacts. "I do not know," he said, "of a single friend I have who did not come to me through the church."

Whether we approve it or not, people do go with their friends to friendly places where they have good times, and they favor those places. The craving of the human spirit for human as well as divine fellowship can be used for building Sunday Church School spirit.

A final suggestion is to exalt the Christian religious motive. *Christian motive* manifest in a school constitutes its major attractiveness. The school that is literally charged with radiant faith, hope, and love, will always thrive. Deadly, dull monotony can scarcely lurk in a true corner of the kingdom of God.

USING AWARDS AND RECOGNITIONS

The use of artificial incentives in the form of prizes, awards, banners, and pins should be reduced to a minimum or eliminated. They appeal to unchristian motives of antisocial and selfish interests. In addition, the regulations are almost impossible to administer with fairness and precision. The Christian educational results will likely be negative.

Modest Christian recognition of eminent service on the part of leaders and of good records made by pupils is another matter. Such recognition should be relatively rare, always sincere and gracious, invariably simple and inexpensive. Above all, it should contribute further to objectives.

Beyond that, the motives of mutual spiritual growth will suffice and should be relied upon to promote the school. Artificial incentives are really "escape mechanisms" for avoiding the hard work of providing a vital program under spiritually minded and competent leaders.

REPRESENTING THE SCHOOL FAVORABLY

If the Sunday Church School is to be highly esteemed, all its members must represent it favorably before the constituency. We can neither make people like us and our school nor exalt our Christ unless they see that we have those same attitudes ourselves.

The pupils should be saying good things about the school. Fathers and mothers discuss with other parents the things their boys and girls have said about Sunday Church School. Likewise, the friends of the pupils want to go where the pupils have enthusiastically reported a vital program. Such reports go a long way indeed.

An instance can be reported. A boy of eight was talking to a friend about Sunday School. The friend said he didn't like to go to Sunday School and he had a reason because, he said, "The kids are all too noisy and fight with each other all the time while the teacher is trying to tell a story." The eight-year-old evangelist replied, "The kids in my Sunday School don't do that. Why don't you come with me to my Sunday School next week and I'll show you." The friend accepted the invitation, became a member of the class, and at the age of thirteen became a confirmed member of the congregation.

The parents, too, should be saying good things about the school. If they can feel that their efforts have been well expended to the advantage of their children, they will continue those efforts. If they see that the children are truly growing in grace under the cultivation of capable workers with whom it is good to have them associated, they will tell others. There is no end to the good which an enthusiastic parent can do.

The workers should be saying good things about the school. Yet there are those who go to their task with the reluctance of sheep to the shearer's. Their way of discussing it is to say that somebody has to do it and it is their duty, they suppose. Such workers are like rotten apples in the barrel spoiling all the fruit. The only worse ones are those who engage in outright negative criticism. Joyous service issuing in loyal support and winsome appeal is to be expected.

Chief among those who should be saying good things about the school are the pastor and superintendent. They should be speaking constantly to various church officers, parents, pupils, and outsiders so as to arouse enthusiasm for the program of which they are the responsible heads.

Contrast a school of which all are speaking well—except, in the proper company, to criticize it constructively—with another school where the members indulge in pessimistic or sarcastic denunciation. Then the possibility of the great improvement to be made in many a school can be seen.

PUTTING EVERYBODY TO WORK

It is to be emphasized again that a Sunday Church School is not properly a situation where leaders *give* to pupils and pupils *get* from leaders. The proper outlook sees leaders and pupils mutually giving and getting for themselves and others.

Earlier it was recommended that workers be given full part in determining the policies and program of the school as a way of securing their response in desired ways. It has been said similarly that pupils should have as large a part as possible in the organization and administration of the school. It is even more essential that they have full participation in all the aspects of the curriculum: planning and conducting worship; contributing to the progress of study-and-instruction activities; engaging in service enterprises; carrying on fellowship activities. People want to preserve that institution of which they are a functioning part. They want to see such an enterprise succeed. Christian work is a satisfaction, an encouragement, and a challenge. The Sunday Church School which puts its people to work at engaging tasks has a full list of investors who want to promote its dividend earning power.

GIVING PUBLICITY

The Sunday Church School will be represented to its constituency more formally through its publicity program. Publicity may be broadly defined as mass education with the end of informing persons so as to enlist them for some cause, develop their loyalty to some movement, or cause them to act in some desired way. This purpose is entirely in harmony with all other forms of Christian religious education. It should, of course, deal in Christian values and scrupulously tell the truth.

A general worker in the church has declared that the people will support its causes generously if only they know the facts about them. How many persons who have been lost to the church might be working busily inside it if they had been kept loyal and enthusiastic by proper information?

Ask the average church member such questions as the following and further need for publicity will appear: How many missionary fields does the church occupy? What is the enrollment of your Sunday School? What is the outstanding project of your youth fellowship? What lessons are the Sunday Church School children studying? What was the per capita contribution to the church last year?

The forms which publicity can take are legion. A dozen leading ones may be listed as follows:

Weekly calendar and monthly bulletin
Posters and bulletin boards
Postcards and letters
Newspaper announcements, articles, pictures, and advertisements
Oral announcements from pulpit and platform
Sermons and other public addresses
Telephone calls
Pastoral and other personal conferences
Church School yearbooks and directories
Radio broadcasts
Pageants, exhibits, and demonstrations
Special bulletins or pamphlets

The "how" of these forms of publicity is a field of study in itself. Fortunately an abundance of material is available in public libraries. These will suggest such things as a committee in charge; young people as reporters; a budget; the use of denominational periodicals and other publications; mailing lists; a duplicating machine or printing press; poster equipment; monthly bulletins; and a host of others.

Active participation in the Religious Education week or month programs of interdenominational and denominational agencies will be one of the most immediately practical procedures for most leaders in publicizing their schools. Rally Day can be made valuable, too.

Good publicity programs, like all other good programs, must follow certain well-considered principles. These are to be studied in the various books on the psychology of advertising and principles of publicity. Briefly, those who undertake publicity work for the church may rather well test their judgment by the following questions concerning each item in the program: (a) *Will it attract attention?* (b) *Will it hold attention?* (c) *Will it obtain good will?* (d) *Will it secure the desired response?*

SECURING INCREASED ENROLLMENT

The question uppermost in the mind of almost every leader concerns ways and means of increasing the number of pupils enrolled in his school. As in the matters of increasing attendance and punctuality, ten suggestions are listed below. Throughout the consideration of this matter, however, it is to be understood that this is, essentially, evangelism. Winning persons for Christ is the total idea, not merely winning members for the school.

General Suggestions

1. Have a definite goal. For the Sunday Church School as a whole, the ultimate goal should be no less than universal enrollment of all Protestant people. For an individual school, it should be the enrollment of every available pupil within that congregation's sphere of influence.

A school can well adopt as its more immediate goal a certain number or percentage within the realm of possibility, perhaps a 10 per cent increase each year. Or, since many schools have less than a hundred members, they might work for that number.

2. Provide for everyone. For most schools this means an emphasis upon provisions for a nursery department and an adult division—these being the two points at which the typical school can most readily increase its enrollment. Present population trends indicate that particular attention must be given to the adult program

3. *Make the school vital.* The school which desires to increase its membership in a substantial and stable way may well devise an adequately vital educational program first. Word about this fine program will be carried by present members to outsiders. Their enthusiasm will kindle the desire to be members. Likewise, when persons have been brought into a vital school, they will remain. "Have an able corps of superintendents and teachers, including substitute teachers," one pastor advises. Another says, "The teaching has to be good and effective, and the material worth-while."

4. *Make the school accessible.* Certain Sunday Church Schools are unfortunately located. Sometimes the members can help by making their cars available on Sunday morning for persons who could not otherwise reach the school. Some congregations have provided bus service. Application to the police department for a traffic officer to protect young children at dangerous crossings may help. Still another and, in some situations, a better idea is to start a "branch" Sunday Church School.

5. *Discover the prospects.* For this enrollment effort the community should be surveyed. Some smaller towns make this a community enterprise every five years. The surveyors, representing the various denominations, call at each home for a report of church interests. When the cards resulting from the survey are collected and assorted, persons expressing preference for one congregation or another become the prospects of that congregation. Such a procedure can also be made as a congregational effort. In any case, churches should make plans for definite and vital use of the data secured.

More informally, any school can secure reports constantly from the members of the congregation concerning new people moving into the community, from the record cards of younger pupils concerning parents or guardians, from the members of the various classes when asked to suggest names of friends who might come to the school, from their former pastors about people who have recently moved to the town. Also, look at the rolls for those who have lapsed, the records of baptisms and marriages, the rosters of weekday and vacation church schools. "Develop a prospect roll" is one pastor's recommendation; that summarizes it.

6. *Go personally to win the prospect with a definite and a trained organization.* Since Jesus went up and down the highroads of Galilee, Christianity has been a matter of personal evangelization. Other publicity has value, but Christianity and church membership are mainly propagated from person to person. There is much in one pastor's statement: "Let the question 'Where do you go to Sunday School?' be on the lips of all members." Another put it well when he said: "Educate pupils to bring every unattached neighbor to Sunday Church School."

Yet, for full results, there should be a definite organization, preferably a standing committee on membership. While membership campaigns may be useful, continuous effort with duly constituted persons definitely in charge will be best. This does not mean that the committee alone shall be engaged in the membership effort. An increase in its membership should be viewed by all as the entire school's missionary enterprise. The spirit of lay evangelism should constantly be inculcated as a part of the educational work of the school. The membership committee can wisely plan to have every member engaging in its program—pastor, director, superintendent, teachers, pupils, and parents.

The organization for securing increased enrollment should be trained. People are not born with the requisite knowledge. There should be definite instructions in the ways of approaching people, the methods of asking them to become pupils, and ways of answering the objections which are sure to be raised by some prospects.

7. *Use publicity.* The use of publicity in Sunday Church School promotion has been the subject of a separate division. Let it suffice to say here that every legitimate form of wholesome publicity should be brought to bear.

8. *Provide a fellowship program.* There is no more agreeable way to get acquainted with people than to play with them. And, if we like the people with whom we play, we want to be associated with them in other activities of their lives. Many young

people, particularly, are won for Sunday Church School by an invitation to an affair where they make likeable acquaintances. Meanwhile, it should be understood that the major purpose of the fellowship program is not to win and hold but to educate.

9. *Avoid contests.* There was a certain school which held a long-range contest with another school in a distant state. The contest ended on a Sunday when all the members of various schools in neighboring churches, whatever their denomination, were invited to help roll up the biggest attendance of all. The school won the contest over its distant neighbor, but the entire session was spent in taking a picture of the group! It is a grave question whether any desirable permanent results accrue from such activity. Indeed, it is probable that many people become discouraged, if not disgusted, with membership solicited in that manner. Thus we undermine the Christian attitudes we are presumed to be building.

10. *Educate all concerned.* In a school the procedures should, it would seem, be educational. Thus in these matters it is desirable to educate everybody concerned. Through regular lessons, announcements, special day programs, church bulletins, and sermons people can constantly be reminded of their obligation and their privilege to win someone for the church's educational program. By the same means, the advantages of the program can be brought before prospective members, while a wholesome background of information and appreciation is cultivated in the members of the school, among the members of the congregation, and among the parents and neighbors of the school. This is the ultimate means of accomplishing the goal set by the slogan proposed in one church: "Want them; find them; bring them; greet them; teach them."

A Denominational Effort

One denomination discovered that its enrollment had declined almost 100,000 in the ten years from 1934 to 1944. After the proper authorities had studied the causes, they determined that the underlying reason was a recession in missionary zeal. All other causes, they believed, could have been overcome if the church had possessed a sufficient "passion for souls" to go out after the un-reached half of the American population.

A competent man was called to direct an enlistment program. The objective of the program was "to win others to the Sunday School that, through it, they may be won to Christ and the church." The specific goal for enrollment was set as "a million pupils by 1950."

General attack was made along the following fronts:

1. Impressing pastors and other leaders with the importance of the Sunday Church School in reaching as well as in teaching.
2. Developing all denominational overhead facilities fundamental to maintaining increased enrollment and attendance.
3. Encouraging and planning for pupils and workers to win others.
4. Appealing for greater home co-operation.
5. Helping leaders and pupils to use the best educational procedures which would result in increased enrollment.
6. Urging Sunday Church School workers to seek the re-enlistment of lapsed pupils.

As one specific method, "Sunday School Enlistment Demon-strations" were held at strategic centers. Local congregational workers were assembled and instructed in methods of lay visitation. Then they went into homes and secured written promises to attend Sunday Church School. Statistics indicate that an average of nearly one promise was obtained in each home visited. A later check showed that approximately 50 per cent of the persons who prom-ised were in attendance after three months had passed.

An important part of this effort was an accompanying attempt to improve the schools and their work. The local workers were led in making an evaluation of their own educational programs. Then they adopted from one to five projects for improvement.

As a second method for attaining the goal, a denomination-wide "Ambassadors for Christ" program was launched. It was devised to "use pupils to increase Sunday School enrollment and attendance." The essence of the program was the development of two types of "ambassadors" in each school. While there were pre-scriptions concerning authorization, training, induction, and pub-licity, the movement rested on the work of "Class Ambassadors" and "Community Ambassadors," described below.

The former were to win back lapsed members of classes and promote regularity of attendance. One (or two) was to be appointed in each class. Community ambassadors were to enlist new pupils; and every pupil in the school could be appointed. One small sampling of the effectiveness of this program showed that ten schools in ten weeks increased their attendance 10 per cent.

The director believes that a by-product of the whole effort may prove to be its major contribution—the knowledge that enrollment can be increased. He writes: "When I came I heard, 'Nothing can be done.' Later the pastors began to say, 'You've shown us that something can be done.' Now, it seems, the whole church knows that fact and we've changed from pessimism to optimism so far as Sunday School enrollment and attendance are concerned."

WORKING AT THE TASK

For a decade before World War II there was concern almost everywhere about decreased enrollments in Sunday Church Schools. During the war one denominational board asked selected pastors to suggest reasons for the increasing decline in enrollments. The following eight causes were the principal ones cited: losses to the armed forces; breakdown of home co-operation; decreased birth rate; moving population; seven-day week and swing-shift hours; transportation; lack of leaders (many are in armed forces and in Sunday or overtime work); and general discouragement.

One might conclude, on hasty consideration, that those causes were largely the result of war conditions. Yet, more people could have attended Sunday Church School if they had really wished to do so. And, here and there, a school reported almost phenomenal growth even during the war. When leaders of such schools were asked to report the secrets of their success they wrote statements like these:

"The key to the whole situation is personal work." "Work with the same enthusiasm as the ward politician." "Have the persistency of an insurance agent."

"Our Sunday-school workers must catch enthusiasm and Christian zeal."

"Our schools must emphasize evangelism."

"A consecrated special visitor will be effective."

"Willingness to work and leadership education explain our growth."

"Our growth (about 100 per cent in one and one-half years) represents just plain, hard work."

"Consecrated, faithful, and trained teachers are needed."

"Everyone must think that this work is important and that it is his high mission to bring others to Sunday School."

"The superintendent tells the new pupils of the joys they will have studying together."

"The feeling of responsibility on the part of teachers and officers will be radiated to the pupils."

"Preaching and teaching are the true means."

"Our leadership personnel has a deepening of Christian spirit in the matter of interesting others."

"We must have less absenteeism on the part of our leaders."

"The whole setup of the school is pupil-centered rather than organization-centered."

"We have more attractive rooms, better prepared teachers, more visiting by teachers; more personal interest in the pupils as individuals."

"We hold regular executive meetings and workers' conferences."

"This Church builds its annual program and carries it out."

"We put our members to work."

"We render valuable assistance to the community in these times."

"You do not win Christians through contests: you win Christians through Christ."

In summary, to the leader who asks himself, "How can I make my school go and grow?" an excellent answer might be:

Engender enthusiasm that is contagious.

Provide a program that wins.

Render a service that is notable.

Tell people about it.

Chapter XVIII

MEASURING IN THE SUNDAY CHURCH SCHOOL

The Sunday Church School leader who has clear-cut objectives, both organizational and personal, wishes to know how thoroughly the objectives are being attained. He has undertaken a task; how is he succeeding? He has developed an organization; how well is it meeting the need? He is fostering a program; is it effective? Are pupils moving forward at a maximum rate into increasingly higher experiences of abundant life in:

Using the Bible fruitfully?

Practicing effective church membership?

Giving supreme loyalty to God?

Maintaining discipleship with Jesus?

Employing the processes and products of Nature beneficiently?

Co-operating in good will with others?

Having personal acquaintance with religion?

Attaining the highest realization of the self?

Furthermore, those questions are asked not as mere inquiries about facts. They are related to the important question, What shall be done next?

The usual way of answering such questions is in terms of enrollment, attendance, pupil interest, offering, and the like. It has been assumed that a Sunday Church School should produce results in somewhat vague terms of Christian profession, biblical knowledge, church membership, and wholesome character. And it has been assumed further that schools which, for example, are keeping up their attendance will produce those results.

Christian educators now have a keener understanding of proper objectives and a scientific interest which insists upon more accurate knowledge about the degree to which they are being accomplished. Also, they demand more careful determination of the means of achieving objectives. Thus they are not satisfied with the usual measures, with guessing, with impressions gained by casual observation, or with hearsay. Here is the pupil with the whole church expecting that he be helped along as effectively as possible in Christian growth. Leaders want to know to the fullest possible extent where he is, where he ought to go, where he can go, and how he can be helped best to arrive there.

Fortunately, certain means of measuring in relation to these things are now available.

Where is the pupil now?

Repeatedly it has been said that Christian education focuses its attention upon persons, finding them where they are and working forward for their Christian growth. Not so long ago there was but one question primarily to be asked in this regard, namely, What does the pupil know already? Now, however, Christian educators are interested in the pupil's total situation, his whole round of behavior. What are his thoughts, attitudes, opinions, feelings, conflicts, and tensions as well as his facts? What are his home, school, work, play, health, and community conditions? In what kind of conduct does he typically engage? Tests, scales, and other measures have been devisd to reveal those things.

Where should the pupil go?

Christian education begins with the pupil's needs and proceeds upon the basis of his interests. Measurement will help to disclose the necessary facts about those things. Perhaps the pupil is lamentably uninformed or misinformed; has bad attitudes; is guilty of misconduct. Perhaps, on the other hand he is already started along lines of very promising development in Christian leadership. He may be in need of simple readjustment or require relief from serious conflict. He may be in a state of high readiness to yield his life to the Christian commitment. There are instruments available to disclose such facts and, when wisely interpreted, point the way toward well-chosen goals for the pupil's highest development.

Where can the pupil go?

What is possible for the pupil? Some things are impossible and so unwise to attempt. Many persons have been discouraged because too much was expected of them; others wasted because they were viewed on too low a level of expectation.

People everywhere have become accustomed to the symbol IQ, meaning intelligence quotient or measure of general intelligence of an individual in relation to other members of an average group. Sunday Church Schools could profitably make use of intelligence quotients although those schools which follow public school grading have, by that means indirectly, a rough adjustment to pupil capacity. It is increasingly recognized, however, that many other factors are at least as important as intelligence in religious development. Many of them, such as social attitudes, personal opinions, feelings, and interests can be measured by standardized tests. Items of factual knowledge are particularly susceptible to measurement. We now have norms of achievement in many such patterns. Thus, pupil capacity in light of intelligence and a whole complex of other factors deserving attention can be revealed by proper measures.

How can we help the pupil arrive most quickly and surely?

That is the ultimate question. Appraisal and evaluation through measuring are not for themselves alone. They are for guidance. In medical procedure, the nurse takes the temperature not merely out of curiosity. The purpose is diagnosis for better treatment. So in educational procedure measurement is to answer the final question, What is to be done? What is to be done about the school itself? Its organization? Its administrative procedures? Its equipment and use of it? Its staff? Its finances? What is to be done about the program? Where should it begin? When and what is the next unit to be undertaken? What pupil activities should be included and what teaching procedures shall be employed? Measurement will point to the answers.

To be sure, no one—leader or pupil—should think that spiritual attainment can be measured quite like an IQ. Yet that fact does not invalidate the general worth of the technique.

MEASURING THE SCHOOL ITSELF

There are two specific ways to answer with some exactness those questions just above and the others with which the chapter opened. The more fundamental way, of course, is to measure the conditions in the lives of the pupils as individuals and groups. That way will be discussed later in this chapter. The other is to measure the school itself. Experience seems to indicate that, everything else being equal, schools of a certain type will produce more adequate results than others. If the leader, then, can make sure that his school approximates the ideal school, he may conclude that he is probably achieving his objectives to a reasonable degree.

Standards

For the purpose of measuring Sunday Church Schools, instruments called standards have been developed. *A standard is a printed statement of the qualities of an "ideal school" with provision for measuring the various features of an actual school in relation to the ideal.*

The more obvious function of a standard, as suggested by that definition, is to disclose how closely a given school approximates the ideal. Actually, the most important work of a standard is to reveal to leaders what strengths and what weaknesses their school possesses.

Standards are available in several different types. Some are provided by denominational boards of Christian education. They may deal with the whole school, a division or a department. The International Council of Religious Education publishes *The International Standard for the Sunday Church School.* This standard covers the following major items: curriculum; leadership; organization and administration; housing and equipment. Among the nineteen sub-topics are worship, training of workers, budget, the pupils, rooms, and the like.

In form, the International standard consists of two pamphlets. One presents in question form the description of items to be considered. For example, there is this question under worship, "Do pupils have opportunity to assist in preparing and conducting the program?" The second pamphlet is a scoring chart in which, opposite the heading of the item just mentioned, there is a place to score the school being measured in the amount of 0 to 8. Additional values may be assigned for other items to a total of 500 units.

The use of a standard can be described by the procedure in one school. The real beginning was the pastor's appointment of a board of religious education. In due time the board had reason to feel that its Sunday Church School should have considerable overhauling. Since there was some difference of opinion about the points where improvements should be undertaken, one member suggested that they apply an International standard to the school. There was ready agreement and the plans were laid. The staff members themselves might have done the work, but several young men of a Christian education class in a neighboring college were asked to undertake it. The superintendent secured the co-operation of his staff and the young men went to work.

After a few weeks of surveying and then of tabulating the data, a report was made to the board and to the school. The score was 315 points on a scale of a possible 500. That was interesting, but it was not the vital thing. The exact points of weakness and of strength in the school were revealed by the many findings, positive and negative. The following sample quotations from the report include both positive and negative items:

"Only 36 per cent of those attending are present at the beginning of the service."

"The supply of Bibles is low."

"Need for an increase in trained leadership is evident."

"The pupils are promoted annually."

"The average attendance in the school throughout the year is but 47 per cent."

"The school has an active Home Department."

"The school has a regular workers' conference."
"The building and fixtures are kept clean."

The total score of the school gave no occasion for discouragement. Yet, the negative findings could not fail to challenge the workers to undertake improvements. That is a typical result of applying standards. They stimulate people to action.

At the same time, standards show people what to do. Thus, upon the basis of the above and similar facts, that school took action to improve its program. Some of the items accomplished were organization of a Junior department, procuring new hymnals for older groups, study of worship techniques by the leaders, and organized effort to increase attendance and punctuality.

Other Means

Several additional means of measuring schools in some of their aspects are employed. There are *rating scales* by which the effectiveness of a worker can be estimated by the superintendent or by other workers, at least three checks being recommended. There are *self-rating scales* for workers—printed forms on which they can check for themselves their personal qualities and attitudes, their method of preparation, their management of the pupils.

"*Studies,*" for example of worship services in a department or school, are possible according to printed forms which may be procured.

"*Supervisory schedules*" can be of great value. A supervisory schedule is a list of questions with which a supervisor might go into a session which he is visiting. He would be seeking answers to those questions while in the session and discuss them with the leader or leaders after the session. While the schedules are meant for use by an actual supervisor, they can be used also by groups or individuals in "*self-supervision.*" Below are a few sample questions which might appear on a schedule for supervising a worship service. Each might have several sub-points.

Were the physical conditions arranged as suitably as possible?
Had all possible preparation been made?

Did the leader exemplify the necessary principles of appropriate leadership in worship?

Was the program fully adapted to the pupils and the occasion?

Did the pupils participate heartily?

What outcomes were being sought? Achieved?

MEASURING THE PUPILS

The most direct way of discovering the effectiveness of a school with a view to its improvement is to measure the progress of the pupils. Ideally, a program of measuring would begin by getting data on the present status of the pupils. Then, after a period of education had taken place, the attainment of the pupils would be measured again to determine their progress. Meanwhile, too, there would be incidental measuring to guide the procedure.

Because of the work and expense involved, very few schools have carried through a continued testing program like that although a considerable number have worked at it a bit. The least a leader can do is to observe carefully the conduct of his pupils as individuals and as groups. Do they give evidence of growing in the direction of the objectives of the school? Most leaders can go beyond that in one way or another.

Examinations

Written examinations of the older or the newer type are used in a number of schools. Sometimes promotion depends upon success in those examinations. In most cases, however, they serve only a diagnostic purpose, revealing the standing of pupils for the informal guidance of the teacher or other leader.

Examinations usually are of the older essay or question and answer type with the purpose of showing pupil outcomes at the end of a course of study. Now and then, as for example in the examination at the conclusion of a confirmation class, there is a public oral examination to demonstrate fitness. Happily, though, that practice is going out. Often the examinations have been specially prepared for and hence deceptive. They are almost always out of key with the fellowship attitude in which the pupil should be entering the confirmation experience.

"New type" or "objective" tests including such devices as those described under "standardized tests" below are being used, too. They have several advantages. They are accepted by most pupils as more interesting, being somewhat like a game. The answers usually are either right or wrong so that teacher opinion is eliminated. They can cover the ground more thoroughly and fairly, and so give a better picture of the pupil's situation. Usually they are easier to administer and, although harder to prepare are easier to score.

There are limitations in objective tests. They often deal with fragments of knowledge out of organization. This is due in part, however, to the particular type of test employed since objective means are available for more balanced measuring. Examinations should be planned to evaluate various manifestations of learning. The basic worth of memorized facts in religious experience is always open to question. Certainly we dare not depend too much upon it as a complete index to reality and depth of Christian growth.

A few directions for those who construct their own tests follow:

Represent a fair sampling of the various elements of learning.
Do not include trivial items.
Use a range of questions to cover the abilities of the group—not too many difficult ones and not too many easy ones.
Guard against guessing.
Use no puzzle, trick, or catch questions.
Employ simple, clear language and direct sentence construction.
Provide for simplicity of use.
Make the instructions brief, clear, definite.
Insure rapidity and accuracy of scoring.

Standardized Tests

Types

All workers in general education and the pupils and parents of modern public schools have become familiar with "standardized tests" of capacity and achievement. The movement for their use has spread to the field of Christian education. Means are available for us, singly or in batteries of tests, to measure:

Attitudes—such as fairmindedness or church interests
Biblical comprehension—the pupil's understanding of biblical verses and passages
Biblical knowledge—such matters as Old and New Testament history and literature, the life and teachings of Christ, Paul and the Epistles
Christian practices—for example, prayer
Conduct—as expressed in such terms as honesty, trustworthiness, loyalty, or reverence
Knowledge of the church—its history, work, and practices
Moral knowledge, judgment, and discrimination—the more immediate ethical problems which confront people daily and others such as race relations or peace and war
Personality—factors like sociability, confidence, dominance, self-control
Psychological status—intelligence, reactions, emotional maturity, and others
Religious ideas and beliefs—in relation to the idea of God, work of Christ, personal immortality, or "other religions"

It is admittedly impossible to measure all of the factors which enter into complex religious experience. Yet a fair sampling made by a judicious combination of the available items mentioned above should furnish trustworthy guidance at most desired points.

Devices

Usually standardized tests employ one or more of the techniques illustrated below. A majority of them deal in mastery of content doubtless because that is most fully subject to measurement.

1. *Best Answer*
   INSTRUCTIONS: One of the statements among the four below tells BEST what the passage means. Mark the best meaning with an X.
   Jesus said, "Let the children come to me, and do not hinder them, for to such belongs the kingdom of God."
   THIS MEANS:
   _____a. Persons who have the spirit of a good child are citizens of the kingdom of God.
   _____b. Little children should not be forbidden to do what they wish.
   _____c. When little children are suffering they can come to Jesus.
   _____d. Even young children can be disciples of Jesus.

2. *Completion*
   INSTRUCTIONS: Complete the story by writing the necessary words in the spaces:
   In the times of the Pharaoh named _____, Moses was born

in the land of _____ in Egypt. His family included his

father _____, his mother _____, an older sister

_____, and an older brother _____ All were

of the Israelitish tribe of _____

3. *Expression of Attitude or Belief*
   INSTRUCTIONS: Put a check (√) if you agree with the statement.
   Put a double check (√√) if you agree *emphatically.* Put an X if you
   disagree.

   ____1. My church is the primary guiding influence in my life.

   ____2. I am loyal to the church, but I believe its influence is on the
   decline.

   ____3. I am interested but only to the extent of attending services
   occasionally.

   ____4. ....

4. *Matching Question and Answer*
   INSTRUCTIONS: From the following list of dates select one to match
   each of the events listed: B.C. 586; 538; 536; 332; 150.

   ____1. The first exiles returning from Babylonia arrived in Jerusa-
   lem.

   ____2. Alexander the Great began to rule Palestine.

   ____3. The book of the Psalms was completed.

   ____4. ....

5. *Multiple Choices*
   INSTRUCTIONS: Only one of the four answers below is right. Mark
   the RIGHT answer by putting X before it.
   1. The first great Christian missionary was:

   ____Luke

   ____Paul

   ____Thomas

   ____Nicodemus

   2. ....

6. *Rating or Ranking*
   INSTRUCTIONS: How seriously wrong is the act? Mark your opinion
   with an X.

	very seriously wrong	somewhat seriously wrong	not seriously wrong
1. Coming late to meals			
2. Borrowing another person's clothes without permission			
3. Forgetting daily prayer			
4. Missing Sunday School classes			
5.			

7. *Scale of Values*

INSTRUCTIONS: As you remember the service of worship in which you have just participated, what do you think about its features listed below? Put a check ($\sqrt{}$) on the line at the proper place to express your view.

1. General effect on faith:

Disturbed   No result at all   Strengthened

2. Appreciation of special music:

Disliked it   Was mildly pleased   Was inspired

3. Result of the sermon:

Irritated   Not very much interested   Found it helpful

4. ....

8. *Simple Recall*

INSTRUCTIONS: Name the prophet to which each statement refers:

_____1. He was the first of the so-called "literary" prophets.

_____2. Wise men were guided to Bethlehem by his words.

_____3. He said: "But let justice roll down as waters."

_____4. ....

9. *True-false Statements*

   INSTRUCTIONS: Encircle T for TRUE; F for FALSE statements:

   T F 1. Jesus was born in Nazareth.

   T F 2. When twelve years of age, Jesus visited the temple in Jerusalem.

   T F 3. It was John the Baptist who first called Jesus "Lamb of God."

   T F 4. The Mediterranean was the sea where Jesus calmed a storm.

   T F 5. ....

10. *Cross Out*

    INSTRUCTIONS: One word in each of the series does not belong. Cross it out.

    1. Amos   Saul   David   Solomon
    2. Matthew   Mark   Luke   Romans
    3. Galilee   Judea   Egypt   Perea

    4. ....

There are numerous modifications of the above, as well as other ingenious devices. They are beginning to appear widely in curricular guides as well as in test forms. In all cases an effort should be made to suit the device to the material, the purpose, and the pupil in the particular situation.

Administration

The administration of such tests is not difficult although adequate preparation must be made. The interest of pupils and workers should be aroused so that their co-operation is secured. It is essential to make certain that no one fears he will be embarrassed; rather, that all are in an inquiring frame of mind. All materials must be ready; there must be enough time; the people should be seated carefully. Then it is necessary only to follow the directions furnished with the test forms.

After the tests have been administered, the scoring is done preferably by a small group of discreet workers, not by pupils themselves. A manual of correct answers and directions for marking is furnished with the blanks by the publisher.

Interpretation

It will be seen that the administration of standardized tests is relatively simple. It is in the interpretation and use of the results that special care must be exercised. We may learn for example that John is the lowest pupil in a certain group and Mary the highest. That information must be used for Christian educational results only. Again, many of the tests can be interpreted by norms of measurement. For example, in using a biblical knowledge test, we may know the average score made by a thousand eighth grade pupils in widely distributed parts of the country. Thus it may be disclosed that the eighth grade boys of the school are below the norm and the girls above it. Consecrated wisdom must be employed in handling such data wisely—in terms of improving equipment, developing leadership, providing motivation, and the like.

Example

One method of using tests was employed by the pastor of a Sunday Church School of some three hundred pupils. The purpose and procedure were explained to his workers and their co-operation enlisted. The pastor procured enough copies of a standardized test on "The Life and Teachings of Jesus" to give to all the members of the school beyond the Primary Department age. On Sunday morning the regular lessons were set aside. Pencils and the blank forms were provided and the printed instructions carefully given. All went to work until by the end of the hour they had finished. A group of interested leaders scored the tests and worked out the interpretations.

Among their interesting findings was the discovery that their general average was below par, although they had considered theirs a quite good school. Also, their twelve-year-old boys and girls equaled the score of the adults in the school!

Two or three years later, a fine new educational building was dedicated by that congregation. Did the testing have anything to do with it? Such indirect results are not impossible. As it discloses present conditions, testing does help to answer the question, What shall be done? Likewise, it gives the people impetus and confidence to act accordingly.

Caution

All standardized tests have been checked for *validity,* which is the adequacy of a test in measuring what it claims to measure, and *reliability,* the degree to which a test can be depended upon for consistent scores. Yet, caution is necessary—for tests are not magical.

They measure only what they measure and that with no perfect accuracy. They are best taken as indicators of general status and not as perfect pictures of any individual. In the field of personality, especially its religious aspects, there is much complexity, subjectivity, and uncertainty. We must not expect to get absolutely exact and complete data on it by any existing or likely paper-and-pencil procedures. In particular, the effectiveness of knowledge in controlling conduct can be easily overestimated. Breadth of testing at a variety of points is important for conclusions of far-reaching import. Always, tests should be carefully chosen to be used for a wise purpose. They should suit the age group for which they are used. It is important to have the testing program in the hands of a trained leader.

Other Means

Sunday Church School leaders can employ various other techniques of which many come out of child study, social case and group work, and public school procedure.

1. There can be *case studies* of individual pupils with a careful descriptive analysis such as might be made by a child-guidance clinic.

2. The *records and reports* of the school have bearing here. Beneath the surface, a discerning leader will find many facts concerning the pupil capacities, needs, relationships, interests, and attitude.

3. Some schools have files of *observation records* prepared by visitors in the home or by teachers and other leaders. These can report, for example: how the pupil gets along with parents and how the brothers and sisters view and treat him; how he spends free time; how he fits into "the pack"; what are the religious practices in the home. Many teachers keep their own personal records

of observation and experience.

4. There are schools where teachers furnish the departmental supervisors *weekly reports on the class session.* The supervisor is thus in possession of innumerable facts of high value.

5. There are many forms of *questionnaire.* A simple form by which a teacher can learn a great deal about a class in short order requires only paper and pencil for each pupil. After making proper arrangements they are asked and given time to write answers to the questions: What three things (a) do you fear most; (b) do you hate most; (c) do you want most to have; (d) would you like best to do with a holiday; (e) do you want most to do as a life work?

6. Another important instrument in this field is the *interest finder*—a check list of items on which young people, for example, can check those things which they wish to consider in a group study. Here is the beginning of one:

INSTRUCTIONS: Your planning committee wants to know your desires concerning topics to be studied in our class. Please check twice ($\sqrt{}\sqrt{}$) the three or four items which interest you most; once ($\sqrt{}$) the three or four others which interest you considerably.

_____1. What does the Bible show us about God?

_____2. How does prayer help us?

_____3. What should we do about our money?

_____4. Why have foreign missionaries?

_____5. ....

A few schools have taken such matters into account. Consequently they can adapt their program more completely to the capacities, interests, and needs of the pupils. They will not expect too much of the less capable and will not waste their opportunity with those on the upper levels, but rather will challenge their capacity. They can provide for more individual guidance and initiate group units of work for Christian growth in wisely selected areas. They can employ procedures more exactly suited to the most effective learning. And in all those matters they will get beyond personal likes and dislikes, prejudices, or even personal opinions.

MEASURING AS LEARNING AND TEACHING TECHNIQUE

Throughout it has been stressed that the basic value of measuring is the guidance and promotion of learning activity. The major emphasis, however, has been upon its worth in the leader's task. It is very significant, though, that measuring also helps the pupil to guide his own learning activity. He, too, discovers where he should and can go and where he needs help.

Learning technique

In many respects measuring is itself a learning technique, for pupils learn in the process of being measured. They learn things concerning themselves. They begin to place themselves more properly in relation to others. They gather facts, meet new ideas, develop attitudes, form purposes, start activities. Listen as a group of pupils discuss the examination they have just taken; watch them search for the answers to the questions they missed!

Teaching technique

Teachers recognize the value of measurement as a learning technique when they follow up tests with discussion and other forms of study based upon the results of a test. Thus it becomes a teaching technique. Further, to diagnose a class situation and discover next steps, to determine the new experience for which a class is ready and arouse interest in entering it, there is scarcely a superior way, valuable alike for pupil as well as teacher.

Leaders may be thinking about launching a unit on the life and teachings of Jesus. What do the pupils already know? That is the place to start the unit. A test can be applied to discover the facts and perhaps indirectly motivate the enterprise. Or the pupils are interested in and seem to need a consideration of some such social issue as war and peace or race relations in the light of Christian ethics. What are their present attitudes? The program for growth will depend upon the answer to that question. Tests are needful.

What religious concepts concerning God, man, sin, immortality, and the like does the learner already have? It is difficult for a religious teacher to proceed unless he knows. Tests will reveal the facts. In conduct matters, how is the pupil acting already and why? For teaching in that area, diagnosis with a view to discovery of readiness is essential. Measuring will be helpful.

There is another important point at which measuring relates itself to teaching technique. Live teachers have a creative spirit, are always restless to be doing things better. To that end they wonder how things are going and want to try something new in the hope that it will be an improvement. Let it be called the experimental attitude.

Measurement makes experiment with teaching procedure possible because measures reveal the truth with regard to objectives and their attainment. What is the relative effectiveness of one teaching method over another? Two groups of pupils with relatively similar capacity and advancement are arranged. Each is tested at the beginning of the experiment. Then two different methods are used. Each group is tested at the end of the educational experience. Which method proved more effective? Similar experiments can be conducted with two types of materials. Thus those who are, in the right way, critical of their work have valid means of arriving at conclusions about it and improving it.

Summary

In all those ways and others, measuring serves a wide variety of purposes as it points the finger toward the solution of such problems as these:

How effective is our organizational setup?

What is the real quality of our staff and its individual members?

What kind of program do we actually have?

What is the truth about our equipment?

Is our church spending enough in money, energy, time, and talent for its educational work?

What are we really achieving in terms of Christian pupil growth?

What is the capacity and ability of our pupils?

What are their interests and needs?

Why did this pupil go wrong: are we responsible?

Am I, teacher or superintendent, doing things in the best possible way?

How can we do our work most wisely to accomplish the best result in abundant life?

Chapter XIX

SOLVING RURAL AND SMALL SCHOOL PROBLEMS

The Sunday Church School chiefly in view now is located in the open country or a small town although it may be in a downtown district or suburb of a great city. The school meets in a "one-room building" with or without a small room or two and a basement or lower floor. It has from twenty-five to one hundred members. In some cases it is part of a multiple parish with one, two, three, or more sister congregations in the pastoral charge. Probably there are several other small churches of other denominations nearby. All in all, it is one of the type which includes, as an estimate, 50 per cent of American Sunday Church Schools.

THE SITUATION

Let it be said at once—many rural schools are not of that type. Some of them are larger, better equipped, and more advanced educationally than their city cousins. Likewise, many small Sunday Church Schools are more exemplary than their larger counterparts. Only the more typical rural and small schools are under consideration.

It is impossible to classify any church as urban or rural, large or small in such a way that anyone knows exactly what kind of church it is. About the only one thing special which can be observed about rural churches is that they exist in the midst of rural life. Their people, therefore, are concerned about soil, weather, crops, and animals instead of other matters. Even so, it must be recognized that there are varieties of rural life, some forms of it being heavily permeated with urban attitudes, practices, and interests. As for the small churches, one can say only that they have small memberships.

Actually, each church is an individual with particular traits and its traits may overlap into several categories. Furthermore, urban-ness and rural-ness, largeness and smallness are but a few of the sources of individuality. Other and more important sources are history, tradition, the personalities of leaders, pastoral guidance, buildings, membership origins, community conditions, and the like. The principles of current Christian education presented hitherto are exactly suited to such a condition. Needs will be met in the ideal way if these principles are applied. A local Sunday Church School then will have objectives which arise from the situation of the people whatever their way of living. It will keep its program ad-justed to the constituency whatever it may be. The organization will be planned not merely to fit some standard procedure; it will be adapted to individual facilities in leaders, pupils, and experi-ence. The equipment will be designed to function in the particular school.

Into these churches the pastor or other leader goes as into a unique situation. He carries with him his experience, attitudes, and convictions about Christian education and his general under-standing of Sunday Church Schools as they are and as they ought to be. He enters the school with its members, traditions, equipment, leadership, and community conditions as they are. Then he studies the school and makes plans to start where it is and lead it toward what it may become.

For his encouragement a weighty word was expressed by Sher-rill in his *Religious Education in the Small Church*. He had made an extended study of this subject. Then he wrote this conviction: "The fundamental principles of the present-day program of Chris-tian religious education can be better carried out, under competent leadership, in a small church than in a large one." [1]   And Dean

---

[1] Lewis Joseph Sherrill, *Religious Education in the Small Church* (Philadel-phia: Westminster Press, 1932), p. 14.

Sherrill might have added—in a rural church better than in a city one.

Rural versus Urban Churches

It has been too long the fashion to speak of "the rural church" and "the city church." The resulting delusion is illustrated in these conflicting quotations from three letters:

Letter One: "Urban church people are more liberal in proportionate giving."

Letter Two: "Giving may be more generous in the rural congregation."

Letter Three: "Rural people and urban people are equally benevolent."

Here, also, is a sentence from the report of a denominational committee on rural churches in the state of Ohio: "Your committee finds no principle which differentiates the rural from the urban church." Further, the chairman of that committee elaborated the viewpoint in a letter. "I have searched diligently," he wrote, "to find the mark which makes one congregation a rural church and another an urban church. I have found none except that used for census purposes—a rural congregation is one 'whose location is in a community of less than 2500 souls.' Exactly the same rural marks might appear in an 'urban' church which, by the way, is located at no great distance from another 'urban' church which did not possess like characteristics."

Nevertheless, an effort has been made below to suggest some main lines of *possibility* of difference. The items are selected from correspondence on the subject, the standards for selection being these two: the items bear upon Sunday Church School work and there is a certain amount of agreement concerning them.

1. The family unit is likely to be a more important factor in rural congregational life and planning.

2. Most rural churches can have more vital civic influence than most urban churches.

3. There is a big city tempo. City church matters are likely to go at a swifter pace, while rural church matters go in a more leisurely fashion.

4. The city church membership is more mobile. City people move so often.

5. In the city a trained or experienced leader can be found or developed for almost any kind of task. There are types of "church work" which do not so readily fit the farm population.

6. Generally speaking, rural people are more conservative. They may be more tenacious in holding to older theological terms and ideas and less disposed to change their methods.

7. In general, a rural church is constantly surrendering its youth to the urban churches.

8. A city membership may include persons of much wider variety in economic, educational, racial, and vocational status.

9. A rural church may be more central in its people's thoughts and lives. It may dominate more phases of living, especially as to fellowship affairs. There may be fewer competing interests and activities.

10. A city church must give more attention to "finish" in its aesthetic and similar accomplishments. It must be more sensitive to publicity values and be more dramatic.

11. While rural people are said often to be more zealous of denominationalism, it is noteworthy that many of their activities can be done only on an interdenominational basis.

12. Typical rural adults are more given to Sunday Church School attendance than their city brethren.

13. Work, particularly for young people and women, will be very different in the country.

14. City churches are less likely to confuse social mores (represented by restrictions upon young people) with true religion.

15. A big city church will likely provide more opportunity for a seven-day-a-week program.

16. Rural people have a stronger interest, readiness, and grasp in the spiritual area. (This is debatable, doubtless, yet frequently expressed in such quotations as these: "There is a greater hunger for the fundamentals of Christian faith." "Religion is considered more worth-while, something to be desired above all else." "They have a stronger sense of real values." "Because of their closeness to nature, rural people are more deeply religious than their urban brothers." "Practical Christianity is better practiced; the Golden Rule is better observed." "There is more spirit to serve, even with sacrifice.")

There will be abundant denials of all such statements. Indubitably it is wisely said: "People are essentially the same everywhere; the basic work of the church is the same always."

Small versus Large Churches

It is almost equally difficult to specify characteristics of smaller churches in contrast with larger ones. There are so many determining factors which have nothing to do with size. However, the items below, like those above, have been suggested in correspondence.

1. The small congregation is more likely to be like a large family. There is a more intimate group relationship.

2. Small congregations are likely to think in smaller terms and be satisfied with smaller results.

3. The small church is more likely to be central in the experience of people as individuals and as groups.

4. Equipment in the small church is usually meager, sometimes so meager that there is no pride in its care and little vision for better.

5. At the same time, a small congregation may have zeal for improvement and growth that is utterly lacking in the membership of larger churches.

6. In the large church, a member may have no particular interest in the church except for its ministry to him. There may be no genuine sense of being needed and zest in helping.

7. Changing leaders in a small church may offend a whole family relationship.

8. Where the membership is small the work cannot be as widely spread. Thus, certain leaders will be overworked to the point where they cannot be efficient.

9. Finances may be seriously lacking in the smaller situation.

10. The leadership in the small church can know its following much more intimately.

Possibly that last item will be highlighted by this plaintive paragraph from the pastor of a great city church: "They come from all over town. Baptisms almost every Sunday; marriages almost every Saturday; funerals without end, sometimes with police escort to get me back in time for a wedding. Even with a deaconess almost the entire time is taken to call on the sick and attend meetings. Scores are just names. Holy Communion is one table after another seemingly without end. And it is very, very hard to 'walk in the spirit' and shun professionalization. Great choirs, excellent music, huge and inspiring congregations are compensations; but one does not have time even to reflect on whether one is happy or not, accomplishing much or little; you just go on and on."

Educational Advantages and Disadvantages

It will be seen that a rural school may possess many special

virtues. The larger influence of the home, the greater centrality of
the church in the life of the people, the possibility of more family
spirit within the group—these lend themselves to effective Sunday
Church School work. There are additional values in the likelihood
that the people are industrious, probably live more simply, have
more stability, possess some creative spirit, and exist more near to
life and the natural manifestations of God.

There are doubtless as many difficulties to be overcome. The
leadership may be untrained, even uneducated. Young leaders
scarcely have been started until they are gone. The equipment may
be meager and lacking in beauty. The people may be slow to talk
and inexperienced in expressing themselves about religion. Extreme
conservatism may be encountered and an equal amount of frugality
especially in religious or educational matters. Transportation problems are not infrequent. There are work schedules which may make
some kinds of educational endeavor almost impossible.

Similarly, there are possibilities of both advantage and disadvantage in the small school. The leader's intimate acquaintance
with his workers and pupils and their interest and needs; the smallness of groups; the family spirit; the sense of having an important
place; all these are genuine assets.

At the same time there are liabilities: too few leaders, overworked; meager equipment and crowded buildings; lack of finances;
a possible tendency to be satisfied with things as they are. All
those lay restraint upon the ambitious leader who wishes to develop
his school rapidly and outstandingly.

There are special problems in the so-called multiple parish,
usually rural. Pastors are known to have as many as five or six
Sunday Church Schools under their charge. The difficulties are
legion. Visits to the schools are infrequent; in some cases the pastor
never gets into a school while it is in session. He will have so much
traveling and so many absolutely essential meetings to attend for
other purposes that he will not find it possible to give the educational work its requisite attention.

Yet something can be done. The proper procedure had been

used in a four-congregation parish recently observed. The pastor concentrated upon the development of the local leadership, particularly the superintendents of the Sunday Church Schools. He was able to visit them in pastoral calls; provide books for them; have them meet from time to time; foster their attendance at conventions and leadership schools. Yet his work in leadership development was by no means confined to the superintendents. On public occasions, he had been able to do some teaching of leadership groups. There were quarterly meetings available for every worker in the school. Besides, this pastor had interpreted his educational outlook to all the members as he had come in personal contact with them in their homes and talked or preached to them.

Finally, although preceding paragraphs may be denied in many parts by those who have lived in some situation which was different; there will be universal agreement on one thing: rural and small Sunday Church Schools are important. This importance arises out of such well-known considerations as the following: the large percentage of churches and schools which are of this type; the basic stability of the group to which they minister; the trend of population back to the rural scene; the place of food and consequently of wholesome rural living in the international order; the percentage of leadership for all walks of life and for the church in particular which comes from these groups.

ORGANIZATION

In achieving the best possible results in rural and small Sunday Church School work, there is a good parallel in medical practice. Health is health, just as disease is disease, wherever you find it. In building for health or in healing disease there may be slightly different prescriptions according to the complications. Nevertheless, the basic aproach, standards, materials, and policies are decidedly the same in all cases. Similarly all these chapters on leading a Sunday Church School pertain in general to work in the rural and small school. Thus it is necessary here to dwell only upon certain special solutions of a few particular problems.

Unity

The major goals as to organization, integration, and unification are as pertinent to these schools as to any others. They may be more easily effected. The closeness or smallness of a group makes for actual unity whether it is expressed in the organizational machinery or not. In a small school, the Sunday Church School superintendent may be a church council member. Whatever the type of school there will be ordinarily no difficulty in establishing a small Church School Committee through which the educational work is directed and reported back to the council. If the congregation is small, there are not many educational organizations; hence the staffs and memberships are more or less identical in the several which do exist. Consequently, it should not be difficult to establish a Unified Church School if the leader determines to lead the people in doing so. Everything considered, it is easier to realize the Church School as the congregation educating itself in the typical rural or small church.

Grouping

Obviously it is necessary to group the pupils of a small school in larger age ranges. Nevertheless, the typical terminology can be employed. There can be at least a children's division, a young people's division, and an adult division. Those divisons may be, also, the classes of the school. There are sometimes a kindergarten-primary class, a junior class, an intermediate-senior class, a young people's class, and an adult class. Any number of other combinations are possible. Sometimes nursery, kindergarten, and primary children are put in one class; junior pupils with the intermediates; senior with the young people. The goal continues to be effective working groups as closely graded as seems feasible. Many problems of leadership and space can be solved by combining the sexes in the classes, although the traditional practice of sex segregation may be harder to break down in a rural school. Whatever the grouping, pupils should be promoted regularly and properly from one department to another.

Staff

In the very small school there will be a staff consisting only of general superintendent, with an associate if possible, a secretary-treasurer, a pianist or organist, and teachers. Very often the officers will serve as teachers, too. One of the first additions to that minimum staff could well be a children's division superintendent and a young people's division superintendent to represent the interests and plan and conduct the program for the larger development of work in those areas. A music leader would be another valuable addition to be made early.

Securing a sufficient number of leaders is one of the most serious problems of the small Church School although it should not be supposed that increasing size will progressively solve the problem. The particular difficulty in the rural and small-town situation is the tendency of the leadership element among the young people to migrate to the city. The only obvious solution is, on the one hand, to make use of the young people early and as long as they are available and, on the other hand, to enlist more of those people who remain. If the small school is in the city, it may have to ask a larger church to share its leaders.

Closely allied is the necessary emphasis upon leadership education. Almost anywhere, a young people's or young adult class, even a senior class, may be operated as a leadership education group for a period of months. (This is the place for the pastor to use his precious time if at all possible.) Other possibilities are available in community leadership schools and classes. There are small towns which co-operate interdenominationally to maintain a young people's class for leadership education. A representative or two can be sent to a summer camp for leadership development. Books and periodicals are fully as useful in these schools as in any others.

Pupil management

Regularity and punctuality of pupils in typical rural schools is largely a family matter for families arrive together as groups. They may be late because of the work. During certain seasons the work makes it impossible for them, as they view it, to come at all. With many rural people, too, being exactly on time with religious services is not considered particularly important. They will start the session when they all get there and stay until it is finished; then they will go home with similar lack of concern for the clock.

The general solutions to these problems are discussed in earlier pages. Here, it may be said, it is possible to place too much emphasis on punctuality. There are conditions under which other things are more important. As for regularity, it may be advisable to shift the time schedule to suit certain seasonal demands. Further, special attention should be given to transportation problems. There are isolated pupils who simply cannot get to the school regularly unless provision is made for them. Also, if it is impossible to do one kind of educational work, there is likely another kind which can be done.

PROGRAM

The major objectives of a program for the schools in view here are identical with those in others. The more immediate goals are discovered by the same process. Curriculum is defined in the same way. There are the same four aspects of the curriculum, namely, study and instruction, worship, fellowship, and service. Ideally here as elsewhere these will appear in a series of units of activity which constitute the school's program. The major principles and procedures relating to the progress of those units of activity are, likewise, the same in all types of schools.

It is commonly lamented that denominational Sunday Church School programs and program materials have the large city church too closely in view. That may or may not be true. It is no occasion for despair. Everywhere programs and materials must be adapted to the situation in which they are to be used, and the existing ones can be adapted to the rural and small school. Furthermore, the Bible abounds in rural imagery and the Christian way is at least as fully suited to the country as to the city. Besides, present-day Christian education sees every church of whatever type building its own program to the best of its ability. The proper attitude is to assess the situation with its advantages and its difficulties, set up objectives, plan a program, and discover or develop the materials needed to carry it through. And let no one assume that there is no possibility of securing the requisite leadership until he has really surveyed the situation.

Study and instruction

These cannot be as closely graded in the small school. The pupils in the group, representing a wide range of ages, will have more varied interests. This has its advantages as well as its disadvantages. Pupils can learn more from association with pupils younger or older than themselves than from companions of their own age. It is necessary, however, to give more attention to the various individuals. Each member needs to have his particular responsibility and opportunity in relation to the total work of the group. There is a particularly fine educational opportunity in having older pupils help younger ones.

Throughout, it is to be remembered that rural and small-church leaders and pupils are fully as capable of getting interested in developmental approach and creative use of techniques as any others. Their very way of life may be preparing them for managing units of activity of a creative nature. Once they get the idea, they do not like to sit and be talked to any better than other pupils. Dramatization, handwork, discussion, visual aids, research and report, and the like will be as generally popular with them as with any other persons.

An interesting point is made by one pastor who writes concerning the introduction of newer lesson books and more progressive methods. "Don't try to change the whole school. Concentrate on one or two teachers. When they are sufficiently convinced of the merit of the new ways to indicate their willingness to try—then let them start and help them in every way to be successful. It worked in four schools where I tried it."

Worship

Worship in the typical small school is more like proper family worship in which each can have his part while sharing with persons of different ages. The lamentable thing is that the worship is so often conducted by adults on the adult level. It would be better to remember that the adults are going to have their special service of common worship. Worship in the school, then, would be principally for children and young people. The young people can plan and conduct it with adult coaching. Even the youngest children can have their special parts such as reciting Scripture, singing a song, or doing some special exercise. The general character of the worship can otherwise be the same as in any other school.

Fellowship

This aspect of the curriculum needs consideration as fully in rural and small churches as in others. A rural pastor writes: "A well-planned social program is essential in every rural parish." Many of the communities are more pitifully lacking in recreational and social facilities than some so-called slum areas of the cities. Many of the members are more starved for social contacts and stunted for lack of play than they realize. Many of the churches harbor tensions which would be eased by proper Christian fellowship activity. This is true for adults almost more than children since the latter have public-school facilities.

For such social activity rural churches have at least the important requisites of people, homes, and the out-of-doors. Understanding, vision, and leadership are the chief additional essentials. Of those, the greatest need is leadership, for the proper leader will help the people to see why, what, and how. To meet the need, a committee or person can be provided with a few books or someone can be sent to a leadership camp or school.

Service

Rural and small schools are not peculiar in that they lack the service element in the curriculum. Nevertheless, it deserves their special consideration. Many of the service enterprises can center in the local church. Indeed, this type of church may have extraordinary advantages. There is so much that needs to be done for the ongoing of the work and so few hands to do it. There is need for evangelistic endeavor, the winning of new friends and members, improving the building and grounds, getting numerous items of equipment and supplies. Those local needs should not, however, blind the people to their wider obligation. They can have their part, however small, in the world-wide work of the church. They will find abundant need for helpfulness, too, among their neighbors.

Thus, a rich program of service is possible for the rural and small Church School. The general outlines will be the same as those for any other school. Yet, as in those other cases, it must be designed for the particular situation. As one writer suggests, "The harness must be adjusted to fit the horse."

The people could meet that demand if they were led to see the need and encouraged to let themselves act freely in meeting it. Rural people are creative; their daily work demands it. The leaders of a small church are courageous, too, or they would not have allied themselves with a struggling cause. Unfortunately, in many cases, a wrong attitude has been developed which leads people to feel that they must hew strictly to the line in their educational program. That attitude needs to be reversed.

EQUIPMENT AND FINANCE

It has been said that the essentials for a Sunday Church School are persons, space, and the Book. Nevertheless, it is well to have those persons grouped according to their interests and needs, the space equipped for educational work, and some materials at hand to supplement the essential Book. It requires money to provide these things. This the typical rural and small school finds difficulty in providing.

Let it be said first that planning should take the place of lamenting. These reprehensible words are uttered too frequently: "But we are a one-room school; we can't do that." One wants to counter: "Do you need much longer to be a one-room school?" And, "Have you tried to do 'that'?"

The one-room school which cannot, by long-range planning, secure at least one additional room is rare. Vision and determination are needed most. Some corner can be curtained off for a children's group, if no more. A balcony can be adapted, even an attic sometimes, for a young people's meeting place. Basements are better than nothing if no better is possible. How many congregations are absolutely sure they could not provide even a small addition within the next ten years if the fund were started, the members would do a considerable part of the work themselves, and community donations of materials were solicited? As one pastor said: "Much work at little cost can be done when the men of the church band together and perform the task for the love of their Sunday School and church."

Meanwhile, how about heat, ventilation, and light? Is it possible to do anything about these simpler conditions for effectiveness? Are there shelves and cabinets for supplies or is it impossible for the men to make them? Is the church kept clean and free from disorder? Are flowers used?—real ones from the fields being better than artificial ones if there are no others. Can there not be at least one good picture instead of the usual abominations? Could not a little painting be done if there is no possibility of doing a thorough job of decorating? How about making some screens to separate the classes and some tables on which the pupils can work? Could not the pews in a corner or two be loosened and turned to face each other around an ordinary folding table? How about stools on which small children could sit as they work upon a pew in front of them? How about a blackboard and maps and a few books for the leaders and for the pupils—books on Bible, teaching, worship, and recreational leadership?

One suggestion always made by every student of the rural and small church is to give attention to the exterior of the building and to the grounds. The property may be ever so small. It can always appear as the temple and school of a Christian congregation. The budget may be strained to the limit. Yet there are many small repairs which can be done by members themselves and even a quart of paint would help in many places. Worst of all, in the country where trees, shrubs, and hardy flowers can be had for the asking, many of the bleakest churchyards are seen. At least 75 per cent of all rural Sunday Church Schools could appropriately initiate an enterprise of landscaping the property.

The ideal in all financial matters is a budget for all regular and special expenses to which each person contributes as he is prospered. The raising of the budget will properly be accomplished by a general program of stewardship education along with special attention to definite needs of the school. The givers should be allowed to participate fully in the preparation of the budget and as fully as possible in the management of the funds. This, too, can be done in a rural school or small school.

IMPROVING THE RURAL AND SMALL SCHOOL SITUATION

A first step for the Sunday Church School leader who undertakes to improve this kind of school is to develop certain new attitudes on the part of his constituency. (That need is not exclusive to rural and small Church Schools; it may apply with greater force to some large and city schools.)

Such a leader will strive to create a desire to try newer and better ways of working and to develop the people's confidence in their ability to improve conditions. He will help the people to get a proper perspective which sees their possibilities and obligations as well as their handicaps. He will certainly emphasize qualitative as well as quantitative standards of work.

One of the chief resources he may use is family relationship. These people are deeply interested in their children and young people. When they are led to see what the on-coming generation needs, they will seek to provide it. Youth, furthermore, can be enlisted in the task of soliciting and helping to provide what is needed. It is desirable, also, to have the school affiliate with and make use of denominational and interdenominational agencies. Such affiliation may foster a feeling of larger significance and surely develop a wider outlook. In the sharing of experience with other schools, the local leadership will be guided in its own development and gain confidence in its own ability. Participation in the larger young people's councils and leadership education programs is particularly to be fostered. Still another desirable way to improve the small school is by an expansion of the educational program to include some of the newer agencies discussed in the next chapter.

Chapter XX

ENLARGING THE PROGRAM

The Sunday Church School may properly demand recognition as the major educational agency of the church. Yet no thoughtful leader will hold that it is a completely adequate agency. The status of Christianity in the present era would refute any such claim. To be sure, the legionnaires of evil never have put themselves in the way of its influence. Still there is pitiful lack of knowledge and lamentable weakness of conduct even among its loyal adherents.

It was the author's privilege to meet annually for a dozen years a significant number of graduates of the Sunday Church School—college freshmen who averaged thirteen years of experience in its classes. They were admirable young people but sorely in need of better moral and religious education. They had only a fragmentary acquaintance with a few Bible stories, mostly Old Testament, excepting the birth, death, and miracles of Jesus. They had only the slightest knowledge of the history and program of the church, a confused medley of rather vague theological ideas, and no clear-cut understanding of Christian ethical principles. Thus their conduct and belief were determined largely by environmental conditions while so much that they might have found of vital worth in religion was not available for their everyday experience.

Why that seeming failure of the Sunday Church School? There is ample reason in the time element alone. Let it be said again: an average member of the church is having not more than one hour of Christian education per week.

Such facts have been moving church leaders to action. Their first effort has been to raise the efficiency of Sunday Church Schools so that the time spent in their sessions will have maximum fruitfulness. Yet, when every possible step in that direction has been taken, the need for more time remains. It is truly a profound evidence of the grace of God working within the movement that so much has been accomplished with so little time.

A second effort has been the development of allied agencies. Many of these are of ancient origin, others are children of this century. Nearly all are weekday agencies. Together they constitute an amazing amount of effort which often escapes the attention of those who are viewing and appraising the educational work of the church. Only an outline and a brief discussion of certain aspects of the situation can be presented.

I. Weekday Church School work
    A. Types related only to educational program of the church (free time)
        1. The congregational Weekday Church School, including confirmation classes and the Midweek Church School
        2. The denominational or interdenominational co-operative Weekday Church School
    B. Types having some relationship to the program of public education
        1. Parochial schools
        2. Bible or other study for high school credit
        3. Dismissed time schools
        4. Released time schools
II. Vacation Church Schools
III. Young people's societies, including youth fellowships, councils and conferences
IV. Leadership education, including education for evangelism
V. Men's and women's societies, including missionary societies
VI. Clubs, including many forms of recreational groups
VII. Camps
VIII. Homes, including parent classes and conferences
IX. Education in church music
X. Weekday services and "prayer meetings"
XI. Pastoral counseling
XII. Home use of radios, recordings, and films
XIII. Community agencies such as YMCA and YWCA
XIV. Publications
XV. Higher schools
XVI. Religion in public education

All the work of those agencies is available to supplement the work of the Sunday Church School. Yet they, too, have reached only a limited number of persons for a limited amount of time. Thus the staggering task remains: to reach the people with, let us say for a good beginning, three hours of Christian education each week. Until that challenge is met more fully, we must expect to live in a world of increasing spiritual ignorance, secularity, immorality, and irreligion.

PROVIDING ADDITIONAL SESSIONS

To enlarge the program of education in his parish, the Sunday Church School leader should interest himself in providing additional sessions. It would have been more immediately practical to say that he should foster the auxiliary agencies listed above; and, until better things are possible, leaders will have to be doing chiefly that. Yet, since the trend toward the simplification of the parish program is reaching at least the overhead agencies and bringing about mergers which will result in ultimate unification of local educational programs, present-day organizers do well to anticipate the coming event.

Sunday afternoon and evening sessions

Church leaders have long lamented the lack of time for their educational work. Some have condemned the public schools for taking all of it. Defendants have remarked that the churches do not make full use of the time they have. They do use relatively little of the time after school, on Saturdays and Sundays for nine months of the year, and during whole weeks of three months each summer.

Young people's societies have wisely utilized a portion of Sunday afternoons and evenings and every Sunday Church School leader may properly promote that work. Better, though, to be in line with the present trend, the various upper classes, departments, or divisions of the Church School should be having supplementary sessions at those times. The same groups with the same staff should assemble to work at a related aspect of their Sunday morning activity or a correlated separate unit.

Weekday sessions

The above outline disclosed that most of the work done by the allies of the Sunday Church School takes place on weekdays. Every leader with a comprehensive vision will foster the continuance or establishment of any appropriate form of it. If he fosters an organized agency, he will seek to keep it always closely correlated with the total educational program. However, the ideal is to have additional weekday sessions which will continue and enrich the work of the Sunday units without multiplying organizations and will provide for integrated Christian experience.

Three particular forms of weekday work merit special consideration.

Historically in several denominations and more recently in others, confirmation or similar classes in preparation for full church membership have been a weekday educational feature. They aim to provide an intensified period of Christian experience which will be fruitful particularly for richer present and future church membership. The period of study sometimes parallels the public school year through sixth, seventh, and eighth grades. More often it covers twenty or thirty special sessions at age twelve or thirteen. Similar classes are sometimes held for adults.

A highly specialized form of weekday work is the Weekday Church School on released time. The present movement which stressed co-operation with public schools is usually dated from 1914 when Mr. William Wirt, superintendent of schools in Gary, Indiana, inaugurated it.

The typical plan was an interdenominational effort in which the school children of certain grades were released from regular public school work at some hour during the week, upon request of their parents. They would then attend a session in a church building or schoolroom where they were instructed in religion by teachers provided by the church and approved by school authorities. Sometimes there was public school and church co-operation also in matters of enrollment, attendance, and discipline.

It was unfortunate that some lack of interdenominational co-operation and financial support curtailed this movement for several years. Yet with returning spirit and prosperity after World War II it began thriving again in many centers. By 1947 there were two million pupils in such schools.

Closely related is "Bible Study for High School Credit," a plan by which high school students study Bible in their Church Schools and receive credit on high school records. Recently also, in several states, this developed into a program of Bible classes usually taught by teachers whom the churches provided in the high school itself.

Then came the Supreme Court action of March 8, 1948. It has been termed "an indecisive decision." Capable students are not yet certain that it does anything more, precisely, than prohibit the type of released time weekday work which had been done in Champaign, Illinois. However, it does seem to increase the weight of opinion against religious teaching in public school buildings, on public school time, or in any other way involving public money directly or indirectly. Time will be needed to recover from the consternation which has resulted, to get a clarification of the ruling, and determine its precise application to the several types of co-operative Weekday Church Schools. Likewise, the meaning of the decision for public school credit in Bible and other religious studies in public schools will have to be determined by a long process of study and, possibly, litigation. Just two things seem clear now: religious forces must scrutinize their plans and procedures more carefully than ever before; and some plans and procedures must be dropped, while others may be retained and new ones developed. Certain more far-reaching implications will be faced in a later section of this chapter.

The Sunday Church School leader may well be a leading spirit of the congregation or community in favoring and securing development and support of such educational endeavors. Further, his work is not finished until he has helped to provide every other feasible educational opportunity in the local congregation and community, has sought to direct the young people into Christian colleges, and has urged upon them the claims of full-time Christian service for which they will prepare in training schools or seminaries of the church.

Vacation sessions

It begins to appear that the church will seize its opportunity to use vacation time for Christian educational work. It is reported that as many as five million pupils attended Vacation Church Schools in a recent summer. These schools minister chiefly to younger children although young people and adults are sometimes included in the enrollments. The usual period is two to five weeks with daily attendance for three hours. Among the unique values are these: marked increase of time devoted to Christian education, development of a contagious spirit; a proper setting for using advanced educational procedures; an everyday contact with religious education.

Another movement which gives promise of being even more important is developing rapidly. While we have had summer camps, assemblies and conferences for a long time, they have multiplied rapidly during the last decade. A well planned camping program provides an almost ideal situation for learning to live the Christian way by living it under guidance. Sunday Church School leaders can wisely seek to help the members of their schools take advantage of these opportunities.

Home sessions

There are those who assert that modern conditions reflect the failure of the home in the task of moral and religious training. This is not altogether true for present-day people live in the whole community as a "larger home." Nevertheless, there is some truth in the statement. Fundamental responsibility does rest with parents.

Thus the family unit must be incorporated in any satisfactory plan of Christian education. A program carried on by the home, fostered and supervised by the church, including literature, visitation, parent and pupil meetings and enterprises could be the most vital factor of all. There is no more insistent need in the entire field today than the demand for great leadership to promote this movement to include the family in Christian educational work.

Sunday Church School leaders do not need to wait until the church undertakes full scale guidance of a home program. Worthwhile beginnings are possible now. They can promote Christian reading in the home. "Story papers," Bible story books and devotional booklets do not exhaust the possibilities. There are denominational and interdenominational periodicals and a flood of religious books which should be made available and urged for reading.

Many homes have favorite radio preachers who are tuned in each Sunday. There are other worth-while broadcasts of stories, dramas, and music which deserve to be included in the family radio fare. A Sunday Church School leader can use oral and printed announcements to foster their use. He can also furnish information which will help the family select the better movies. Finally, he can foster the use of the excellent phonograph recordings of religious readings, stories, dramas, and music now available.

EXTENDING THE SUNDAY CHURCH SCHOOL SESSION

Another method of securing additional time is the expanding or extending of the Sunday morning program. Come to think of it, there is something a bit odd about getting children up, dressed, and away to the church for just an hour. Why should not the older people, too, plan for a longer session?

One possibility is the simple addition of a quarter hour, half hour, or hour to the present Sunday Church School schedule. Some have provided for a total of three hours. Another procedure which gives somewhat similar results without requiring more time is the combined teaching-preaching service mentioned in Chapter V. Its essential nature, for older persons, is an hour of study and instruction under the educational staff and an hour of worship, with preaching, in charge of the pastoral staff. Elimination of duplication in repeated sessions of worship will give additional time for the more specifically educational activities. For the younger children, many would make the program a two-hour teaching service except periodic visits in the adult services of worship.

Two major problems face those who wish to inaugurate such plans. First, what shall be done in an expanded session? Where only a quarter or half hour has been added, a period of departmental instruction and a slight lengthening of the class instruction period will suffice. For a two-hour program, the new views and practices in education can be introduced more fully—informal procedures, pupil participation, and units of activity.

In most cases, especially where the expanded sessions of the school parallel the church service for part of the time schedule, we shall have to think of a dual program. The first hour may be much like the present. A second can be "Junior Church" or a special study or group enterprise. Suggestions like these have been made for the latter: making things for the sick of the congregation; working out services of worship for the following Sunday; a study of the home land of Jesus; a discussion of the problems of right living; study of the hymns of the church; study of the various forms of work done by the church. Some schools are finding this the best place to introduce the new audile and visual materials which have proven so valuable.

The second major problem which arises in relation to such an expanded session is the securing of workers who are capable of the different work required and are willing to give additional time, particularly if it keeps them from church services. The problem may be met in part by raising the question whether we are church members to serve or to be served. Some will find that their most fruitful way of living the Christian life is to do this needful educational work even if they cannot attend services of worship at the usual hours. Again, there is the relay system in which certain workers serve for a quarter, then return after another quarter passes. In that case, a trained leader like a deaconess or director of religious education who can give continuous oversight and guidance to the program is almost essential.

A combined teaching-preaching program, providing an expanded session for children through the junior age (intermediates being included until they reach the confirmation age in churches which have that practice) will be described as it might be done in a typical larger church. At 9:30 all members of the congregation assemble for an educational program. Persons of intermediate age and older will go to departmental assemblies for a short devotional service and any business or departmental instruction planned for the day, then to their classrooms. Younger children go to Kindergarten, Primary, and Junior departments where they will remain for two hours. The first hour will be a rather typical Sunday Church School program. The second will be in charge of the director of religious education for the Junior Department, another worker for the Primary Department, and the regular Kindergarten superintendent for that group. Each will have helpers serving on the relay system for three months at a time. At 10:25 closing bells ring in all classrooms of older pupils and the organ in the church auditorium begins playing. At 10:30 the processional is followed by the common service for all but the Children's Division, which attends periodically when special provisions have been made for their participation in the service.

The similar sorts of things which can be done are exemplified in three actual programs outlined below.

PROGRAM NUMBER ONE

The Church School is described as follows:

The Primary Department meets at 9:30 A. M.

The Service for Boys and Girls (grades 4-8 inclusive) is held at 9:25 A. M. in the church. Classes follow the service.

The Service for High School Young People is at 9:55 A. M. Classes follow.

The Church Hour Group for pre-school and kindergarten children meets at 11 A. M.

The Young People's Class meets at 10 A. M.

The Men's Class meets at 9:45 A. M.

The Women's Class is held at 7 P. M.

The most unusual features of this program are the services for children and high school young people. They are conducted in the congregation's main place of assembly for worship and use the same pews, organ, chancel, and altar. Children's and young people's choirs serve in the respective groups. Here are sample orders of service:

Service for Boys and Girls
    (25 minutes)
Prelude
Processional Hymn
Call to Worship
Hymn Response
Responsive Reading
Hymn
Scripture Reading
Offertory
Dedication of Offering
Hymn
Prayer
Recessional Hymn
Benediction and Organ Amen
Postlude

Service for High School Young People
    (35 minutes)
Prelude
Hymn
Dedication to Worship
Choral Response
Responsive Reading
Prayer
Offertory
Dedication of Offering
"Meaning of Worship"
Closing Prayer
Hymn
Benediction and Choral Amen
Postlude

PROGRAM NUMBER TWO

(Chiefly Sunday)

Elementary Grades: Sunday Morning, 9:30 to 12:30—a varied program of activities: discussions, stories, arts and crafts, rhythms and dramatics, music and recreation, worship.

Junior and Senior High School Departments: Sunday Morning, 9:30 to 10:45—departmental services of worship and classes for study and discussion of the Bible, religion, and personal problems.

    Friday Night, 7:30 to 10:30—various activities integrated with the Sunday program; special groups for arts and crafts, dramatics, music, scouting; recreation; special service projects.

Special Group for Undergraduate Students: Sunday Morning, 9:30—a group whose discussions seek to clarify the place of religion in personal living and of the church in social life.

General Group for Young People: Sunday Morning, 9:30—a discussion group with topics that reflect the personal interests of its members.

Adult Groups: Sunday Morning, 9:30—three classes for parents—initiated by, conducted for and by parents, divided according to the particular age group in whose problems parents are most interested. Outside experts and members of the Church School staff are used freely.

    9:30—group for Bible study, open to both men and women.

    9:30—a group for men and women who are interested in discussion of current issues.

(Chiefly Weekday)

Parents' Fellowship: All parents with children enrolled in the Church School are assumed to be members. It arranges Parent-Teacher conferences and promotes other meetings of special interest to parents. There are usually four or five meetings a year.

Wednesday Evening Lectures
The Nursery School
The Vacation School
Arts and Crafts
Physical Recreation
The Symphony Orchestra
Young People's Activities
    Sunday Night Program
    Thursday Night Program
Men's Activities
Women's Activities

PROGRAM NUMBER THREE

First Period—9:15 to 10:10: The first worship service with music by
the Youth Choir. This is for adults and for young people from the
sixth grade up. The first Sunday School for children up to the fifth
grade inclusive.

Second Period—10:15 to 10:45: Bible classes for adults and for young
people from the sixth grade up. There is no worship period for these
age groups under a Sunday School superintendent; their worship for
the day is at the first or second church service. Children of the Church
program for children up to the fifth grade inclusive.

Third Period—11:00 to 12:00: The second worship service with music
by the Senior Choir. This service also is for adults and for young people from the sixth grade up. The second Sunday School for children
up to the fifth grade inclusive.

Note: The church services are listed "for adults and young people
from the sixth grade up," not because younger children would not be welcome, but because younger children would probably prefer to be in departmental rooms where, at the same hour, there is graded worship (as well as
education) suited to their age level.

It will be observed that such programs have some resemblance
or relationship to the Junior Church or Young People's Church
idea, mentioned also in Chapter V where a somewhat unfavorable
evaluation was given. However, one pastor writes: "One of the
fine things we have done toward enlarging the program is the work
in our Children's Church. As you may know, we have a lovely
chapel for the children's use. They have their own deacons, litur-
gists, council, offering envelopes, bulletins, ushers, choir, organists,

and all. While I had an assistant pastor the service was entirely in his charge. Now we have a competent young lady who tells a story sermon while one of the youngsters acts as the liturgist. We have around eighty boys and girls—aged 6 to 12—enrolled in the program. The attendance, on a per capita basis, is better than adult attendance; so is the giving."

There can be no question about educational value in such an activity. Yet it is possible to inquire whether a different use of the time might serve the objectives more fully. A writer recently urged these weaknesses of the Junior Church plan: boys and girls are not yet ready for an adult type of service; because the children do not understand its meaning, they are only "playing at" worship; usually the age groups are too inclusive; the pupils do not graduate into adult worship services as something new.

But why should the Sunday Church School leader trouble himself about additional sessions, expanded sessions, or any such things? If he does his immediate task well, why not be satisfied? The Sunday Church School leader's task is not merely to conduct efficiently a Sunday Church School hour with all its ramifications. It is to get the people of the congregation and community as well educated in morals and religion as possible. That requires more than the usual hour a week. So, when the leader has taken the major steps for the highest efficiency in his Sunday Church School hour, he will give yet more thought, energy, and support to the enlargement of the whole congregational educational program.

PUBLIC INSTRUCTION IN RELIGION

A still more fundamental development has been getting attention in recent years. Its future is uncertain, especially since the Supreme Court decision of 1948. Yet, as a long-range proposal, it deserves earnest consideration instead of the hasty dismissal so often accorded it.

The benefit of historical surveys discloses that religious instruction in early America was conducted on weekdays within the general educational program. In present-day America it is in danger of being rather meticulously excluded. There are those who hold that the departure from the early practice was unnecessary and undesirable while a return is possible and essential.

Religion has never been officially and legally eliminated from the public schools of the United States. Dean Luther A. Weigle some years ago listed certain "factors of circumstance" by which we "drifted" into the separation of secular and religious education. He mentioned the growth of knowledge, the expansion of the Sunday School movement, revivalism, the centralization of public education, and sectarianism.

For such reasons the country is now reaping the fruits of secularized public schools: contentment with the condition; religious illiteracy and moral laxity; a secularized point of view; fragmentary educational experience; the persistence of sectarianism; loss of confidence in the public school system on the part of certain elements in the population; and an endangered democracy.

There are three other possibilities for the increase of religious culture, yet all together do not seem to promise sufficient relief, particularly when we think of a total and unified Christian personality as the goal. Parochial schools for all, even if feasible and desirable, would be impossible except in certain special circumstances. We have not been able to equip, staff, and finance the Sunday Church School properly! Besides do we want, can we endure, a dozen or more school systems paralleling the public school system in this democracy? As for the second possibility, the various local Church School agencies described above are not meeting the issue. For example, the Sunday Church School movement has been promoted in a state like Pennsylvania since 1795, yet only about 20 per cent of its citizens are enrolled in Sunday Schools. A third possibility is to expand the work in which public schools and churches co-operate. Yet, although Bible study for high school credit has been in existence since 1911 and the Gary type of weekday church school since 1914—a generation—neither had touched a very considerable part of the public school constituency even before the present anomalous situation developed.

There remains no alternative to giving every possible consideration to the expansion of religious work in the public schools. They are not now and never have been godless. Bible reading is required in many states and permitted in almost all. There are other religious exercises in public schools, such as prayer, singing of religious music, festival programs, and baccalaureate services. A great deal that is religious in content already has been integrated with such subjects as history, literature, civics, and art.

A movement to build upon those foundations is gathering strength. Recent studies and publications, along with appointments of committees, for example, in the International Council of Religious Education, constitute a beginning toward more religion in general education. Another long-range effort would put religion consciously back into the curriculum of instruction.

An important objection is the practical one which recognizes the wide variety of pupil and parental opinion about religion with which it would be necessary to deal. Against this objection it is urged that teaching need not mean indoctrination in the distinctive convictions of some particular sect. The new approach in education and the new techniques are suited to that demand.

Again, cannot the basically religious and the sectarian be distinguished in providing the content for public instruction in religion? It would seem that a great portion of important material could be handled with a reasonable degree of freedom from dogmatic bias and organizational interest. Such items as the following have been proposed:

The history of Israel and of Christianity
The influence of Judaism and Christianity upon government, art, literature, and music
The present status and work of the various churches
Forms of worship and devotional literature and music
The English Bible and the story of its development by synagogue and church
Ethics and the ethical implications of Judaism and Christianity
Men and women of the Bible and other outstanding religious contributors
Masterpieces of Biblical literature
The other religions

It should be observed that there is already a large body of experience along such lines within higher education. Professors in church colleges have long been teaching groups as widely divergent as any which would be met in a typical public school classroom. Increasingly, too, state and municipal colleges and universities are developing departments of religion where Protestants, Catholics, and Jews mingle in a fellowship of study concerning the religious culture and enterprises of the race. It is proposed only to extend such experience downward into secondary and elementary levels of public education.

The major objection to public instruction in religion is the question of public policy involving the principles of religious freedom and separation of church and state. Many will assert that these principles forever exclude religion from the public schools. On the other hand, careful students have concluded that those principles have assumed a negative meaning which was not in the minds of those who evoked them. If they are right, the teaching of religion which is free from creedal emphasis and sectarian purpose need not be considered incompatible with them.

What does freedom of religion mean? Clearly the individual opportunity to hold such beliefs and to worship in such ways as one will, without dictation by government; and the corporate privilege of developing any church body which is not obviously subversive of good citizenship. What does separation of church and state mean? Clearly that there shall be separate executive or administrative control for each, church and state.

Both principles do require that a citizen shall not be forced to accept views of religion alien to his conscience and that public funds cannot be used to foster a particular branch, denomination, or sect of religion. Does either mean that religion must be excluded from the education of a child or that public funds cannot be used to foster religion in general?

The whole matter is being studied carefully by such bodies as the Federal Council of Churches and the International Council of Religious Education. Quite as important, experiments are being conducted. There are centers where the work is actually being done. Thus a body of experience will be available in a few years.

Forward-looking leaders in Sunday Church Schools will be watching this development with interest. It is rightly to be expected that they prepare themselves to express intelligent judgments about it and lend it their aid. Their work will continue to be important even if public instruction in religion should gain acceptance. The Sunday Church School will need only to shift its emphasis to the more distinctively ecclesiastical objectives.

The present difficulty can be a blessing if it sharpens, as it should, the church's larger view of its educational task. The Sunday Church School should be lifted to a higher level of effectiveness, with an extended time schedule. Additional sessions or, if more practical, allied agencies should be fostered incessantly, including those which are related to public education. Perhaps, also, some new form needs to be developed; for example, one leader is advocating co-operative Saturday schools of religion. Whatever the developments, the Sunday Church School leader may be re-assured that Christ's commission has been revitalized: *"Go therefore and make disciples of all nations, baptizing them in the name of the Father and of the Son and of the Holy Spirit, teaching them to observe all that I have commanded you; and lo I am with you always to the close of the age."*

INDEX

INDEX

Type used in this book
Body, 11 on 12 and 9 on 9 Garmond
Display, Tempo and Vogue